THE TRUTH
IN THE LIGHT

*An Investigation of over 300
Near-Death Experiences*

Peter Fenwick
and Elizabeth Fenwick

www.whitecrowbooks.com

Dr Peter Fenwick, MB BChir (Cantab), DPM FRCPsych
Dr Peter Fenwick is an internationally renowned neuropsychiatrist
and a fellow of the Royal College of Psychiatrists. Dr Peter Fenwick
is Consultant Neuropsychiatrist emeritus to the Epilepsy Unit at the
Maudsley Hospital, which he ran for twenty years. He is presently ap-
pointed as a Honorary Senior Lecturer, at the Institute of Psychiatry
and Southampton University, and Honorary Consultant Clinical Neurophysiologist at Broadmoor. Dr Fenwick has a longstanding interest
in the mind/brain interface and the problem of consciousness. He
is Britain's leading clinical authority on the near-death experience.,
and is at present carrying out a research project in hospices in the
UK, Holland and Japan into the experiences reported by the dying
and their carers around the time of death. He has co-authored several books with his wife, most recently *The Art of Dying*.

Elizabeth Fenwick, MA (Cantab)
Elizabeth Fenwick is a professional writer on health and family matters. She is married to Peter Fenwick. They have three children, eight
grandsons and a granddaughter, and have written several books together. She has worked as an agony aunt advising on sexual problems
on radio and in *Company* Magazine and has been involved in sex education in two schools in London. She also worked for three years as
a telephone counsellor for Childline.

The Truth in the Light

Published and printed in the United States of America and the United Kingdom
by White Crow Books; an imprint of White Crow Productions Ltd.

For information, contact White Crow Books
at P. O. Box 1013 Guildford, GU1 9EJ United Kingdom,
or e-mail to info@whitecrowbooks.com.

Cover Designed by Butterflyeffect
Interior production by essentialworks.co.uk
Interior design by Perseus Design

Paperback ISBN 978-1-908733-08-5
eBook ISBN 978-1-908733-09-2

Non Fiction / Body, Mind & Spirit / Parapsychology

www.whitecrowbooks.com

To Irene
And to
Annabelle and Gareth, Natasha and Jonathan,
Tristram and Annemette

Contents

Acknowledgements

W E would like to thank the Committee of IANDS (UK) who helped devise the questionnaire used in our study, and in particular its founder, Margot Grey, who first drew our attention to the near-death experience, and whose example and support encouraged so many people to 'come out' and talk about what had happened to them.

Our special thanks are also due to David Lorimer, Chairman of IANDS (UK), always a good friend and supportive colleague. David, with Margot, has done more than anyone else in the UK to generate interest in the topic of near-death experiences, and it was through David and Margot that we were able to contact many of the people whose experiences are described in the book.

Finally, we want to give our very sincere thanks to everyone who took the trouble to fill in our questionnaire, or who agreed to contribute their story, or who agreed to lend us photographs. It was because they were willing to do so that we were able to write this book. Our only regret is that we have not been able to meet them all to offer our thanks in person.

Peter and Elizabeth Fenwick

Introduction

MOST of us at the very least wonder about our own immortality and many people are convinced that there is something beyond death, beyond the blackness of the grave. In Western Judaeo-Christian culture we absorb from an early age the idea that virtue now has its own reward - later. We are taught that the universe is essentially moral and that there are absolute human values.

But increasingly, science presents us with a picture of a much more mechanical universe in which there is no absolute morality and man has no purpose and no personal responsibility except to his culture and his biology. We no longer live in an age when faith is sufficient; we demand data, and we are driven by data. And it is data - data that apparently throws some light on our current concepts of Heaven and Hell - that the near-death experience seems to offer.

The near-death experience (NDE) is intriguing for two major reasons. First, it is very common and secondly, it is cross-cultural. The results of one NOP survey in America suggest that over 1 million Americans have 'seen the light'. Any experience that is so common must have had some influence on the way we think about life and death. Indeed, it could be the very engine that drives our ideas of an afterlife.

Many people believe that in the NDE we are given glimpses of Heaven (or Hell). But it is just as reasonable to assume that it is the NDE itself which may have shaped our very ideas about Heaven and Hell.

It is natural that we should want to examine such experiences in detail and subject them to scientific scrutiny. But it's also important to bear in mind that we may not be using the right tool for the job. The scientific method of analysis is essentially objective: are we justified in using it to analyse data which is mainly subjective? One aim of this book is to give space to those who have experienced the beyond and to give ourselves time to listen to them without preconceived prejudices. Then we may be able to decide whether their experiences can be explained by an entirely scientific approach or whether it is only by taking a wider view of man and of the universe that we can find any satisfactory answers.

The experiences described in this book are all first-hand accounts from people who wrote to me or to David Lorimer, chairman of the International Association of Near Death Studies (UK), after a television programme, radio broadcast or magazine or newspaper article made them aware of our interest in near-death experiences. People wrote from all over England, though the greatest number were from the southeast. There were fewer responses from Wales; fewer still from Scotland, and only one or two from Ireland.

We asked 500 of those who wrote to answer a detailed questionnaire about their experiences. Our aim was to gather in a standardised format as much detail as we could about the NDE, the people who have experienced it and the effect that the experience has had on their lives.

Over 350 people replied. Of these 78 per cent were women and 22 per cent men. Eighty per cent were adult (over eighteen) at the time of their experience; 9 per cent were ten or younger. About half described themselves as Church of England, 12 per cent as Roman Catholic, 19 per cent as other Christian denominations and 1 per cent were Jewish. Eight per cent described themselves as agnostic and 2 per cent as atheist. But few were regular churchgoers - only 16 per cent went to church every week, though just over a third had been to church in the previous month. Asked whether religion was important to them, 39 per cent said it was, 41 per cent that it wasn't, and 20 per cent replied 'Maybe'.

As well as asking about the near-death experience itself, we tried as far as possible to discover when it occurred, and what state of consciousness the person was in when it began. Many people had their experience during an operation, while they were under anaesthetic. Others were asleep at the time of the catastrophe that induced the

NDE. Just over a third were taking some form of drug at the time of their experience. It was common for patients who were having a heart-attack to report that the NDE began while they were awake.

Most experiences occurred during illness. The illnesses varied very widely but were usually severe though not always life-threatening. We had two accounts from people whose near-death experiences occurred at the time of an attempted murder when they were unconscious. Two per cent of our sample had NDEs during a suicide attempt.

Most (79 per cent) had had one NDE only, though a surprising number (12 per cent) had had two and a few (9 per cent) said they had had three or more. Clearly the NDE does not confer lifelong immunity - in fact it looks as though there may even be an NDE-prone personality or that one experience in some way facilitates another.

Kenneth Ring, an American psychologist, has suggested that NDEs are most likely to occur in people who have had a difficult birth and so are possibly mildly brain-damaged, or in people who have had a particularly unhappy childhood. We tested these ideas and found that in our sample they did not hold true. Only 27 per cent said they had had a difficult or prolonged birth, and only 17 per cent said their childhood had been unhappy: indeed, 50 per cent described their childhood as 'very happy' or 'happy'.

We asked about the effects that the NDE had on the subject. Seventy-two per cent said that the experience had changed them in some way. As might be expected, attitudes towards death and dying were often changed by the experience. Although the great majority (82 per cent) said that they now had less fear of death, it is interesting that fewer than half (48 per cent) believed in personal survival after death. Forty- two per cent reported that they were more spiritual as a result; 22 per cent claimed to be a 'better person', and 40 per cent said they were more socially conscious than before. An increase in psychic powers is often reported in people who have had NDEs, and 47 per cent of our sample said they felt the experience had made them more psychically sensitive.

We also wanted to know how many people had read about NDEs before their experience. This was important, since if the subject already knew about the experience before it occurred, then it would be reasonable to suppose that his or her NDE could to some extent be coloured by this. We found that only a tiny proportion (2 per cent) said they had first become aware of NDEs before their own experience. The vast majority (98 per cent) knew nothing about the phenomenon and became aware of what had happened to them only much later, when they happened to come across accounts of other people's experiences.

It is from this database that the statistics quoted in this book have been drawn, and the accounts given to me by these people and by others who have written to me since then form the basis of the book. But their accounts provided much more than mere statistics. Each one was special in its own way, and provided a personal testimony which I found both moving and utterly sincere. It is very seldom that an author can so truthfully say that without others a book could not have been written - in this case, without these people there would, indeed, have been no book. I feel privileged to have been allowed to read their accounts, and I am grateful to everyone who, by being willing to share their experience with me, has helped in this search to find the truth in the light.

Peter Fenwick
London
December 1994

Chapter 1

What is it Like to Die?

THE man who told me the following story was Peter Thompson, who'd been a patient of mine for many years:

I think the guy doing the operation still had his L-plates on. At any rate, he wasn't being supervised properly - the consultant was out of the room. I remember holding out my arm for the local anaesthetic so that they could cut my skin for the cardiac catheter to be inserted. God knows why he didn't put in any local anaesthetic, but there was the most searing pain in my arm and I looked at the doctor and I could see his brow was covered in sweat. Then I was aware I was losing consciousness and of people rushing around me, knocking things over in their efforts to get emergency equipment set up. Then there was nothing - no pain at all. And I was up there on a level with the ceiling - I say 'I was there', because that's how it was. It wasn't a dream, it wasn't imagination. It was as real as me sitting here talking to you. I could actually see myself; me, my body, down there on the bed. Doctors scurrying round it, a general air of panic, but it didn't worry me at all. I suppose it should have done - I knew it was me down there but it didn't seem to be me if that makes any sense. The me that was really me was up there, out of it all.

Then I was floating in what seemed to be a tunnel; dark, but not frightening at all. I could see a light at the end and I felt as though I was being pulled towards it. I had to go - there was no alternative. But still I wasn't frightened. Rather the reverse - I had the most wonderful feeling of peace, more than I've ever felt before, at any time in

1

my life, as though everything that was happening was right. And you know me - this isn't anything like my usual self. The light at the end got brighter and brighter, but it didn't hurt my eyes. Although it was brilliant, it wasn't dazzling. I felt I was being drawn into it and the feeling was well, the only way I can describe it is pure bliss and love.

He looked slightly embarrassed and dropped his eyes as if to apologise for saying such a silly thing, then he went on.

There was someone there in the light, waiting for me. And then suddenly I was pulled back, away from it, back, slammed into my body again, back with the pain, and I didn't want to go. I just wanted that peace.

The next day the surgeon came round and said, just as if nothing had happened - he didn't even apologise – 'Well, we didn't have much luck yesterday, did we? We're going to have another go this afternoon.' I just couldn't believe it. He had sent me up to the ceiling and now he didn't even ask how I was. All the other doctors with him were looking at each other and not wanting to catch my eye. I became very angry at their lack of care and started breaking out into a cold sweat, I was really frightened of going through all that pain again. So I discharged myself on the spot. I just felt I couldn't trust them. I've been terrified of falling into the hands of doctors ever since. But death? This is the strange thing, I've got no fears about that at all. If that's dying, it's nothing to be afraid of. It's wonderful.

Peter Thompson was a man I liked and respected, and there was no doubt in my mind that he was telling the truth. Since that episode he had developed an anxiety neurosis and sweated whenever he came into hospital, but the experience of love had changed him; he felt he knew what happened after death.

He couldn't explain what had happened to him. Neither could I. But I didn't doubt for one moment that he had experienced it, whatever it was, whatever it meant.

I had already come across descriptions of similar experiences collected by Raymond Moody, an American doctor. Dr Moody was a philosophy student when he first met someone who had 'died' and gave a fascinating account of what had happened to him while he was 'dead'. Later, when Moody was teaching in a university in North Carolina, a student told him about an amazing experience his grandmother had had when she 'died' during an operation. These two accounts were so similar that Dr Moody started actively to search for others. The result was his book Life after Life, published in 1973, the first book to describe in detail the tales told by people who had survived a brush with death.

The response to the book in the States was fantastic. To begin with, although Dr Moody himself never claimed that anything he had found was proof of a life after death, he was often misinterpreted. Many of the accounts he recorded were from people who had been resuscitated after a cardiac arrest; some had even been said to have been 'clinically dead' for a short while. Medically speaking, these people had not died - by definition they could not have died because they were now alive. But the notion that these were experiences described by people who had actually died and then come back from the dead became widespread. For many these experiences were read as a literal description, not just of what it was like to die, but of what happened after death.

I had been fascinated by these accounts, but as a scientist, I was sceptical. I suspected (as European scientists tend to do) that the 'Californian factor' might be operating: some experiments and some experiences just do not seem to cross the Atlantic. My initial feeling was that near-death experiences might be only another one of these. Now here was someone who'd had just such an experience sitting on the other side of my desk. 'Flaky' was about the last adjective I would have chosen to describe Peter; I had to take what he said seriously, and that meant I might have to revise my views about near-death experiences in general.

In fact, there is nothing particularly new about the notion that people can 'die' and live to tell the tale. There are written descriptions of similar experiences in myths and legends going back well over 2,000 years. It is likely that for as long as man has been aware of the certainty of death he has contemplated the possibility of survival and wondered, what happens next? The most ancient burial sites contain artefacts which suggest belief in the survival of some aspect of the human being after bodily death. Plato (427-347) at the end of The Republic tells the story of a soldier, Er, who was thought to have died on the battlefield. He revived on his funeral pyre and described a journey out of his body to a place of judgement, where souls were sent on to Heaven or to a place of punishment, according to the life they had lived on Earth. Before reincarnation they were sent across a river, where their experience of Heaven was wiped from their memory. But Er himself was sent back to tell others what he had seen.

Moody's first contemporary reports of near-death experiences raised all sorts of interesting questions. Does everybody who comes near death have one, and if not, why not? Do you have to come near death to have such an experience? Are the experiences described specific to a near-death situation or do they occur in other circumstances? Could they be dreams or hallucinations, and if so, why should so many people dream more or less the same dream, or have more or less the same hallucination? If they are true glimpses of an afterlife, then why are there any differences in the accounts - why doesn't everybody glimpse the same afterlife? Is there any relationship between the kind of experience you have and the closeness of the encounter with death - that is, do you experience more the nearer you actually come to dying? Kenneth Ring, a psychologist at the University of Connecticut, was one of the first people to make a scientific study of these experiences and to try to answer some of these questions. He interviewed 102 people who had come close to death, and what he found confirmed many of Moody's observations. Some people, though by no means all, had had similar experiences to the ones Moody had reported, and these experiences did seem to follow a consistent pattern. In 1980, Ring listed the five features which appeared most commonly in their reports, and which he found usually occurred in the same order. He found that at the beginning of the experience, when the person might be frightened or in intense pain, he or she would be suffused with feelings of peace. This happened in 60 per cent of the people he studied. Then they would suddenly find themselves leaving their bodies - 37 per cent reported this out-of-body experience (OBE). Next, 23 per cent reported that they entered darkness, saw light (16 per cent), and entered the light (10 per cent). Ring called this consistent pattern of events in the near-death experience the 'core experience'.

Many people's experiences were even more complex than this so Ring went on to develop a more detailed scale which included many other components of the experience: some people saw dead relatives, others saw beautiful colours or heard music, some encountered a 'being' or presence, and some underwent a 'review' of their life. He gave different weights to these features, so that an NDE could be scored - the higher the score, the 'deeper' the experience, according to Ring.

The first people to attempt any kind of statistical analysis of near-death experiences were two American physicists, Russell Noyes and Donald Slymen. They asked 186 people who had survived serious illnesses or accidents about their feelings during their experiences. What they found was much the same as Ring had discovered, but they categorised the experiences reported slightly differently, and found three general underlying factors. The most common was a 'hyper-alertness' factor - thoughts were speeded up and became sharper and more vivid, vision and hearing seemed to be more acute. The second factor was one of depersonalisation, a feeling that the 'self was apart or detached from the body and felt strange or unreal; that objects seemed small or far away. There is a loss of emotion and an altered sense of the passage of time. In about a quarter of subjects they found a third, 'mystical' factor. Mystical feelings included feelings of great understanding, a sense of harmony and unity, feelings of joy and revelation. Memories might be evoked and sometimes there was a feeling of being controlled by some outside force.

What actually happens in a near-death experience? No two are identical and yet, as anyone who has studied them has found, there are uncanny similarities between them. Certain features crop up again and again, regardless of the person's sex or age, or (even more intriguingly) of their religion or culture, so much so that Bruce Greyson, another American psychiatrist and NDE researcher, laid out a blueprint of a characteristic experience. The events described don't always occur in the same order, and few people experience every event. But virtually everyone who has had a near-death experience will recognise some features in the following brief outline, and will be able to say, 'Yes, this is what happened to me.'

Feelings of Peace

For many people overwhelming feelings of peace, joy and bliss are the first and most memorable part of the experience. Any feelings of pain that the earthly body may have been feeling drop away.

Out of the Body

Often the experience begins with the person leaving his or her body. He feels as though he is slowly rising out of it, weightless, floating, and can look down on himself from some objective vantage-point, usually near the ceiling.

Into the Tunnel

The person may enter darkness, usually a dark tunnel. They seem to pass very rapidly through this without making any physical effort.

At the end of the tunnel they see a pinpoint of light which, as they approach it, grows larger and larger. For some people the whole tunnel is a tunnel of light, not darkness.

Approaching the Light

For many people, the light is one of the most significant parts of the experience. Nearly always it is described as white or golden, a very brilliant light but not dazzling, so that it doesn't hurt your eyes. Very often the light seems to act almost as a magnet, drawing the person towards it.

The Being of Light

At this point the person may meet a 'being' of light. If the person is himself religious, this may be an obviously religious figure such as Jesus; sometimes it is simply a 'presence' which is felt to be God or God-like. This is nearly always an intensely emotional experience, so much so that often the experiencer cannot find the words to describe his feelings. But the experience is nearly always a positive one. The descriptions that are given are of a presence that is warm and welcoming and loving.

The Barrier

Sometimes people sense that there is some sort of barrier between them and the light, a barrier which in some way marks a point of no return. Several see this as a physical barrier - a person or a gate or fence - sometimes it is simply a feeling that they know this is a point beyond which they cannot pass.

Another Country

Experiences often say that they have visited another country - usually an idyllic pastoral scene, brilliantly coloured, filled with light - or that they have glimpsed such a place beyond the barrier.

Meeting Relatives

Occasionally other people are encountered too, usually dead relatives, more rarely friends who are still alive, or strangers. In some instances these figures beckon to them, in others they wave them away, signalling that they should go back.

The Life Review

At some point in the experience the person may see events from his life flash before him; a few people have felt they are being weighed up, experiencing a sort of Day of Judgement in which their past actions are reviewed. Some have a life preview - events are unfolded to them which are to take place in their future, and sometimes they are told there are tasks ahead of them which they must go back to complete.

The Point of Decision

Often people want to stay, more than anything they want to stay. But in every case they realise that this is impossible, that it is not yet their time to go. Sometimes they make the decision to go back themselves, usually because they realise that they are still needed by their families. Sometimes it's made for them; they are sent back either by the being of light, or by the friends or relatives they have met. Often they are given a sense that they have unfinished business to complete before they are finally allowed to 'cross the barrier'.

The Return

The return to the body is usually rapid; the person often shoots backwards down the tunnel at tremendous speed, and 'snaps back' into their body as if on the end of an elastic cord.

The Aftermath

For most people the near-death experience is one of the most profound they will ever have. It is vividly remembered for years - often for a whole lifetime. And very often the person who has had it reports that he or she returned changed in some way, often, though not always, permanently. Virtually everyone reports that afterwards they have no fear of death, though they don't particularly want to die - it's as if they value life even more and have a renewed sense of purpose. Their attitudes change. If they already have some religious faith the experience tends to confirm it. Even if they have no particular religious faith, many, probably most, return believing that death is not the end. A small proportion believe that they have been given psychic powers, precognition or the gift of healing, following their experience.

As a neurophysiologist and neuropsychiatrist, I have always been interested in different states of consciousness. We know so little about the mind and whether or not it is entirely limited to the brain. The scientific evidence so far suggests that it is, but the question still remains open. It looked to me as though near-death experiences might be another way of looking at the relationship between brain, mind and consciousness.

Near-death experiences also seemed to have a lot in common with other kinds of mystical experiences, for example those in which the subject feels that he has seen through the very texture of the universe into its ultimate structure. Often people feel that the experience is one of universal love, that the structure of the world is love. People who have NDEs often describe similar feelings of being surrounded by universal and complete love.

These mystical experiences had always interested me because they seem to lie at the frontier of science; we can find partial scientific explanations for them, but they can't be explained entirely by the mechanisms we already know. And yet as an area of research they are unsatisfactory because they occur at random and totally unpredictably. Of course it is interesting when people say they have felt that they are part of the universe or report that visions of the Virgin Mary regularly appear to them. But they can't make these experiences happen to order; they just occur.

This makes it impossible to set up a situation in which you can actually monitor what is happening to someone's brain during a mystical experience and correlate this with what they are feeling, their subjective experience. If you could do this then you would be able to set up a prospective study, that is a study in which you can watch things as they happen and so know what has actually occurred. If you cannot do this then you have to rely on the person's memory of what he thinks was happening to him at the time he had his experience. Such retrospective studies are inevitably distorted by memory, and this makes them much less reliable, and, scientifically, of much less value.

Yet it looked as though in the near-death experience one might have a mystical experience which not only seemed to conform to a consistent pattern but occurred only in special circumstances, and as these circumstances were known there was real chance of predicting it and therefore of setting up a prospective study.

Who has near-death experiences and how common are they? In 1982 the Gallup organisation published a national survey, 'Adventures in Immortality', which set out to examine what adult Americans

8

believe about life after death. One of the questions asked was, 'Have you yourself ever been on the verge of death or had a "close call" which involved any unusual experience at that time?' An astonishing 15 per cent of the respondents said that they had. Almost certainly this overestimates the true number of near-death experiences. The type of experience isn't specified, and a close call with death can mean different things to different people. It is very likely that a good proportion of the people who answered yes were, clinically speaking, not near death at all.

Even so, near-death experiences are by no means rare. When researchers questioned only people known to have come near death (for example, because they have had a cardiac arrest), they found that although not everyone near to death had the experience, somewhere between a tenth and a third did. This was cheering news for science - if it occurs that often then a prospective study was certainly feasible.

There remained the major difficulty that until I had talked to Peter Thompson all the experiences, and indeed all the research, seemed to lie on the other side of the Atlantic. I knew of no evidence to indicate that NDEs occurred on anything like the same scale in Britain. It was about this time that I first met Margot Grey, a psychologist who had herself had a near-death experience, which had had a profound effect upon her. She had interviewed many other English people who had had similar experiences in a hospital in England, and in 1985 published Return From Death, the first piece of English research on NDEs.

After the book was published she was contacted by so many other people to whom the same thing had happened that she decided to form an association which would act both as a way of putting these people (many of whom had never talked about their experiences to anyone else) in touch with each other, and possibly also as a vehicle for collecting accounts of the experiences so that they could be studied systematically. She invited me, together with several other people whom she knew were interested, to help her set up the association, the UK branch of the International Association of Near Death Studies.

Margot's book sparked off even wider interest in NDEs, and in 1987, shortly after it was published, I was approached by Tony Edwards, a gifted BBC television producer, who wanted to make a QED popular documentary film about the subject. The film was eventually shown at prime viewing time, but even so we didn't expect the enormous response we got from people who wrote in to tell us about their own experiences. Nearly always their first and overwhelming emotion on seeing the programme was one of relief that they were not alone; they were not Moony' - other people had had these experiences too.

'You can imagine my delight when I saw your programme and realised that I was not the only person who was out of step with what is termed normal.' 'I was delighted to hear other people have had the same experience. I was not a "nut" or a liar even to myself.' 'How thankful I am that I am not on my own with this experience.' Secondly there was a feeling of relief that they felt they could now 'come out' and at last talk about what had happened to them. Letter after letter expressed these feelings.

'It's something I haven't wanted to discuss with anyone other than a few that I am very close to, but it's something I desperately want to clarify.'

'Ten years ago 1 could not tell anybody about my experience, even my husband, because I thought people would think I was crazy.

'It comes as some relief to me to be able to actually share my experience after all these years.

'At the time [1947-8] I did not mention it to anyone. In those days they would have thought the worst had happened'

'I guess we all think others are inclined to laugh, so we keep silent.' The third reaction, and the one which made these experiences so compelling, and so moving, was that although they may have been in themselves extraordinary, they had happened to people who were ordinary human beings. If something like this could happen to them, you felt on reading their letters, then it could happen just as easily to you or me.

'I am a quite normal, level-headed human being in my forties.' 'I am quite a normal person and yet this certainly happened to me.'

'Before I tell you what happened I must tell you that my husband was a tool and die maker and tool designer. He was a man not given to fantasy, very down to earth, very honest and straightforward, an extremely hard worker, and well read and intelligent.

'My friends are mostly shipyard workers or local miners, so you will understand why I have not attempted to tell anyone of my experiences; one does not discuss the idea of afterlife and reincarnation with coalminers and shipyard workers, not if one wants to keep one's friends and sanity. Football, women, and greyhounds maybe, but not the afterlife.' The special value of these accounts is that, by and large, they came from people who were recalling something that happened to them years ago - twenty, thirty, sometimes as long as fifty years ago, long before anyone had heard of NDEs, and certainly long before such experiences had captured the popular imagination in the way they have done today. These people had no preconceived ideas about near-death experiences: indeed, they didn't even know about them and most had not the slightest idea what it was that had happened to them. Contemporary accounts will always be open to the criticism that they are contaminated by preconceptions, that people see what they expect to see. If they expect to travel through a tunnel, to meet their long-lost loved ones as their journeying souls leave this world for the next, then, the critics will say, that is exactly what is likely to happen. The people who wrote to us were quite simply describing their own experiences, without embellishment. They would have liked an explanation but usually felt quite unable to offer one. Is it surprising that these experiences were so clearly remembered so long after they happened? I don't think so. You do not easily forget something which leaves you absolutely baffled.

Chapter 2

Virtual Reality -
How Real is the Real World?

THE first question people ask about near-death experiences is always 'Are they real?' Sometimes what they really mean is, are people making it up? The answer to that is quite definitely no. If the experiencers had simply made it up, why would they have been (as most of them were) so reluctant to tell anyone else about it? For most people the experience is something they talk about only diffidently, and only to people they trust. They fear ridicule - why would they court it by inventing the whole thing? They are describing exactly what happened to them as they remember it. Also implicit in the question is, are they mad? And again the answer is no. They were quite sane before it and just as sane after it.

But the question still remains: is it real? Did it happen? And if it did happen, did it take place in what we know of as physical reality? Reality isn't always as real as we think it is. In fact, everything we see around us is perceived entirely through our senses and filtered through them. The objects we see when we wake up in the morning seem familiar only because our memory tells us that they were there when we went to bed the night before. If we feel the duvet cover, it is memory that recognises it as a cotton-polyester mix, and memory that provides the additional information that we bought it in Marks & Spencer a year ago. If we shut our eyes the visual perceptual world disappears into darkness, but this isn't particularly alarming because memory (experience) tells us that when we open our eyes again the same world will reappear.

Until the seventeenth century there was no clear consensus about the true nature of the world, and much confusion. Whilst many philosophers argued that the world existed independently of the observer, this degree of certainty was not shared by every philosophical school. The Platonists held that the world that we see around us is only part of the true world, and that a true vision of reality is restricted by our senses and our understanding. Aristotle, on the other hand, believed that we see an object only because it alters our physiology in some way. Indeed, Aristotle attributed any sensation to an alteration of physiology - feelings of anger, for example, he put down to the blood boiling around the heart.

It was Galileo who brought some order into this confusion, and who is largely responsible for the modern scientific view of the world, which is much more Aristotelian than Platonic.

He postulated that the universe was composed of two types of primordial stuff: matter-like stuff which could be weighed and measured and had shape and form, and energy-like stuff which acted on the matter. He went on to divide the world into a primary, objective world, which had primary qualities, and a secondary, sensory world of perception, which he said had secondary qualities. He distinguished between these two worlds like this:

> To excite in us tastes, odours and sounds I believe that nothing is required in external bodies except shapes, numbers and slow or rapid movements. I think that if ears, tongues and noses were removed, shapes, and numbers and motions, would remain, but not odours or tastes or sounds.

We can all share Galileo's commonsense view of an objective, external world which is independent of the individual. We expect that if we shut our eyes and open them again the world will be just as it was a few moments before. But the problem with Galileo's world is that it lacks subjective qualities; it has no meaning or value because these are subjective qualities that we impose upon it. Indeed, Galileo was unhappy with subjective qualities and did not pretend to understand how to incorporate them into his scheme:

> ... vision, I say, is related to life itself. But of this sensation and the things pertaining to it I pretend to understand but little; and since even a long time would not suffice to explain that trifle, or even to hint at an explanation, I pass this over in silence.

Thus the foundations of Galilean science were set. It was to be the science of a world without any subjective qualities, value or meaning. Descartes, too, had a similar view of a world composed of two kinds of matter:

> There are two radically different kinds of substance: physical extended substance (the res extensa), that which has length, breadth, and depth and can therefore be measured and divided - and thinking substance, res cogitans, which is unextended and indivisible. The body and brain equals res extensa, the mind, res cogitans.

This Cartesian world, in which mind is separate from body, and the objective external world from the subjective, internal, thinking world, has plagued science ever since. For nearly three centuries it has not mattered greatly, as science was so largely concerned with the physical properties of the external world. But it does matter very much now. As far as the biological sciences are concerned, the body now holds few unsolved mysteries; the last frontier is in the mind, or rather at that junction between mind and brain where perceptions come into consciousness - the very area over which Galileo wisely 'passed over in silence'.

Let us consider for a moment what science allows us to do. Science says that there is an objective independent world ruled by physical laws. We know what many of these physical laws are and they hold throughout the universe. Particles will behave according to these laws, and experiments carried out in England or Australia or even on other planets will all conform to them. It is thus a fact of science that if I carry out an experiment and you carry out a similar experiment, we should both get the same results. It does not matter that we may each have a different subjective view of the world, or different personalities, because the world is independent of both of us, and is not altered by our view of it in any way.

What happens when we try to describe subjective qualities (love, anger, beauty) in a scientific way? We can do so only in terms of an objective description which would be given by a third person. In scientific terms, anger is activity in a particular group of cells in the temporal lobe of the brain - not, after all, so very different from the Aristotelian view that anger is the blood boiling round the heart.

Science now can say little more about the mind than could Descartes and Galileo in the seventeenth century. It recognises the mind entirely in terms of brain function - neuronal populations and collections of neurones connected together in a special way to make neuronal nets, which are the basic building-blocks of subjective experience. If I am to describe the colour red scientifically I have to describe the wavelength of the light as it hits the eyes, and then the progress of the electrical impulses through the brain, and finally, the firing of neuronal populations in the association area of the cortex, but nowhere does the colour red as you and I experience it come into this description.

This leaves out a vital part of the world as we know and understand it. Daniel Dennett, an American philosopher, has said that once you have described the way the brain works in every detail, then you have given a full description of the consciousness of man and nothing more is required. In his view, love, truth, beauty - all the higher emotions - are simply patterns of electrical activity traversing different brain areas; nothing more. Mind is totally a function of brain; there is no question of the mind existing beyond or outside or in a different way from the brain. Mind and brain are forever welded into precisely the same thing. When brain dies, mind dies, and that is an end to it.

The Canadian philosopher Tom Nagel takes a different view. He argues that a scientific objective description of the world will never be complete. To give a full picture we must include the secondary, subjective qualities of Galileo. Imagine a bat. We know scientifically about a bat's radar, understand how a bat bounces sounds off objects and constructs a world from these radar echoes. It is theoretically possible to know everything there is to know about a bat's brain and the type of world it lives in. But Nagel says that however much we know about a bat's brain, we will never know what it is like to be a bat. This question of what it is like 'to be' is one of the most important questions that the science of the brain is now facing.

Kant was one of the first philosophers to suggest that both Galileo and Descartes were wrong in postulating an outside world which was independent of our subjective selves. He pointed out that unless the brain contains structures to perceive, there can be no perception. Quite simply, unless we have a visual system we won't be able to see objects. He then added that the objects which we see may not be the objects themselves, but simply a reflection of the way the visual system works. Kant's view was that the world outside is a subjective world and whatever we do we will never be able to understand or see 'the thing in itself. We will always see the thing as it is interpreted by the brain.

Of course there is a real world out there, an independent, objective external world, one which can be weighed and measured, and is subject to all the physical laws of nature, but it is not the world we actually see. The world we see is a very subjective psychological experience. It depends on the mood we are in, the circumstances surrounding us, and on the intact functioning of our brains. The 'thing in itself - the 'real' world - is forever hidden beneath this internal model created for us by the brain.

This model is, of necessity, a limited model. Information is continually coming into the brain from all the sense organs. From this the brain selects some bits which it processes and makes into a model of the world for us to understand. But this model which finally comes into consciousness is based only on selected data.

Daniel Dennett talks about a 'multiple draft theory of consciousness'. What he suggests is that the brain is continually updating the model of the world according to our psychological needs. If we need to switch our attention to something else, then a new model of the world is produced for us, and this process continues all the time. Thus our feelings about ourselves, our emotions, our understanding, in fact everything within our minds, is all created for us by the brain.

The NDE is a subjective experience. It includes sensations from an external world, and an internal world of thoughts, emotions, feelings of absolute truth, absolute knowledge, and of pure love. When we look at the NDE we can interpret it in three ways. We can give it a physiological interpretation, the Dennett treatment: what is actually happening in the brain, where is the sensory information coming from and what brain centres are active during the experience? We can give it a psychological interpretation: is this the brain's interpretation of a model primarily arising in the 'real' world, or is it a psychological model created entirely by the brain? Or we can interpret it as a transcendental mystical experience, something which suggests that mind and brain are separate and gives positive evidence of a transcendental reality beyond the brain. Each of these interpretations is valid in its own right and none will invalidate the others. Each may hold some truth, but there is no guarantee that any will give us the whole truth.

So it follows that when we talk about the subjective experience of the NDE, we cannot and should not use only the ordinary scientific method to validate it. We give labels of true or false to a subjective experience according to whether or not we happen to share it. The best analogy I can give is falling in love. It can be described quite well in physiological and psychological terms. Your heart and breathing rate increase when the telephone rings or the mail arrives. Your stomach lurches and your palms sweat at the sight of the loved one in the far distance. Your perception of this perfectly ordinary, maybe even rather plain, person is quite different from that of someone who doesn't happen to be in love with him or her. Like an NDE, being in love can have a lasting effect and change your life. It can change your behaviour, make you give up (sometimes for quite lengthy periods) biting your nails or humming under your breath or staying too long in the bath or the pub. It can even make you, for a while, a nicer person - so much nicer that those around you notice it and say, 'Aaahhh, he must be in love.' The presence of the lover is a source of bliss, his loss a cause of devastation. No one can doubt that being in love has meaning and value to the people involved.

And yet we can only really understand this if we have been in love ourselves. Most of us have, so being in love is held to be a 'true' experience. If it had never happened to you it would be very difficult for you to understand the peculiarly obsessive behaviour of the lover, his attachment of special significance to some other quite undistinguished human being in an apparently random fashion. You couldn't really 'believe' in it. You might even think he was a nutter.

MYSTICAL EXPERIENCE

Being in love is clearly a very common - almost a universal - experience. Mystical experience is less common, but it still happens to more people than you might imagine. If we are going to entertain the idea that the NDE might be a mystical experience, we need to define what a mystical experience is.

Its essential features seem to be:

1. *An intense realness. It comes with the conviction of absolute truth, so the experiencer is overcome by the validity and meaning of the experience.*
2. *Feelings of unity. The experiencer feels he has seen through to the fundamental nature of the universe, perceives and understands it and is united with it.*
3. *A feeling that the experience is 'ineffable \ There are no words to describe it. All sensory experience would fall into this category if language did not contain terms to describe it.*

   As soon as some new or unusual sensation is experienced, then it becomes ineffable.

4. *Transcendence of space and time.*
5. *A sense of sacredness.*
6. *Deeply felt positive mood. Feelings of joy and peace.*
7. *Paradoxicality. The feeling that something which is 'impossible' is in fact true.*
8. *Transiency.*
9. *Positive changes in attitude and behaviour.*

None of these feelings is unique to the mystical experience. Feelings of unity and intense realness, for example, are common in many drug-induced states. So are transcendence of space and time, and positive emotions. Feelings of ineffability are often reported by people with epilepsy who say they have a funny feeling they cannot describe just before an attack. No amount of questioning can elicit the particular feeling, as there are no words to express it.

Many studies have attempted to gauge exactly how many people have had mystical experiences, and their results have varied widely, depending on the populations studied and of course the questions asked. Most of the surveys have used questions such as these:

Have you ever felt you are in touch with the universal or at one with the universe?

Have you ever been aware of or felt an influence from a presence or power different from your everyday self?

Have you ever felt close to a powerful force that seems to lift you out of yourself?

The answers received have shown that this kind of mystical state is well within the range of normal human experience - in fact it is relatively common. Mystical experiences quite often occur in athletes during and after great moments. Greeley and McCready found that 35 per cent of a very large sample of people had had a mystical experience. Another study (Wuthenow, 1976) found an even higher figure -50 per cent of a sample of 1,000. The highest estimate was the 65 percent which David Hay found in a 1976 study of postgraduate students at Nottingham University.

Religions have always relied heavily on faith, and consequently on dogma, because they are short on proof. Miracles, visions and stigmata are highly valued because they are the nearest one can get to third-person objective proof of a personal subjective experience. A symbolic resurrection is for many people not enough to confirm their belief - only the doctrine of a physical resurrection will do.

It has always seemed odd to me that physical confirmation is thought necessary to validate spiritual belief. How can it? We are talking about two different worlds, two different realities, and two different kinds of experience. When we use science to test the mystical experience for reality we are almost bound to come to grief. In the following pages we are going to try to explain the NDE in terms of biology and psychology, to test it for 'reality' in a scientific way. This means that we start with the assumption that the mind does not operate independently of the body. But we will have to be prepared for the fact that science may not take us all the way. If we come to the conclusion that there are aspects of the experience which seem to be inconsistent with this, that the NDE is not a physical or even a psychological phenomenon, but a mystical experience originating in a transcendental reality, then the only way to validate it is through experience. Otherwise, it has to remain an act of faith.

Chapter 3

Out of the Body

IN March 1987 Dawn Gillott was admitted to Northampton General Hospital, seriously ill with microplasma pneumonia. She was put into intensive care, and doctors eventually decided to remove the ventilation tubes and do a tracheotomy because she could not breathe.

The next thing was I was above myself near the ceiling looking down. One of the nurses was saying in what seemed a frantic voice, 'Breathe, Dawn, breathe.' A doctor was pressing my chest, drips were being disconnected, everyone was rushing round. I couldn't understand the panic. I wasn't in pain. Then they pushed my body out of the room to the theatre. I followed my body out of the ITU and then left on what I can only describe as a journey of a lifetime.

I went down what seemed like a cylindrical tunnel with a bright warm inviting light at the end. I seemed to be travelling at quite a speed, but I was happy, no pain, just peace. At the end was a beautiful open field, a wonderful summery smell of flowers. There was a bench seat on the right where my Grampi sat (he had been dead seven years). I sat next to him. He asked me how I was and the family. I said I was happy and content and all my family were fine.

He said he was worried about my son; my son needed his mother, he was too young to be left. I told Grampi I didn't want to go back, I wanted to stay with him. But Grampi insisted I go back for my children's sake. I then asked him if he would come for me when my time came.

He started to answer, 'Yes, I will be back in four,' and then my whole body seemed to jump. I looked round and saw I was back in the ITU.

I honestly believe in what happened, that there is life after death. After my experience I am not afraid of death as I was before my illness.

Can the 'self separate from the body? When people describe what it feels like to come out of their body and see themselves, they are in no doubt that the body they see is not the 'real me'. Whatever is real, whatever is true and vital for them is nothing to do with their physical body. That is simply the vehicle, as one person put it, for the real self. This is how Mrs Doreen Wood saw herself after a heart-attack:

I actually felt myself come away from my body. I twirled so fast up in the air, so free, no pain, weightless, then I felt myself go back in my body and thought, was that old body with her knees curled up, facing the wall, was that me? I didn't see any lights, just whizzed round and round, so fast, and so free. Now I am not so afraid of death. I know this body stays here and was so disappointed that I came back, and wondering, why.

This feeling that the 'me' up there and out of the body is the real me, infinitely more real than the body it leaves behind, is described over and over again. Avon Pailthorpe, whose experience is recounted in Chapter 4, was surprised 'how clearly I felt myself to be myself without my body'.

Mrs Frances Bamshey: 'I couldn't see any kind of body belonging to me. I seemed to be mind and emotions only, but I felt more vital, more myself than I've felt in my life at any time before or since.' Ella Silver: 'I realised I was looking at an immense space, black, velvety. My mind seemed terribly clear and alert - more so than ever before. I was warm and comfortable. I seemed to be lying on my back, but when I tried to look along my body I found I couldn't move. I felt as if I didn't have a body, but was all mind.' Sarah McAdam: 'I "woke up" to find myself floating near the ceiling of the hospital room looking down on my peaceful body. I wondered why I was there in bed if my feelings and self were up on the ceiling.' The out-of-body experience is one of the events most often mentioned by people who have had a near-death experience. About two thirds of the people in our survey said they had seen their own bodies at some time during their NDE. They saw themselves just as they were - lying on the bed or operating table - but quite dispassionately, divorced from all that was happening to them, and free, too, from pain. W. C. Ball describes what happened to him when he was in great pain after an operation:

> I was exhausted and felt I could no longer bear the pain. I fell backwards on to the pillows. And then I seemed to be looking down at myself, I could see all about me and looking over towards the window I could see children playing in the garden next door. Yet that was something I couldn't possibly have seen from my bed. I looked so peaceful, and I can't describe the marvellous feeling I felt . . .

Compare this experience with Anne Allcott's, quoted below, which occurred after an operation in 1949. She was in great pain and was being given penicillin, and possibly other drugs too. Anne's experience is unusual because of the order of events: most people leave their body and then go down the tunnel and into the light. For Anne the OBE was the final event, just before she 'poured' back into her body. Anne is also one of the very few people who don't feel that they were free from pain right from the start of the experience. Mr Ball, who left his body straight away, reports a marvellous feeling of peace; Anne was still in pain, still feeling ill while she was in the tunnel going towards the light.

> I can remember floating in a very dark tunnel with a brilliant light at the end. When nearing the light I called out - I thought - 'please let me die quickly.' I felt so ill and had much too much pain. A deep voice which seemed to echo in the tunnel said, 'Who are you to decide when you die?' and I turned and floated away from the light. I then had this looking-down-from-the-ceiling feeling, knowing it was my body people were working on. They appeared to be lifting an eyelid. Then a male voice said, 'She will make it now,' or similar words, and I realised I was to live, so quickly 'poured' - it is the only way I can describe it - myself into the body on the bed.

Escape from pain is an almost universal feature of the NDE. But usually the release is only temporary. For most people, back in the body means back with the pain. A few people, though, describe a more dramatic and more permanent effect. For them the NDE brought a resolution of their illness, which usually seems to have been quite unexpected and caused doctors and relatives some surprise. Joan Hensley, who gave me the following account, was only fifteen when she had this experience. It was 1967. Joan was seriously ill with glandular fever. She had a high fever and was delirious. This particular night her mother was sitting with her, as the doctor had told her Joan could die. She says she was not aware of either her mother or the doctor in the room.

> It's very hard to put my experience into words. Initially I felt very frightened. I was only fifteen and knew I was dying. Gradually I relaxed and felt very calm, an acceptance of what was going to happen. My fear vanished. I saw a distant light that was friendly and warm, and felt myself drawn towards it. There was just a feeling of tremendous peace. 1 felt I was floating, weightless, I appeared to see only a tunnel. I think I looked down on myself in bed, but this was very brief. There was a light or glow at the end of a tunnel, a beautiful gold like the sun rising. I felt it was warm and pleasant. It made me feel very secure and loved. I saw someone, but no one I knew. He held out his arms to me, he was smiling and called my name. I seemed to know what he was saying but he didn't appear to talk to me. It was more a sort of telepathy. I felt very comfortable and secure. At the time I felt it was Christ. There was no evil, nothing frightening.

I reached out to touch his hands, but he told me I was not ready to join him and I must go back and I would recover. I knew I only had to touch his hands and I would join him.

There was definitely some threshold I had to cross. At the time I thought it was betwixt Heaven and Earth. I felt reluctant to go.

I felt I had experienced something wonderful. My mother certainly thinks I experienced something that night as she witnessed it all. According to her, I sat up in bed. Minutes before I had been delirious and throwing myself around the bed. My temperature had gone and I improved rapidly from that night. The doctor was amazed at such a dramatic recovery. I have told my fiance and one or two close friends - most people, I fear, would brand me a nutcase, or say I dreamed it.

Alf Rose's NDE (see Chapter 12) produced a similar dramatic recovery from a feverish illness, in his case pneumonia, a serious illness in the 1920s, especially for a small child - Alf was only four or five at the time.

He describes how, after his experience 'I suddenly found myself back in bed again, opening my eyes and telling my mother I was hungry ... When I asked for food my mother knew I was going to recover.' Mrs Holyoake's experience twenty-five years ago is described in Chapter 4. She was ill with pneumonia and pleurisy, and in intense pain. She described her meeting with Jesus in a beautiful garden with a strong smell of flowers, and her realisation that she could not leave her family. When she came back to her body, she 'got out of bed to find that all the pain had gone'.

Dennis Stone (see Chapter 12) was another who apparently made a miraculous recovery after having an NDE during an attack of meningitis. Dennis was thirteen years old, and the year was 1938. 'I remember thinking what happened to the terrible pain that I had been in, for it had gone and I felt so well. Then I reawoke in the hospital bed with Dr Galpine bending over me. Mother told me that he had suddenly turned back to the bed and could not believe I was alive and conscious.' Mrs J. Johnston had a similar experience. Her OBE occurred when she was very ill with 'flu. As she finally floated back into her body 'I opened my eyes and I thought, I feel much better.'

Ten years ago I could not tell anybody about my experience, even my husband, because I thought people would think I was crazy.

It was back in the early 1960s. I was a young housewife with three small children and at the time I was very ill with 'flu. I remember feeling really bad and thinking I was going to die. Suddenly I floated out of my body, it was a lovely feeling, and I looked down and saw myself lying in bed. I floated upwards to a beautiful vivid green field. There was a huge tree with a brilliant white light on top. I saw my father all in white with his arms outstretched towards me (he had died a few years previously) and I floated towards him. But as I got near he waved his arms and gestured for me to go back. I then floated backwards down and down into my body. I opened my eyes and I thought, I feel much better. But the strange thing was I put my hands up in the air and there was steam coming out of my hands.

I really believe I died for a second or so, but I remember thinking, 'I can't die and leave my children when they are only little,' and I think this is what pulled me back.

These rapid recoveries are interesting, but I think we should be cautious about attributing the recovery to the NDE. In each of these cases the illness was an infection, accompanied by a high fever. Fevers do resolve, often quite dramatically and suddenly (the resolution of a fever crisis was an often- used dramatic device in Victorian novels).

Are these people confused? Are they hallucinating? Certainly the very strong sense of personal identity so many of them describe is not something that you would expect to find in someone who is in any way confused or disorientated. There are some hallucinatory qualities about Mrs Johnston's experience - the steam coming out of the hands, for example - and the obvious explanation is that it was simply the product of a high temperature. But the interesting point is that Mrs Johnston thought she was dying, and then had an experience which had so many of the hallmarks of the NDE - the out-of- body experience, the vivid imagery and brilliant light, the meeting with a relative who waved her back, and finally the feeling that she had to return because of her children. We have to consider whether it was the belief that she was dying that triggered the experience.

I Know What Happened'

Out-of-body experiences are potentially the most fascinating feature of the near-death experience, simply because of the many people who claim that while they are out of their body they have gained information which they could not possibly have acquired except in the normal way through their normal senses. W. C. Ball, for example, 'saw' his neighbour in the next-door garden from his vantage-point on the ceiling. Mrs Mary Errington told us about the following experience which occurred in 1961, just after she had had brain surgery to remove an aneurysm. She was thirty-six years old and had three children, the youngest just two years old.

I had returned from surgery and was still unconscious when my spirit left my body and I was up on the ceiling watching myself on the bed and the nurse bending over me as though she was stroking my face, but of course I couldn't feel anything. I then left the ceiling and went through the dark tunnel out into a beautiful bright meadow. It was so peaceful - a peace that I can only describe as heavenly - and I was floating on this meadow towards a tree that had its branches outstretched like arms waiting to welcome me. I was thinking that once I got to the tree I was safe, but I didn't get there because I came back down the tunnel, very fast, and on to the ceiling where the nurse still seemed to be doing something to my face. I had these huge bandages on my head which to me, on the ceiling, looked like Yuri Gagarin's space helmet - I'd had the operation shortly after Gagarin's voyage into space.

Suddenly I was back on the bed and my face was feeling very cold. I regained consciousness and found that the nurse was bathing my eyes with ice bags to reduce the swelling. It was three days before the nurse brought me a mirror and asked me if I wanted to see how I looked. I was surprised to see the bandages exactly as I'd seen them when I was up on the ceiling. I was informed they were pressure bandages and also told that for a while I had been close to death.

It was a long time before I told anyone of my spiritual (or heavenly) experience. Now, thirty years later, I can still remember it clearly.

What I have wondered over the years is why was I sent back. Has God rejected me so that when I do eventually go it will be to somewhere else? I hope not!

One of the things that is striking about this account is that although Mrs Errington could see her face being stroked, she could not feel it. In the first account in this chapter, Dawn Gillott smelled 'the summery smell of flowers'. If the senses are working at all, why should some be able to acquire information and not others? This is yet another of the oddities of the NDE that we shall have to try to explain.

Michael Sabom, an American cardiologist, was intrigued but sceptical about reports from patients who claimed to know details of what had happened to them when they were unconscious after having had a heart-attack. The most likely explanation, he thought, was that they had been able to hear fragments of sound and conversations, and from these their brains had reconstructed a scenario which they believed they had actually seen. He taped a hundred interviews with people who had had OBEs after heart-attacks, and compared what they told him with details of their resuscitation procedures obtained from their medical files. He was not expecting what he found, which was a surprising degree of correlation between the two sets of data. Many people gave him specific physical details unique to their own resuscitation that they couldn't have known about, and couldn't have gained any knowledge of from television.

It is extraordinarily difficult to prove or disprove such accounts. It's difficult to know, for example, the level of consciousness of someone who has an OBE. It is possible that he may still be picking up a good deal of information with his physical senses, even though he is unaware that he is doing so. Extreme pain, for example, seems to be one trigger for an OBE, though in itself it may not cause total unconsciousness. Lightening in levels of anaesthesia can occur, so that occasionally people have more awareness of what is happening to them than their surgical team might like, and may even pick up comments made by the surgeon and operating team. There's also the problem that most people nowadays have a pretty good idea from innumerable television films and drama documentaries of what an operating theatre looks like, and even what happens in procedures such as resuscitation. But even so some of the accounts we .were given are difficult to explain and are very persuasive indeed.

Audrey Organ, who as an adult had two near-death experiences during operations, relates how in 1923, when she was five years old, she had a tonsillectomy. The next day she horrified her mother by describing just how they did the operation. They had 'funny scissors with long, long handles and they go snip-snip in your throat'. Was this an OBE? It seems highly unlikely that anyone would have tried to prepare a five-year-old for a tonsillectomy by describing the operation to her in quite such graphic terms, and just as unlikely that she had managed to see the surgical instruments before the operation. Audrey herself believes that she has always been a 'bad anaesthetic subject', but while a reaction to anaesthesia might explain the OBE, it wouldn't explain how she came by this information.

Several other people who wrote to us felt that they had acquired information when they were out of their body which they couldn't possibly have gathered in any other way. Mrs Jean Giacomozzi had this experience in 1977, when she was aged forty, and suffered heavy haemorrhaging after a hysterectomy. Her experience is unusual in that she met not only her dead father, but her partner, who was alive, and very close to her.

> I was outside my body floating overhead. I saw doctors and nurses rushing me along the corridor, back towards the operating theatre. On arrival there, the gynaecologist who performed the operation, was thumping my chest. Later repair work to my wound was going on and I remembered a doctor was inserting a long cotton wool plug.
>
> I recall floating in a very bright tunnel. Everything seemed so calm and peaceful. At the end of the tunnel my father, who had died three years previously, was holding out his hand and calling me to come.
>
> As I said, the feeling of calmness was indescribable. I heard music and there was a beautiful smell. I stopped floating a few feet before I reached my father and then I heard someone calling me. I turned and saw his face at the other end of the tunnel. It was Fabio [the man she was living with]. I remembered the doctor removing the cotton wool plug. When I later saw this doctor I told him everything. Although he seemed rather shocked at my story, he had no explanation as to how I knew so much about the events of the previous night. Like most people I had a tremendous fear of death. Now, believe me, it's the last thing I want, but I have lost that fear of the unknown because I truly believe I have had a preview.

In 1976, Mr John Parkinson was having an operation in Blackpool Victoria Hospital. The operation went wrong; he had a massive haemorrhage and was given a blood transfusion.

> During this time I seemed to leave my body and look down on the medical staff. I would have put this down to loss of blood to the brain except for the following reason. I was surrounded by screens and couldn't possibly see the rest of the ward. I saw the doctor enter the ward and go to another patient before coming to me. I could not have possibly

29

seen this from my bed and I confirmed what I had seen with the doctor.

Here is another very convincing story told by Maurice James, who suffered two cardiac arrests while he was in intensive care.

> It was as though I was standing on the wall of the ICU defying gravity and looking down at my own body. I was shocked at what an ugly corpse I was. I was naked and a nurse was taking down a drip out of my ankle. I vividly remember how purple my face was and how blank my forehead seemed. I appeared to have a black triangle from my hairline to my nose. My wife later confirmed that was how I looked once when she was allowed in to see me.

Derek Scull is a retired Army major. He describes himself as 'a pragmatic down-to-earth sort of person'. He is the kind of person you cannot help believing - however unlikely a story he told you, you would know with absolute certainty that he wouldn't have made it up, and wouldn't have imagined it.

He is just not that sort of man.

Major Scull had never told anyone, not even his wife, about the experience he had in 1978, and he had never understood it, although he still remembered it vividly. Then, driving home one day and listening to the radio, he heard a programme about near-death experiences which ended with a request for listeners to write in if they had had similar experiences. He thought, 'My God, that's what happened to me.' At the time of his experience Major Scull was in intensive care after a heart-attack. He had been in hospital for forty- eight hours, in a side ward which had windows around the top of the wall, just below ceiling level. The door to his room was closed. Major Scull would be the first to admit that he is not the world's easiest patient and that he has a low pain threshold. This is what he told us.

> I was lying there feeling terrible - absolutely at my lowest point, I'd never felt so low. Then these women just descended on me like three witches. They had to insert a catheter. I'd never had anything done like that and they gave me no warning, nothing. I didn't know what they were up to. I can remember shouting, 'Who's that dreadful woman in the white coat?' and

someone saying, 'That's the doctor.' I felt this enormous tension, as though I knew something was going to happen. Then I felt absolutely airy-fairy - as if I was levitating, quite serene, withdrawn from my body. I floated up into the top left-hand corner of the room. I looked back and saw my own body, lying there with its eyes closed. It didn't seem at all surprising for me to be up there. I could see through the windows at the top of the room to the reception area outside in the ward. Suddenly I was conscious of my wife waiting at the reception desk, talking to someone who was sitting down behind the desk so I couldn't see them properly. She was wearing her red trouser suit. I thought, my God, what an inappropriate time to arrive. It's not visiting hours, I haven't shaved, I'm looking dreadful, and anyway, I'm up here and she's down there, and there's the body. What's going to happen? The next thing I was conscious of was being back in my bed, I opened my eyes and there sitting beside me was Joan in her red trouser suit. I wasn't a bit surprised, because I knew she'd arrived, I'd already seen her.

Was this a coincidence? Was the image of his wife just a figment of Major Scull's imagination? In that case you would have to postulate a double coincidence: that he imagined her not only wearing the correct clothes, but did so at a time when she was actually there, although he couldn't have expected her to be there because it wasn't visiting time. He wasn't familiar with the layout of the ward or the reception area - he had not been out of his room since his arrival there, flat on his back, forty-eight hours previously. The door to the room was shut so he could not have seen his wife, and neither he nor his wife think it is possible that he could have heard her voice. We asked the Sculls whether the red trouser suit had any special significance - whether Joan wore it often or whether it was a particular favourite of his, something that, if he had been 'creating' an image of her, he would have been likely to include. But this doesn't seem to have been the case at all. Joan is a painter, very aware of colour, and she says that she deliberately chose to wear the red suit that day, although it wasn't something she often wore, because she felt red was a cheerful vibrant colour and it would suit the occasion and cheer him up.

So what was going on? Did all these people see what they think they saw? Unlike the medical and surgical techniques made familiar by television, many of the details mentioned in the stories above are so specific, so personal, that it's hard to explain them away: Major Scull's wife's red trouser suit, the 'space helmet' bandages seen by Mary Errington, the purple face and black facial triangle of the man in intensive care, the cotton wool plug that Jean Giacomozzi saw being inserted and then removed. It's difficult to believe that they could have got this kind of information other than by somehow 'seeing' it. And yet whatever did 'see' it was on the ceiling: it was not their physical eyes, not their visual system.

Certainly Major Scull has no doubt at all that this experience was real, that he did indeed see his wife outside the door and was able to get information about what she was wearing that he couldn't possibly have obtained if he had been simply lying in his bed. His explanation?

> Something, call it your soul, call it whatever you like, detaches itself from your body and goes to a vantage-point. Everyone's fearful of death, because of the unknown. But if what happened to me is a forerunner of death, then death won't worry me.

Spontaneous Out-of-Body Experiences

As well as being such a common feature of the near-death experience, OBEs also occur on their own, quite frequently and quite spontaneously, to people who are not near death at all. They can be induced by drugs (LSD and other psychedelic drugs, for example). Sometimes an OBE occurs when the person is resting or meditating, when he or she is stressed and anxious^ or even when they are just going about their ordinary everyday business. Leaving one's body seems to be a knack which comes more easily to some people than to others. Several of the people who had had NDEs which included an out-of-body experience also told us that they had had OBEs on other occasions too. A few people manage to induce them at will, and (because, by and large, it is a pleasant experience) some people have devised methods to induce the experience which they say can be taught. In some Western mystical traditions this ability to leave the body is called astral projection: it is claimed that there is an 'astral body' which in life can leave the physical body temporarily and travel independently, and in death is permanently separated from it. A silver cord connects the astral body to the physical, and indeed a few people who told us about their out-of-body experiences did describe seeing something which attached them in some way to their real body. I would have predicted that such a psychological safety harness would be more likely to figure in a spontaneous experience, but in fact of the three examples below, only one, Frances Barnshey's, was spontaneous, although none was near death. James Carney's occurred during dental anaesthesia, and Mr E. A. Hearn-Cooper's when, aged thirteen, he was ill during the 'flu epidemic of 1918. E. A. Hearn-Cooper:

> I felt myself rise up, float into the highest part of the room and look down upon myself lying there 'asleep' on my bed. I felt marvellous, no pain, free from all ills, just floating there. But I realised that I had a 'cord' linking me with my body below me, and while I felt very happy floating there, I somehow knew that if I moved too violently I would break the cord and I would never be able to return to my body. I decided to return, and did.

Mrs Frances Barnshey:

> I felt like a kite on an endless string, which I could feel attached between my shoulder blades ... I had to go back, and then I felt this cord on my back - the biblical silver cord? - pulling me back and the next thing I knew was that I was back in my body.

James Carney recalled: 'When I looked down, although I could not see my body, I could see I was attached by a light grey rope.'

It is worth looking closely at some accounts of OBEs which were given to us by people who were not near death at the time that they had them, to see what similarities there are between these and the OBEs which occur in the near-death experience. If the phenomena seem the same, even though they occur in different circumstances, then the chances are that all OBEs have an underlying common mechanism. A seventy-year-old ex-police and Army officer told us the following story.

> One Saturday night when I was ten I had been given permission to stay up late, until 10 p.m., to listen to the wireless. I was very healthy and not ill at the time. My two younger brothers were upstairs asleep. Everyone else was out. In the room we had a round mahogany dining table. I sat with my

back to the fireplace facing towards the outside wall of the house. On my right was the kitchen door, to my left the door to the hall and stairs. I remember clearly thinking that it must be possible for your spirit/ soul to detach itself from the physical body and roam free. I sat still, I don't know for how long, when I suddenly realised that all was still and silent. I was truly free and I was not frightened. I decided to look at myself. This I did and was in fact studying myself. I was intensely curious.

All of a sudden I was conscious of a movement on my left-hand side. The kitchen door opened and my sister walked in. She looked at me, that is my physical self, and screamed. Without any effort or desire on my part I found myself 'whole' again. I remember asking my sister if she was all right. She was very upset and told me she thought I was dead. She told me I looked totally 'empty', just a shell. I was going to tell her when she became very angry and accused me of trying to frighten her. She threatened to tell my parents. I reached a 'pact' with her but did not tell her what had happened.

This account is interesting because of the third-person reaction we are given. To the onlooker, the person who is out of his body does not look asleep (as one might expect), or lost in thought, or daydreaming, or 'away with the birds'. He looks 'empty', as though some vital part really has left the body, leaving an empty shell behind.

A similar account was given to us by Dora Parker, who had also had an out-of-body experience when she was ill with 'flu as a seven-year-old child.

I left my body and felt relief that I was free ... I heard a noise and my nanna coming upstairs... I continued to float and the light at the bottom of the stairs was brilliant (we only had gas). I was inquisitive. I needed to see why the light was so bright. I got to the curtain (we had a curtain at the bottom of the stairs) and I heard my nanna scream and scream. My body started to shake. I was tangled in the curtain. I had to go back - my lovely nanna wanted me - so I floated back and as she let my head on the pillow I came into my body feet-first.

Whatever the grandmother saw, it clearly terrified her, just as the sister of the boy in the previous account was terrified. There is obviously something about an OBE which to an observer seems like death - a body without its vital force.

In some instances, leaving the body seems to be a way out for people who are in great physical pain, or even great emotional distress. Some of the people who wrote to us had had an OBE in these circumstances and were subsequently able to reproduce it as a mechanism to escape pain. Mrs Christine Hopkinson describes what happened to her when she was in severe pain (though not near death) due to an undiagnosed gall bladder problem.

> I remember saying to myself, all right, take me, I can't go on any longer - here I am. I spent some time out of my body and then felt I had a choice of whether to go back or not. I chose to go back. For several weeks the same thing occurred, but I controlled the experiences. At the onset of pain I relaxed and 'floated out' until it was 'safe' to return and the pain was gone. I was able to roam about the house, check that my baby was sleeping, look at the cat and dog, see my husband asleep. I could see my body sitting there waiting for me to return to it.
>
> I have always felt that if I 'needed' to I could do it again - but only if I 'needed' to - and consequently have never been afraid of suffering acute pain. I have always felt guilty about not sharing these experiences as I feel if the techniques could be taught they could help people who suffer pain.

The OBE can be as effective an escape from psychological pain as it is from physical pain. Mrs G. Robinson had the following experience at a time when she was deeply depressed. Again there is this same feeling that the real 'me' is not contained in the body but can be separated from it.

> I was in that deep abyss of depression where I yearned to disappear into a hole in the ground and pull over the cover. That not being possible, I did the next best thing and went to bed, wrapping myself tightly in the blankets for comfort.
>
> I don't know how long it was before the 'real me' was floating close to the ceiling, face downward, looking down

with great interest at the body lying on the bed. The interest was because the mind in that body was a total blankness, a complete darkness, like a TV screen switched off.

'Real me' was ethereal, had no shape, no substance, but had a mind, enjoyed sensation, could see everything in the room in detail, was a power over and above the body that lay inert. The body had no mind, no feeling, no eyes, no life.

I cannot believe it was just a dream - dreams are soon forgotten - but I could not say that I had or that I had not gone to sleep.

Back to the Body

The actual return to the body after an OBE is not always described. Usually the person just finds himself back in his body, back in bed, without any real sensation of returning. One person described it simply as returning to the weight of her body.

The return seems to make more impact, and is usually described more vividly when the OBE occurs in isolation, not as part of the NDE. When a return is described it tends to be fairly abrupt. Judith Smith describes her return as being 'whisked back (I can only describe it as being like when you blow up a balloon and let the air out)' to find herself in the recovery room in hospital with a nurse saying, 'She's not coming round, she's not coming round - oh, it's OK, she's all right.' For Audrey Organ it was being 'pushed like a returning space rocket - or maybe how birth feels to a baby? - and back I came'. Mrs Dawn Gillott says: '... then my whole body seemed to jump. I looked round and saw I was back in the ITU.' Anne Allcott describes her return as being 'poured' back into her body. Other people have said that they 'snapped back', or 'slammed back'. Eleanor Cleator remembers 'being horizontal, above my body in bed, back in my bedroom, when I slowly "clicked" back into my body, and eventually tried moving an arm, a leg'.

An interesting point emerged from some of the letters we received from people who had had a spontaneous out-of-body experience, unconnected with illness and not in the context of a near-death experience. None of the people who had an OBE as part of an NDE were frightened by the experience.

They accepted it totally: it felt right for them to be out there - in fact, usually much more right, much more 'real', than being in the real body from which they had escaped. This isn't always the case when an out-of-body experience occurs on its own, out of the context of an NDE. Then it doesn't necessarily have this quality - indeed, it can be frightening, and people who have had both types of OBE have commented on this difference. Isabella McLeod, whose NDE is described in Chapter 6, also told us about a spontaneous out-of-body experience she had a few years later which did frighten her.

'I was walking along a main street and became aware I was not in my body. My spirit/soul said or thought, what am I doing out here? This was very frightening, although it appeared to be over in seconds.'

Similarly, it seems to be rare for someone having an NDE to worry about the practicalities of getting back into his or her body (although Major Scull was certainly conscious of the inconvenience of being up on the ceiling when his wife came to visit him). But in general this seems only to happen during a spontaneous OBE. Mrs Ivy Davey had three out-of- body experiences during her second pregnancy. On two of these occasions, she says, 'My spirit (or whatever) floated off to the right-hand corner of the ceiling, and stayed about a foot away for a time, and then came happily back into my body.' The third occasion was more unnerving. 'I had the greatest difficulty getting into my body,' she says. 'I can still remember the sensation vividly. I gave three "shudders" before my body "locked" into position.' Mrs Davey adds that although she was up on the ceiling, she did *not* see her body.

WHAT HAPPENS?

So what does happen during an OBE? Does 'something' - soul, spirit, essence - really leave the body? And can it, whatever it is, pick up information while it is away from the body? Let's deal with the second question first. From a scientific point of view, this cannot happen. Even if I am on the ceiling, 'my' eyes and ears, which gather information, and 'my' brain, which processes it, apparently remain sedately down there in my body. Unless there is a whole new information-gathering system up here with the 'me' on the ceiling, what am I seeing with? And how do I transfer what I see to the brain down there, whose memory is clearly able to recall it later on? The most straightforward explanation is that the out-of- body experience is a trick of brain function - that it is totally explicable in terms of human physiology and psychology.

As explained in Chapter 2, the brain is quite capable of making a whole new synthetic world for you. The brain can reset the coordinates of 'self, re-running them so that the brain definition of you moves from behind your eyes to the ceiling. However, if this is indeed what happens, if you are in psychological space and not real space up there on the ceiling, we should expect there to be major discrepancies between the psychological image - what the person sees from up there on the ceiling, which will be constructed by the brain entirely from memory; and the real image - what is actually going on at ground level. Mrs Ivy Davey, for example, did not see her body, although her body was clearly there. It is to be predicted that the more factual images the person has been able to gather about the room beforehand, the fewer these discrepancies will be. The faster the situation changes in the room, the less likely it is that the psychological model created by the brain would be accurate.

The quality of the body image should give us another clue as to whether when someone is out of their body they are in real space or psychological space. Body image is created by the brain, and damage to different brain areas can result in alterations in body image. For example, if someone has damage to that area of the brain which recognises faces, not only will they be unable to recognise familiar faces, but they will dream of people without faces. People who have damage to a special part of the right half of their brain tend to ignore the left side of their body. They may not recognise their left hand, and may not shave the left-hand side of their face. A brain that is malfunctioning should not produce a clear body image, and there is no indication from any of our accounts that this has occurred.

There are two sorts of body image. There is our own conception of ourselves - how we feel inside, which is usually a young adult of about twenty-five - and the image we see when we look in the mirror, which unfortunately is usually rather older and more haggard. A psychological body image should tend to the former rather than the latter. Later in the book we will see that when friends and relatives are met in the NDE they are quite often seen as younger than their chronological age. In this respect, Mrs Doreen Wood's description of herself is particularly interesting. "Was that old body with her knees curled up, facing the wall, was that me?" That does sound very much as though Mrs Wood was seeing her real self and not the more idealised body image one might expect, if this was just a psychological model.

Our view of anything is always coloured by our psychological viewpoint, which is one reason why witnesses to an accident seldom give identical reports of the incident. They will each select the facts which made a particular impact on them. If what is experienced is entirely of the psychological world then one would expect to see an even more marked selection of facts - you'll see only those things that seem to be psychologically relevant to yourself. A lovely account by John Bowers illustrates this very clearly. His experience occurred in 1942, when he was thirty and serving with the Sudan Defence Force in the North African desert. His unit came under attack from four Heinkel bombers. He takes up the story:

> As we withdrew from the oasis of Jalo, the squadron of Heinkels that had harassed us for the past six days pursued us like swooping falcons, their cannon fire spattering the sand and occasionally hitting one of our trucks with a sharp clang. I was driving at a steady thirty miles an hour over a flat expanse of hard sand when I became aware that a turtle dove was flying beside my truck, some ten yards away from my right shoulder. It kept with me for about a mile and then veered off westward into a wide rocky wadi. It was the season of migration and birds were crossing the Sahara in their thousands, but this was the only turtle dove I had seen in all my months in the desert and it lifted me into my superstitious mode. The Spirit in the form of a dove or just a weary winged traveller? The Heinkels left us to refuel and we steered our pack of fifty trucks into the wadi for a midday halt, seeking concealment in the steep rocky gulleys in the valley's wall. Before we could spread our camouflage nets the German pilots had picked up our tracks and now had us as sitting targets. Making noise is a good antidote to fear so I grabbed a Bren gun and lay in the cover of my truck, shooting at the planes as they roared past. The battery cook (a devout Muslim) came running in panic towards me, with little jets of sand spurting around him from the Heinkel's guns.
>
> 'Come over here,' I shouted, 'Lie here; don't be afraid. It is written.' He lay down, touching my right elbow, and calmed himself. The Bren gun had jammed so I laid it aside. It was little use anyway against well-armoured bombers. As I looked up one of the Heinkel pilots executed a tight turn over the rim of the wadi and lined up on us. No bombs had

dropped so this was probably his bombing run. I am not sure whether I saw the bombs leaving his belly but at that moment I had a vivid impression of my Irish grandmother telling me what to do if a Zeppelin dropped a bomb on you. Just a sudden memory from my wartime childhood? Probably, but it electrified me into action. I flattened out like a lizard on the sand, scooped out a hollow for my head (a personal refinement on Granny's advice), put my fingers in my ears and opened my mouth.

Instantly I was enveloped in a cloud of beautiful purple light and a mighty roaring sound as if a great Atlantic roller was breaking over me; and then I was floating, as if in a flying dream, and watching my body, some dozen feet below, lifting off the sand and flopping back, face downwards. I only saw my own body. I was quite unaware of the two Sudanese lying beside me. I was talking to myself with a quizzical sense of humour; 'Just like a rabbit,' I said - or thought - recalling, I suppose, my early days out shooting with a farmer friend. And then I was gliding horizontally in a tunnel. It reminded me of the entrance to the Pharaoh's burial chamber in the Pyramid at Giza, but it was not dark and rectangular but rather like a giant, round, luminous culvert, constructed of translucent silken material, and at the end a circle of bright, pale primrose light. I was enjoying the sensation of weightless, painless flight but I remember saying to myself: 'If this is death, it's rather dull.' But I had a feeling that it would be more interesting when I reached the light.

I would like to think that I felt some nostalgia for Sheila and the son I had never seen but I cannot be sure of this. However, I became aware that I was being 'sucked' back through the tunnel and then into a body that felt rather unpleasantly 'heavy', that the sun was burning my back and that I was trying to pick out a small piece of gravel that had penetrated the flesh below my thumb. I suppose I cannot have been 'up there' for more than a few moments because the Heinkels were still firing at us and a cannon shell knocked a saucepan off the truck above my head. This troubled me not at all; indeed I seemed to have lost all sense of fear, but my back felt wet and slimy so I looked over my shoulder to investigate the cause. My back was a red mass of blood and raw flesh. 'If you

aren't dead,' I thought, 'you will be soon.' Then I realised that
I was looking at all that remained of Osman the cook, who
had been lying beside me. I noticed also that my Bren gun-
ner, who had been close to my other side, had disappeared. I
felt a little light-headed but quite happy.

It's quite clear from this account that John Bowers was in 'psychological space' and not 'physical space' when he was out of his body. It
was (understandably enough) his own body he was most concerned
with, and it was his own body he saw. He was unaware of the cook,
who had been lying beside him - and was now not simply lying beside
him but spread all over his back, where he could hardly have failed
to be seen. John Bowers himself puts this whole experience into a
wonderful perspective when he says of it

> I have not regarded my NDE as proof of its own reality,
> though it felt convincingly 'real'. I am sometimes asked
> whether it made me more 'religious'. I suppose the answer
> is yes, though [I would regard it more as] an important epi-
> sode in my spiritual training. My NDE did, I think, enhance
> my capacity for 'superstition', for standing above and outside
> events, and the range of my religious experience. I have al-
> ways thought it strange how any experience can be recalled
> and described from two quite distinctive aspects: the first,
> a mundane view as a natural sequence of events - effect fol-
> lowing cause, complex and puzzling, perhaps, but entirely
> 'normal'; the second a 'superstitious' or religious view, stand-
> ing above the events and outside oneself, seeing or imag-
> ining a 'cosmic' pattern behind the mundane scene. The
> devout Muslim habitually takes this second view, regarding
> all events as the will of God - *maktub* as he would say.

A prominent feature of OBEs is that pain is entirely absent. Pain
has always intrigued philosophers because it is a sensation which is
constructed entirely by the brain. There is no pain world out there,
the only pain world is internal. Any sensation can become painful
when it is too strong, or when the body is deformed in some way so
that the nerve endings in the tissues are stimulated.

If pain is constructed entirely by the brain then it seems logical
to assume that the brain has special mechanisms which can switch it

off. And indeed, there is a psychological mechanism known as dissociation in which the switching off of pain does occur. There are some ceremonial and religious tribal dances, for example, in which people drive sharpened sticks through tongue and cheeks, and dance on, apparently oblivious of the pain.

It is also possible to switch off from emotional feelings, and of course quite often emotional and physical pain are linked. Thus it is not surprising that if the out-of-body experience is purely psychological, aspects of the psychological world that the individual finds unpleasant would be switched off. In many accounts we received, either intense unhappiness or intense physical pain seems to have been the trigger for an out-of-body experience. There is, of course, an alternative explanation, which is that pain can be synthesised only within the body, and that in the OBE 'something' really does leave the body and pain is not part of its repertoire of experience, of what it can do.

Does all this supply a complete explanation for the out- of-body experience? Well no, not entirely. It does provide a very good explanation for almost every aspect of a simple OBE which takes place spontaneously, or is triggered off by pain or emotional stress. But what about the OBE which occurs as part of the near-death experience, when someone is unconscious, or their brain function is compromised in a significant and serious way? Physiology tells us that in these conditions brain processes will be distorted, and the model created by the brain will lose precision and become confused.

A truly disorganised brain should not be able to produce clear psychological images. And yet what emerges from all these accounts is the startling clarity of the images seen. If the OBE is indeed only a product of brain function, then we need to look for clear evidence that a disorganised brain is capable of maintaining a psychological process with the degree of clarity that is reported. At the moment this is still lacking.

More fundamental and more difficult to explain is the remaining problem of information-gathering and transfer. If it could be proved that information really can be acquired in this way, that the mind is not local, that consciousness is not limited to the brain, but can become separate from it and exist outside it and independently of it, then a great many scientific concepts will have to be abandoned. Then we will have discovered something entirely new and very fundamental, and Nobel Prizes will be there to be won. We'll explore this possibility further in later chapters.

Chapter 4

The Darkness and the Light

AVON Pailthorpe is a social worker who describes herself as 'Christian but not churchgoing'; she finds organised religion 'difficult to take', and is quite sceptical about spiritualism. In other words, she is not the sort of person who would expect to have the kind of experience she describes here.

I was in a serious car accident in June 1986. I was driving in the central lane of a motorway, it was raining and although only just past midday, very dark. I realised a car in front of me had slowed down sharply, and I didn't want to brake for fear of skidding, so I steered right to the fast lane, and my car aquaplaned and went into a spin. I was struggling to control it, when suddenly I was not in the car any more.

I was in a black tunnel, or funnel, shooting through it incredibly fast. I was spinning, too, yet it was a different movement from that of the car. I felt I was shooting through this tunnel, head first, spinning round the edges - like water going down a plug, or like a coil. There was a loud roaring - it was very noisy, like the moment of birth. I had no time to feel afraid. I was very interested in what was happening, but I felt completely safe.

While I was shooting through this tunnel, which was completely black to begin with but seemed to be getting less dark and less clearly defined further on, I was aware of a terrific debate. This part is very difficult to describe because all

43

the words I can think of to use seem limited and therefore inadequate. Even 'terrific', as I just used it, I thought about for some time - great does not seem big enough, and I certainly don't mean 'terrifying' because it was the opposite of that. So the words I am using are only the nearest I can get to what this was, not a definitive description.

Around me, as the tunnel began to lighten, there were presences. They were not people, and I didn't see anything but I was aware of their minds. They were debating whether I should go back. This was what made me so safe; I knew that I had absolutely no responsibility to make any decision. This is an almost unknown situation for me, and it was wonderfully liberating. I also knew I could not influence what decision they made, but that whatever it should be it would be right. There was total wisdom and goodness in them.

I did not hear voices or words, so I don't know how I was aware of this discussion, but it was not only one presence: it was as if there were many minds gathered on each side into one, and these two debated the decision about me. I didn't know the outcome, but I was intensely interested and peaceful.

Then there was nothing.

Then I opened my eyes; I was astonished because I was in my body, in the car, and I hadn't expected to be. I thought, 'Oh, they've put me back!' and I think I was a little disappointed and I heard a sort of echo from the minds which gave me to understand I didn't have permission to go yet, because my children only have one parent. It was quite right, of course, but I have to admit I hadn't thought of them at all.

I can only have been away from my body for a short time, but it was strange to be in it - almost as though I had to reacquaint myself with it. It was a surprise to me to realise how clearly I felt myself to be myself without my body. I don't know if that makes sense, but what I am trying to say is that I had not known before that I was divisible from my body. I suppose I had believed that an individual, as that one unique person, is a soul and body combined, and that when the soul leaves the body it may still exist but not as that person any more. But when they put me back in my body I realised it was the vehicle for my being; I was still me when I wasn't wearing it.

So now I was back in the car, which had come to a standstill across the fast lane, with the driver's side towards oncoming traffic. I saw a white car approaching fast, and knew we would be hit, but because I knew I would not be killed I had time to think that my mechanic had told me of the steel-reinforced bar through the door and to wonder how it would save me.

In fact I learned afterwards that this car swerved and avoided us, but the car behind crashed into us. The crash knocked me deeply unconscious but when I came round the second time I was not surprised because I knew it was all right. I was only surprised, later, in the hospital, that the doctors were so worried and dashed around and worked so feverishly on me, because I knew it had been decided I should live. I tried to tell them it was all right, and I wasn't going to die, but they didn't understand.

In the popular imagination, it is the image of the light at the end of the tunnel that seems most to epitomise the near-death experience. Often the tunnel is seen as the passage, literal or figurative, to the next world. And yet it is by no means a universal part of the experience - only just over half (51 per cent) of our sample found themselves in a tunnel.

Avon's experience is also interesting for a quite different reason. It won't have escaped your notice that it occurred before the impact that led to her injuries. At that moment she was not dying. So why did she have a near-death experience? Was it the knowledge that she was close to death? Was it simply induced by terror? Time is often changed in near-death experiences, and some people describe the period of the experience as being almost an eternity. In Avon's case we are lucky, as it is possible to gauge both mental time and chronological time. There can only have been a few seconds between the spin and the impact - just about time for her to have the rational thought that the reinforced steel bar in her car might save her - and yet the time in the experience was clearly in a quite different framework. Approximately fifteen to twenty seconds must have elapsed from the time the white car went round her to the moment she was hit and lost consciousness. The time that it took the car to spin must be of the same order, possibly even shorter. Avon's whole experience occurred during this short period - less time than it takes to read about it.

45

This stretching-out of time is also seen in OBEs where accidents are involved. The person leaves his body, sees the accident about to happen but feels there is as much time as he wants before it occurs. Ms N. Baker, whose experience is described later in this chapter, says: 'The seconds that went by as the car was turning for me seemed an eternity.' When someone has a serious head injury, memory is sometimes lost for the time just before the accident. Indeed, it's possible to gauge the severity of a head injury by the length of time memory is a blank before the accident happened. In Avon's case the pre-traumatic amnesia, as it is called, starts as the white car is coming towards her. She must have seen that it avoided her but does not remember this, any more than she remembers the following car hitting her.

Avon is one of the few people who describes 'spinning' down the tunnel. This may be because she was indeed spinning in reality, and some component of this real experience was incorporated into the tunnel. The spinning may have destabilised her psychological world as she entered the tunnel, so that the brain would have no coordinates of her surrounding world to make a mental 'model'. The spinning down the tunnel seems a reasonable best guess for the brain to make about what was going on.

The sensation of rushing through the tunnel at an incredible speed is common. Mrs S. A. P. Thirlwall:

> I started zooming down this really black tunnel at what
> seemed like 100 mph. Then I saw this enormous brilliant light
> at the end which seemed to take on the shape of an angel.
> When I reached the light I heard a voice saying, 'Go back,
> go back,' and seeming to will me to make the return journey.
> I then came back along this tunnel, but very slowly.

Mrs Dawn Gillott recalled in Chapter 3 going down 'what seemed like a cylindrical tunnel with a bright warm inviting light at the end. I seemed to be travelling at quite a speed.' But more usually the sensation in the tunnel is more like floating or drifting, sometimes without direction, usually forwards. Very few people drift backwards, except sometimes when they return back into their body, which they usually do feet first. People who have lucid dreams in which they drift through space also report that it is easier for them to go forwards than backwards - although they also say that the only way they can

pass through a brick wall is to turn around and go through feet first!
Linda Gordon relates:

> I remember seeming to float through a long tunnel, which
> was dark from my end but became lighter. I know someone
> was calling me towards the light, but I didn't really know
> who it was. The voice was very comforting, I wasn't afraid,
> but more unsure of what to do ... suddenly I felt I wanted to
> go into the light. I was in no pain, my body felt warm and
> comfortable ... I was about to let myself be drawn deeper
> into the tunnel but then I remembered I'd just had a child,
> and suddenly I panicked, I wanted to go back, so I could
> look after her.

Mr R. J. Fletcher is one of the few people who traversed the tunnel in a more pedestrian way: 'I felt as though I left my body and
went walking towards a very bright white light which was at the end
of a long tunnel.' Although only half the people who wrote to us described a tunnel, over two thirds said they had experienced 'darkness' - a darkness that is seldom frightening, but is usually described
as soft, velvety blackness. Ella Silver:

> I realised I was looking at an immense space, black, velvety...
> I looked at this blackness with some interest and noticed
> there were no stars. I didn't feel suffocated, as if this velvet
> was close to me or claustrophobic. Behind my right shoul-
> der came a very gentle golden light (like old-fashioned oil
> lamplight)... I 'knew' I had to go through this blackness and
> I would know such joy unimaginable.

David Whitmarsh 'seemed to be floating in a beautiful velvet- like
darkness, feeling completely at peace away from the frightening flashes. I seemed to be going through a tunnel angled slightly downwards.'
And Judith Smith was 'in a velvety dark tunnel, incredibly soft darkness and surrounded by voices -1 could see no shapes - who were all
very pleased to see me. There was a tremendous sense of peace, love,
compassion and understanding. At the end of the tunnel there was a
very bright luminous light.' Sometimes the passage to the light that
people describe is not really a tunnel, though it usually has tunnel-like
features - and nearly always the welcoming light is seen shining ever

more brightly at the end. Sheila Berry was aware of moving down 'a dark country lane with high hedges. At the bottom of the lane there was a cottage with a light in the window.' W. C. Ball felt himself being drawn through 'a dark round corridor with a light at the end'.

Could it be that some people interpret an image of darkness with a distant light as a tunnel (like a railway tunnel), while others do not make this connection? That is certainly a possibility, but it would not explain the tunnel in the following experience, which is unusual in that it takes such a definite 'tunnelly' form. It was the long hot summer of 1976, and Mrs Jenny McMillan, who was twelve weeks pregnant, was admitted to hospital with a threatened miscarriage. It was a Sunday afternoon, the sister was off duty and the ward short-staffed. She was examined, put in a side ward on a saline drip, and told that they would keep an eye on her and might have to operate later.

My husband stayed with me and the bleeding became heavier and heavier. A couple of times he went out and told the SEN that I thought I was losing blood faster and she told him it was quite normal and not to worry. He was too shy to make a fuss and I was too faint to do so.

Eventually, when I was hardly conscious, he more or less dragged the nurse in to look at me whereupon all hell broke loose and the room was instantly full of people. He was sent out but I vaguely remember the conversation through a haze.

'What's her blood pressure?'

'I can't hear it.

'Let that drip run as fast as it'll go. What's her pulse?'

'I can't feel it.'

After that I faded out and found myself up at the top left-hand corner of the room against the ceiling, looking down in quite a detached way at all the people fussing about round my body. I realised that I must be dying and the odd thing was that I didn't mind in the least. I remember being very interested in the experience in a very unemotional academic way and feeling that it was quite an adventure - no regrets at all. While I was there, I was very surprised at myself for feeling like this. My husband and two-year-old son were everything to me and I was shocked and amazed at myself for not minding the thought of leaving them, yet I was overwhelmed by a feeling of peace such as I had certainly not known in all my adult life. I knew how devastated they would be at my death but even this did not really move me. I felt extraordinarily comfortable, relaxed and free of any cares at all.

Geographically, as I have said, I was up at the top corner of the room. There was a big sash window below me which was open at the top and through which the blazing light of that hot summer was coming in and I was vaguely surprised to discover that that was not the way out. Against the ceiling beside me was a wide-bore pipe or narrow tunnel through which I was obviously meant to make my exit and in the distance at the end of that it seemed to be even brighter. Bright light was nothing exceptional that summer, but this did seem to be actually like the sun itself up there. The pipe itself was corrugated or ridged in some way, rather like the sort of tube that you can attach to a tumble-drier to let the damp air out of a window.

I never actually went past the entrance to the pipe. I seemed to hover quite comfortably near the entrance for what seemed like a few minutes. Certainly there was no feeling of hurry or panic of any sort, nor of any force pulling me in either direction. It was just peaceful and interesting and detached. I cannot say that it was an intensely mystical or religious experience. It was not, but I did feel that whatever was at the other end of the tunnel would be very pleasant and in no way frightening.

A remarkable feature was the complete silence. I was only a few feet away from the people round my body whom I could see were very busy and who must have been talking in fairly agitated voices, but I did not hear any of their conversation once I had left the bed. They seemed very far away. Neither did I hear any traffic noise or any of the other general hospital noises that there must have been. However, unlike the window, this did not seem at all odd.

The next thing I was aware of was that I was very much back in my body and being rushed along the covered ways that joined the building of the old hospital on my way to the theatre. The whole experience seemed like a bad dream but the 'near death' in the middle of it stood out clearly as a bright light in the middle of a grim year.

Seventeen years on, the whole experience is still quite clear in my mind. Although it had a dream-like quality, the memory has faded far less than some very important events, both happy and sad, in my normal life, despite the fact that I have rarely discussed it and only written it down once and never read it since. I had never heard of anyone else who had experienced anything similar until about ten years afterwards and felt that no one would believe me anyway and might put it down to hysteria, hallucinations or something similar brought about by my rather depressed state at the time. It has left me with a complete absence of fear of my eventual death itself, although the horror of an untimely parting from my family has returned to the normal level.

Mrs McMillan became unconscious because her blood pressure was low and her pulse very weak - in essence, this was a faint. But her individual consciousness continued, and this does not happen during a faint; consciousness returns only when the faint is over. There are other odd characteristics about this experience which don't fit the pattern of a faint. For example, vision remained although hearing disappeared - Mrs McMillan remarks on the 'complete silence' - and hearing is usually the last sense to go in a faint. People who faint shut their eyes, and I would suspect that Mrs McMillan's eyes were also shut. The world that she then entered contained visual data of people scurrying about but without sound.

However, vision was more psychological than physical; the ceiling became distorted and a tunnel appeared in it. Why should she imagine (or fantasise, or hallucinate, or dream) a tunnel? Mrs McMillan herself is surprised at this - the logical place for her to escape is through the conveniently open window, and yet she realises that it is through the tunnel she has to go. It is as if the experience blends two streams. One contains elements of reality - the doctors scurrying around beneath her, the open window; the other, the appearance of the tunnel, is clearly psychological.

Mrs Margaret Dinkeldein also describes a tunnel of concentric circles which sounds very similar. Margaret, a registered nurse who describes herself as a 'basically down-to-earth person with plenty of friends and outside interests', had this experience in 1979, while giving birth to her third child. It was a difficult and protracted labour, with the baby in an awkward position, but she was given no drugs, only gas and air.

At the time I had read nothing about the subject and remember feeling somewhat loath to talk to anybody about
it for fear that they would dismiss it as hallucination. For
me it was the most glorious and uplifting experience and it
utterly convinced me that death was certainly not 'the end'
but the beginning of something else. I clearly remember
thinking at the time that it was ironic to be actually giving
birth at the time, when in fact I myself was being born into
another existence.

However, I felt a very intense pull back from the threshold to this other 'place' mainly because of my strong feelings of responsibility to the baby and the rest of my family. I
was aware of this indescribable light after the typically rapid
journey down the tunnel of concentric circles. I heard one
of the medical students say, 'She's stopped breathing.' Before
they had time to take action I had made an almighty effort,
taken a few very deep breaths and pushed out a hefty 9lb
10 oz baby boy. My husband was by my side and confirmed
that I seemed to have stopped breathing for fifteen to thirty
seconds, although I did not actually have a cardiac arrest. I
felt absolutely no physical desire to breathe again.

Again, one can see the mind and brain interacting to produce the
imagery of the NDE. It seems as if the mind has the 'feeling' of going through a tunnel; what the brain does is to create an image to fit
this feeling state. Sometimes, it seems, it does not do this too successfully. Jane Dyson had an NDE while in intensive care on a life-
support system after a serious car accident. She says:

I had the incredible experience of knowing I was dying and
going through a bright shining tunnel towards dazzling light
at the end. I felt quite calm, apart from feeling surprised that
the tunnel was made of polished metal, jointed and held together with something like rivets. Although I was not aware
of the phenomenon [of the NDE] before my own experience,
I felt it should have been more ethereal somehow. When I
got to the point where the light was so bright and I knew I
was at the end, I had this feeling that I had to return back
- probably the thought of leaving so much unfinished at
home, and my three daughters needing me - so with great

and positive effort I turned back. My feet felt like lead but as I walked back to life the light threw my shadow on to the floor of the tunnel as I walked away from it.

Mrs Dyson's awareness that the tunnel conjured up by the brain was not quite right, did not quite correspond with the way she was feeling, is fascinating. It shows once again that what often seem to be the most exciting parts of the NDE - the adventures, the complex visual imagery - are only a side issue, the product of the individual brain. What we can learn from the NDE is probably less to do with what seems to happen than with the feelings experienced.

Maurice James, who suffered two cardiac arrests in intensive care, told us about a series of fascinating experiences he had during this time. He too went through a tunnel, but a quite different, more colour-ful tunnel than those we've looked at so far.

The sensation was of being weightless and falling down or into a kaleidoscope of ever-changing colours. The colours were pleasant and I was not in the least bit frightened, but I sensed that I did not want to go at the moment. I fell down the kaleidoscope tunnel many times, sometimes going deep-er than others.

I felt I was on a yo-yo but that the force which brought me back was mine to control. I also have the feeling that as I gained confidence I was able to descend deeper. Several times I went beyond the end of the kaleidoscope tunnel and was able to see the world beyond. It was as though I was at the entrance and was able to have a good look but also to be able to go in or stay was my decision. I had the sense that I still had work to do and could go in a minute - a similar feeling to those one had as a child when one had to make a decision about whether to go out to play or stay and finish one's home-work. The land beyond the entrance was beautiful and like a grassy meadow in a valley bounded by low hills. It was very green and pleasant and warm and filled with a golden sunlight - I could feel the warmth from where I stood at the entrance. A faceless figure who was alone kept asking me in -'Come, come' - and he would reassure me constantly. He seemed to have human form but his face was indistinct. I would have no fear of dying and leaving this world as I believe I glimpsed a small view of what lies ahead. I had the feeling of peace and beauty and utter serenity. I also had the feeling of guilt if I had gone alone without my wife and did not feel I could leave her in the cold world I was about to desert.

What is unusual in this experience is the degree of control Mr James felt he had about entering his kaleidoscopic tunnel - as he grew more confident, he could go deeper. For most people there is no element of choice about entering the tunnel, though decisions are often involved later, when the time comes to return. But in fact for Mr James the decision to go deeper was very much bound up with the decision about whether to go or stay in 'the world beyond'. His direction of travel through the tunnel is unusual too: as we've already mentioned, it's rare for the tunnel to lead downwards, perhaps because in our culture 'down' is usually associated with Hell. But this is clearly not so in this experience: the sensation of going deeper was for Mr James a positive step towards what lay ahead of him.

The Light Holds All the Answers

We were coming home from a party and my boyfriend was driving. I was tired and closed my eyes, so I never saw what happened when the car left the road and turned over and over before landing in a field.

The seconds that went by as the car was turning for me seemed an eternity. The first thing I recall is feeling very light-headed, almost like being in a drunken state. My body tingled. I had butterflies in my stomach. My mind was worried. Then, suddenly, I became detached from my worldly body - I was seeing my life flash before me, recalling my family, friends, the man on the bus, the lady in the shop - and feeling confused but happy. At this time I was in a tunnel-like black space. Just beyond a light was glowing invitingly. I was encouraged by a strong feeling to enter the light. I approached without haste as I felt the light was part of the jigsaw to which I rightfully belonged.

I was peaceful, totally content, and I understood I was born on earth and knew the answer to every mystery - I was not told, I just knew, the light held all the answers.

Then there was sudden confusion. I had to go back to the tunnel, quickly; something was wrong. I was upset and scared. I thought of my family and friends and earthly life. I was travelling. I regained my body and all emotions; I panicked and felt pain, tremendous pain, all over my body.

I believe I died for a short time. I am not a particularly religious person, but this experience has totally changed my life ... I know there is some form of life after death and it is a truly wonderful 'Heaven'. I love life and live it to the full. I'm just happy to be allowed to live on this Earth for this comparatively short time.

In most religions and mystical traditions, light holds a special significance, equated with consciousness, with God, with knowledge. It seems as if light is a fundamental part of our psychic structures. People who meditate regularly find that no sooner have they turned their attention inwards than they enter into a band of consciousness which is primarily composed of light. The light experienced in meditation has many of the qualities of the light of the NDE, such as that reported above by Ms N. Baker. It often contains total knowledge, but its predominant quality is that of bliss and universal love. For those who meditate, a few minutes spent resting in this internal light changes the structure of the day.

Certainly, for those who have an NDE it is the experience of light which seems to hold most meaning. It is also one of the elements of the NDE that occurs most frequently. In 72 per cent of the near-death experiences we were told about, light was a predominant feature. Its qualities are always described positively. 'The light was all love and peaceful. It seemed a beautiful place to go but it wasn't my time to go.' The light is compelling, and has a magnetic quality so that you are drawn towards it.

'I could see the light at the end and knew I must get to it.' 'I saw a distant light that was friendly and felt myself drawn towards it. There was just a feeling of tremendous peace.' Although the light is nearly always described as brilliant, it is never dazzling. Often the point is made that it can be looked at directly, although if it was seen in everyday life it would be bright enough to hurt your eyes. Usually it is described as white or golden, and nearly always it has a quality of warmth. 'The light was lovely and warm', 'everything became warm and bright and light and beautiful'. Although some people describe entering the light and feeling themselves enfolded in it, enveloped in warmth and love, for others there is a realisation that the light marks a point of no return - they are aware that if they enter it, they will not come back.

Richard Hands experienced 'a blackness with a pinpoint of light far off in the distance. I feel drawn towards the light, but there is a terror and a feeling that I do not wish it to pull me towards it. My mother is with me in this scene, trying to pull me back from the light. There is also a wind rushing past, towards the light.' Richard Hands' experience is not typical, because although the magnetic quality of the light is there, and Richard feels drawn towards it, it also seems to hold a threat. He does not want to go there. Richard's experience, recounted in Chapter 12, occurred during a childhood illness and it could be argued that at some level he is aware that his mother is trying to hold him back. But this is not a particular characteristic of childhood experiences. From other accounts we were given (detailed in Chapter 12, which deals with children's NDEs) it seems as though even when children are aware that their parents are grieving for them, and even though they love them, their attraction to the light is far more compelling.

Most adults mention this, and are puzzled by it, too. So strong is their longing to get to the light that the people they love the most cease to matter to them. The most likely explanation of Richard's ambivalent feelings is simply that he did not experience the strong positive emotions which are so often reported.

Usually, but not always, the light is perceived at the end of a tunnel, drawing nearer and nearer and growing brighter and brighter. We came across no one who experienced the darkness of the tunnel without also seeing the light at the end, but it seems that it's perfectly possible to experience only the light, without the darkness. David Verdegaal, for example, remembered:

> Then I saw a light that seemed to grow brighter and brighter until its brilliance had completely encircled me, as if my very soul had been transformed and enveloped in love.
>
> It was then that I had the sensation of being gathered up and held like a newborn child. Nestling in the warmth of this loving embrace, I knew that nothing could ever harm me again. Whether I was to live or die, I knew I should be given the strength to continue on. At the time I didn't know who I was or what kind of life lay ahead, but now I had the certainty that God would be leading the way. It was then that the Lord took me by the hand ...

A few people simply describe a tunnel of light.

Hazel Graham: 'I felt "floaty" and then I was in a tunnel of light...' Audrey Organ: 'Here I was in a tunnel of glorious golden light...' Jean Giacomozzi: 'I recall floating in a very bright tunnel.

Everything seemed so calm and peaceful.' H. N. Smith: 'There was an intense white light all around, so bright that I could not see any colours.' Elizabeth Rogers is another experiencer whose NDE strongly featured light.

> Fifteen years ago when I was fifty-nine I had a heart-attack. An iron band around my chest was getting tighter and tighter. The doctor came, and when he left to ring for an ambulance he warned me not to move on any account. Then everything became warm and bright and light and beautiful. The iron band was gone and I was travelling along a tunnel. It was light, light, light. I didn't move my feet, I just 'floated' I suppose. But it was calm and peaceful and just lovely. Gradually there was a brilliant light at the end - really brilliant - and I knew I was going right into the growing heart of that light, but then I saw a group of people between me and the light. I knew them; my brother, who had died a few years before, was gesticulating delightedly as I approached. Their faces were so happy and welcoming. Then somehow my mother became detached from the group. She shook her head and waved her hand (rather like a windscreen wiper) and I stopped, and I heard the doctor say, 'She's coming round,' and I was in my bed and the doctor and my husband were there. My first words to the doctor were, 'Why did you bring me back?'

'Something Beyond the Light'

Henry Foster, a college lecturer, had been under a long period of stress and was feeling extremely tired. At work one day a student asked him a question he felt he should have been able to answer himself.

> This was for me the last straw. I suddenly felt all my strength draining from me and there was a sensation of sinking. When the head of department arrived I was slumped back in a chair and, in his words, apparently lifeless. I experienced a feeling of utter peace and was conscious that I was smiling.

56

Around me was an overall brightness (not brilliance) and there was a distant bright light to which I was drawn. I was moving through a tunnel of beautiful light towards something which I can only describe as a presence (either the light or something beyond the light). I had no sensation of being called or beckoned, the presence was simply waiting for me. Something inward told me 'not yet', and the light began to recede. I came round to find myself lying back in the chair.

The doctor told me later that at the time I collapsed my blood pressure had plummeted and I came very near to having a stroke.

My head of department told me that when he came into my office and found me slumped over the chair he immediately felt for my pulse and looked into my eyes and his first-aid knowledge indicated to him that I had died. He was on the point of rendering first aid when I breathed very deeply and said, 'It's all right, I'm coming back.' I cannot remember saying anything but I believe that this indicates that I had made the decision not to go, and not any other person or presence.

This 'presence' - 'either the light or something beyond the light', as Henry Foster put it - is something many people feel. It seems to be this which has the power to draw people towards it, and for some people the NDE culminates in a meeting with this 'being of light'. Mrs A. Burns reported:

Then everything went very dark and there was the feeling of going down a tunnel with a teeny speck of light in the distance which gradually got larger until everything was very white, very bright, but there was a softness to it. It was almost like mist gradually dispersing. As it got clearer I knew instinctively that in just a moment I would come face to face with my 'maker', as I thought of him, rather than God.

The positive emotion, the strong feelings of love and joy which the experience of the light in the NDE so often evokes are described very movingly in the following account, sent to us by Mr G. Thomas, a seventy-year-old man who had a near-death experience during

57

a heart-attack when he was fifty-five. He was taken into hospital and given an injection. The pain slowly left his body and he fell asleep.

> Now this is where I had the most wonderful experience. I slowly floated down a tunnel, not afraid in any way but looking forward to something. When it came I was absolutely at peace and going towards the most wonderful light; believe me, it was great. No worries, problems or anything, just wonderful. At the centre of this light there stood a figure with hair down to his shoulders, dressed in a robe with wide sleeves which reached down to the floor. I was going to ask him something, but another being came into this glorious light and spoke to him first. Then he went away so I was waiting - I didn't want to leave this man. I wanted to stay with him and stay in this wonderful glow, but slowly he waved towards me in such a way as to indicate, go away, go back, but when he did this I felt, oh no, I don't want to leave, please don't send me away, let me be with you forever. I woke up and found I was wired up to the heart machine. I was told by the man in the next bed that earlier the nurses had been very worried about me and there had been a lot of rushing around my bed.
>
> I did go to church when I was a little child, but I was never a regular churchgoer. So I wonder and wonder what did I see and feel. I feel very positive that I must have been 'over'; it was the most wonderful thing that has happened to me. When I got home ten days later I had to tell my wife what happened. I got so excited to tell someone that I nearly burst into tears because I wanted everyone to have the same experience. It was wonderful.

About a quarter of the people who told us about their experiences were aware of some spiritual 'presence'. Although the 'being of light' always has spiritual significance, it is only seldom that people describe seeing a particular religious figure such as Christ. Even those people whose Christian faith is strong don't always see Christ. Much more often there is a feeling of 'coming before one's maker': the being is felt as 'God' in a very broad sense. Perhaps 'neutrally spiritual' is the nearest one can get to the feelings the being evokes. Mrs Holyoake is one of the few people to whom the being of light seemed to be Jesus. This is how she describes her experience.

All of a sudden my eyes were drawn to the corner of the bedroom door. A brilliant light appeared - it was taking over my bedroom and as it did so I floated above my body.

This place was amass with beautiful flowers - the perfume from them was very strong - and then Jesus came walking up to me with arms outstretched. He was dressed in a long white robe, his hair to his shoulders, ginger-auburn, and he had a short beard. The nearer he got to me I could feel the warmth from his body and as his hands almost touched my face he said, 'Come!' and again, 'Come!' This time I felt myself beginning to step over, and yet I was trying to speak to him but I could only croak because my mouth was dry and my tongue swollen. I was trying so hard to tell him that I couldn't leave until I had kissed my husband and three children goodbye. Jesus heard me and understood, he smiled and started to walk backwards, taking his magnificent garden with him and the light.

As this is one of the few accounts we were given of an experience in which Christ is seen as the being of light, it's worth looking at it quite closely. Most of us, whether Christians or not, have an 'identikit' image of Christ, and it is usually very similar to the one described by Mrs Holyoake. But it is simply that - a composite image based on the different versions of Christ depicted in countless religious pictures.

No one has any notion of what Christ actually looked like. There is no description of him in the New Testament. We have no idea whether he was fair or dark, short or tall, even whether he had a beard. It is highly unlikely that his hair was auburn, a colour quite atypical of Mediterranean races. In fact the first Christian images bore much more resemblance to the Roman sun god Apollo - blond and beardless - than to the consensus we have finally arrived at after more than a thousand years of artists' impressions. I think we have to make a distinction between the feeling of the presence of Christ in the experience, and the image which the perceiving brain creates to fit it, which is simply drawn from the picture-bank of memory.

It is noticeable how many people describe the light as growing brighter and brighter, even if they do not see it as a light at the end of a tunnel. Is it possible that the tunnel might be some kind of optical illusion, that the mind assumes the tunnel simply because of this perception of light at a distance, growing larger? One explanation which has been put forward to explain the tunnel-and-light phenomenon of the NDE is that it is due to lack of oxygen (anoxia) in the brain. The visual system is organised in such a way that there are many more cells devoted to the centre than to the outside of the visual field. Dr Sue Blackmore has suggested that a lack of oxygen will cause random activity throughout the visual system, giving the impression of lots of bright lights flashing in the middle where there are lots of cells, but fading out towards the periphery of the visual system, where there are fewer. This will give the impression of a bright light at the end of a dark tunnel. As the oxygen level falls even more, and the brain activity goes up and up, so this bright bit in the middle will get bigger and bigger, and you will get the effect of rushing through a tunnel towards a light. Eventually the whole area would seem to be light, giving the feeling that you have actually entered the light. However bright the light it will not hurt your eyes, because it isn't seen with your eyes, only by the part of the brain that 'sees'.

If the oxygen supply is restored, then the random firing stops, the light dims, and the sensation of movement is reversed so that you feel that you shoot backwards down the tunnel again.

This is an enticing model, but it has a major flaw. Random firing just does not hold water as an explanation of the tunnel-and-light phenomenon. To the perceiver the experience is too organised, too structured - there is nothing random about it. Mrs Thirlwall, for example, (see Chapter 12) saw light taking on the form of an angel, and many others describe seeing the being of light. Could it be that random firing is interpreted by the brain as an angel or a being? Probably not, because if such a structured pattern is seen, then this means that the brain is functioning adequately and random firing would not occur.

It is difficult to reconcile this explanation, too, with the fact that the light often seems to have physical properties. Jane Dyson, whose experience appears earlier in this chapter, describes the walls of her tunnel as being like 'polished metal', as though the light was reflected off them. Mr H. T. Mill saw light spilling out from behind a rock, as if the rock was blocking the light. Light generated by random firing would not be able to take on structure in a visual field containing well-formed objects. Mrs Hover (Chapter 14) describes seeing 'ordinary' sunlight outside a window at the same time as she saw the light at the end of a tunnel which suddenly appeared in the ceiling, and she makes a clear distinction between the two. It is difficult to see how random firing and cerebral anoxia could account for this.

Finally, there is the real stumbling-block that the tunnel-and-light experience also occurs in its entirety in situations in which there is no question of the brain being devoid of oxygen. So destruction of cerebral mechanism by lack of oxygen cannot be the mechanism. The perception of inner light is a very common feature.

People who have pathological states such as hypomania, in which there is an elevation of mood, sometimes perceive an internal light, though often they will project this outwards so that they describe the doctors or nurses looking after them as being surrounded with light.

This inner light is also associated with strong positive emotions in experiences which are not pathological. It can be induced by drugs, but it is also a hallmark of all kinds of mystical experience, whether they arise spontaneously, during meditation or in the NDE. Internal light seems to be part of a spiritual dimension; spiritually developed people are said to emit light - in stereotypical Christian iconography light is seen as the halo over the saint's head. It is as if when you probe the mind in a particular way you come down to a bedrock of light and positive emotion. The light does indeed seem to be 'part of the jigsaw to which I rightfully belong'.

Chapter 5

Coming Home

THE following account is taken from a letter I received from Mr J. Inman, who wrote to me after seeing the QED television programme 'Glimpses of Death' because, he said, of the 'complete dissimilarity of my own experience from the classical tunnel experience shown on the programme'.

In December 1969, when I was thirty-six, I crashed through a wall at high speed. I can recall, vaguely, lying on my back in the roadway for a brief moment, trying to tell an indistinct figure bending over me that I felt cold. I felt no pain at all, although I have been told since that my injuries were very serious. I have no further recollections for, I believe, twenty-eight days, although I have been told that I drifted in and out of consciousness for brief periods. I had to be resuscitated on five separate occasions during the first few days. Obviously I cannot say when I had my 'experience'. I can recall, however, a 'state', for how long it lasted I cannot tell, but surmise that it must have been of short duration. This 'state' cannot really be described, for words are inadequate. Suffice to say that at no time before, or since, have I experienced such a feeling of complete release. I did not see anything, nor was I aware of being of solid matter, having a body, hands, feet etc.; nor even conscious thought: it is only with hindsight that I can interpret. I was merely, for want of a better word, a feeling, a sensation of serenity,

timelessness, warm and comfortable in total darkness, floating high above a distant cacophony of indistinct voices, the
sound of feet, metal objects being dropped or knocked over.
I have no recollection of returning; the next memory I have
is of lying in a bed looking up at the ceiling.

I have tried over the years to keep this incident in objective perspective. It would be all too easy for me to put images to the 'state' itself and to the voices and sounds that
intruded on the 'state' I had become. With hindsight I can
only liken that condition to a feeling similar, I would imagine, to that of being wrapped up in soft black velvet, a sense
of complete release from care, no thoughts or memories, no
concern or fear and a sense of utter timelessness.

My own belief - and I am not a religious person (I did
not believe in an afterlife before this happened) - is that
we leave this life as easily as passing from one room to another, into a state - a period of waiting, and that state, be
it the soul, electricity or whatever energy, then passes into
another receptacle, perhaps shortly after conception to be
born again.

Before my experience I had wondered, like most, about
death, and, like most, was afraid of the unknown. I now
count myself among the privileged in that I now know that
there is no pain, there is nothing other than the ending of
one chapter and the turning of the page.

Is this really so very different from the 'typical' near-death experience? True, it does not have the vivid visual imagery of some experiences. And yet it seemed to me that in essence it was very similar
indeed.

It is interesting to compare this experience with that of Mrs Langschield, who had a near-death experience during childbirth. She,
too, watched a television programme on NDEs and was struck by
the ways in which her own experience differed from those depicted. She says: 'I saw no person or persons. I did not hear sweet singing or music. I did not see magnificent gardens and landscapes etc. I
did not look down on my bodily self.' For her, the truly memorable
thing about the experience was 'the absolute peace, the oneness, the
completeness'. She too felt that no words were adequate to describe
or explain the experience, and describes a sense of timelessness. She

felt as though she were being 'transported back into another dimension which had been there all along, as if I were going home, so familiar was it to me.' She sees her experience as 'a very real journey into the realm beyond. The knowledge of it has never left me, never faded or diminished over the past years.' Neither of these two people, one of whom describes himself as 'not a religious person', the other a practising Roman Catholic, had any of the visual imagery or the encounters which are part of the world of many other experiences. And yet for both it was a deep spiritual experience with lasting significance. Both mention something which is primary to the NDE: not only is the experience felt as complete, but this completeness is a 'coming home'. It is as if they had always known this state and that birth, life with its pain, and death, are all a departure from an underlying consciousness.

To me, it seems probable that this emotional state is primary and spreads into whatever imagery arises. When strong imagery is present it is coloured by fundamental feelings, and becomes an intensely emotional experience. The essence of each of these experiences was the 'feeling state' of absolute peace which lay at its heart. It is this feeling state more than anything else which seems to me to shape and define the near-death experience, and which makes the most lasting impression on the memory. If these feelings are present, they give meaning and emotional or spiritual significance to the experience: without them it may be neutral or occasionally frightening; interesting enough to remain in memory and yet still not felt to be of any great spiritual significance.

One of the accounts which seems to demonstrate this very clearly is that given to us by Richard Hands, whose childhood NDE is described in Chapter 12. Richard is a scientific journalist and an atheist. He is also one of the few people for whom an NDE had no spiritual or religious significance. Reading through his experience, the absence of any of the positive feelings so many people describe is striking, and so too is the lack of strong imagery. Richard recalls an image of blackness with a pinpoint of light, far off in the distance. He felt drawn towards the light, but there was also a feeling of terror and a desire not to enter it. His mother was also in this scene, trying to pull him back from the light.

About 88 per cent of those who filled in our questionnaire described feelings of calm or peace or joy during their experience (82 per cent mention peace and calm, about 40 per cent feelings of joy). This means that these positive feelings are far more common than the light or the tunnel, or indeed any of the other phenomena of the NDE.

James Carney: 'The peace and happiness was overwhelming.'

Henry Foster: 'I experienced a feeling of utter peace and was conscious that I was smiling.'

David Whitmarsh: 'I felt a complete sensation of happiness and contentment.'

Constance Cawthorne: 'I felt utter joy as I knew when I reached it I would find what I had been seeking.' Hilda Middleton: 'My experience of death was wonderful. I was floating high up, no pain, great joy, and no fear... I was overwhelmed with joy.'

When happiness is experienced it seems to be overwhelming, something quite different from ordinary, everyday happiness. The following accounts all convey the quality of this joy beautifully. First, Mrs C. Proctor:

> During the night after a serious operation I was aware of being above myself looking down at my body lying on the bed, nurses and doctors leaning over, checking blood pressure and blood transfusion. My 'mind' seemed then to be travelling down a long corridor at the very end of which a brilliant yellow light shone. I was filled with elation and pure joy. The nearest description of the feeling was what I felt as a child on the last day of the summer term, knowing that six weeks' holiday loomed ahead full of freedom and sunshine. I felt absolutely no fear at all, just utter pleasure, as if I was off somewhere wonderful.
>
> It was therefore with some astonishment that I awoke to find myself still in a hospital bed and very much earthbound. I cannot tell you how long I was in my state of bliss and I have never experienced anything like it since.

Ella Silver:

> I realised I was looking at an immense space, black, velvety. My mind seemed terribly clear and alert - more so than ever before. I was warm and comfortable. I seemed to be lying on my back, but when I tried to look along my body I found I couldn't move. I felt as if I didn't have a body, but was all mind.

I looked at this blackness with some interest and noticed there were no stars. I didn't feel suffocated, as if this velvet was close to me or claustrophobic. Behind my right shoulder came a very gentle golden light (like an old-fashioned oil lamplight). I tried to look at it but as I said I couldn't move my head. I 'knew' I had to go through this blackness and I would know such joy unimaginable. All my will was concentrating on 'going'. I never once thought of my husband or my children, who were quite young then. It all seemed terribly personal, nothing to do with anyone else.

I was aware at this point of muffled voices to my right. I still couldn't move and yet I could 'see' them. I assumed it was two men, although both had long hair to the shoulders. They were in the gloom a little way off from me. They wore long garments, white, with a cord around the waist. I 'knew' they were discussing me very deedily (sic) although I couldn't hear what they were saying. They stood close together and seemed to be looking down at something in their hands. One suddenly looked towards me. I didn't know him but he seemed to have great presence and authority. His face was very serious. He returned to the discussion and then in a beautiful voice, very loud, he said, 'She must go back.' Oh, the terrible feeling. I felt resentment. I didn't want to go back. I didn't feel they rejected me, because I knew they loved me. It just wasn't for me to decide.

My Christian name was being called by a different voice. I was suddenly cold and heavy and what I thought was a worm was being pushed up my nose. I struck out at the sister I recognised. The next day I felt I should explain and apologise. I thought she would scoff but she didn't.

She listened very quietly with her hand on my shoulder.

She told me they had been very concerned about me because they could not pull me out of the anaesthetic. I had been out for hours and my pulse was very low.

That day I was riddled with guilt because I had not considered my family, and I told my husband about it when he came in that night. He thought it was a dream because of the anaesthetic. I felt the sister believed me, strangely enough. I think I still believe it really happened. It's crystal clear to me. I have not heard a human voice so loving and yet so authoritative.

I have never before or since had such a feeling of 'knowing' for sure I would know joy. It was totally different from happiness. I felt my heart would burst with the excitement of expectation.

Ashley Coleman:

The pain was replaced by this wonderful feeling, such a contrast to the pain and suffering; I was convinced no living person could experience such joy. The only way I can explain it is think of the happiest moment of your life, and when you do, that happiest moment is awful pain compared to what you feel, and I will swear to that. You really want to stay where you are, even though you are aware something has changed or is changing. I'm convinced it was only my family that really brought me back. If I live for a thousand years I will remember it.

Religion, no matter what denomination, plays no part in it whatsoever. I would like to encourage people to be unafraid of death. I have a completely different attitude to life after death after my experience.

Deep joy of this ecstatic quality does seem to be different from ordinary happiness and pleasure. It carries with it, as already mentioned, the feeling of completeness and utter rightness. Similar states are described by people who have experienced altered states of consciousness, either those which occur spontaneously, as in the deep mystical experience, or those induced by meditational practices.

Fragments of this feeling are found in drug experiences and in people who have a pathologically elevated mood. The mystics claim that this feeling of 'coming home' with total joy, and the certainty that one has all knowledge of the universe, reflect the fundamental ground state of the universe. Even if one assumes that it arises through malfunctioning of the brain, it is difficult to explain why these feelings should be encoded in the brain. However they arise, they lead to the feeling of a transcendent reality beyond everyday experience.

Mrs Doreen Shingles reported her husband's NDE.

My husband was a strong, sporty and industrious man of fifty-seven, who had worked for the Ford Motor Company for forty-three years. In 1984 he was diagnosed as having stomach cancer and given one month to live. He said he would beat it and never accepted that he would die, referring to the cancer as 'Tubby the Tumour'. He suffered greatly but kept going and did live for six weeks. He became a Catholic on 12 September 1984, having thought about it for several years. On 13 September he paid the consultant for what was to be the last time, and when we returned home he was weary and went off to bed fairly early. When I went upstairs later he looked very peaceful and relaxed and I thought he might be dead. I'm a nurse and wasn't afraid and realised he was alive but in a deep sleep and breathing very quietly. At 11.30 p.m. he stirred and said he had died. I asked what it was like; he replied, 'Ecstasy.' He described the tunnel and light, then said they had sent him back to me as his work wasn't finished. Then he insisted on sitting on the edge of the bed saying he wasn't taking any chances (that being the 13th). I said, 'But we are not superstitious.' However, he stayed there until midnight and then got back into bed. A couple of days later I asked if he remembered what had happened and he repeated everything word for word, adding, 'If anyone asks if there is a God I shall say yes, I have seen him.' He went into hospital for the last days of his life and the nuns from the local convent went in relays to be with him up till his death. They all said he walked with God and I found that a great comfort, knowing what a good person he had always been.

Now here is a fully formed near-death experience in which there seems no possibility that brain chemistry was altered because the brain was in the process of dying. Can one find a psychological explanation? Mr Shingles certainly realised he was soon to die, and although he had a strong will to live he seems to have made psychological preparation by becoming a Catholic. It makes no sense to suggest that it was fear of death that triggered his experience. He was, however, certainly preoccupied with death, and if he had simply fallen asleep one might have expected the content of his dreams to have reflected this. But don't forget that this happened ten years ago, when very few people were aware of the phenomenon of the NDE. It seems too much of a coincidence that a dream would have incorporated the light and the tunnel and the encounter with God, and the instruction to return because of unfinished business. It clearly had the stamp of reality too: Mr Shingles was quite certain that he had actually died, though it is worth noting that however ecstatic the experience, he did not wish to repeat it there and then.

At the same time that people are experiencing these blissful feelings, they are also often aware that they are dying but totally unconcerned about it. They feel, as one person put it 'no regrets at leaving, nothing only pure joy and peace.' Another woman, recalling an experience she had as an eleven-year-old child with acute appendicitis, remembers: 'I longed to be able to tell my parents not to grieve, that if they could only know how joyously happy I was they would rejoice instead. For that is the dominant feeling, the memory and knowledge of ultimate, total peace.'

The Key to the Universe

With the peace often comes a feeling of profound knowledge, a realisation that you have been given the answer to all the secrets of the universe, as explained by Ms N. Baker in Chapter 4 - 'I was peaceful, totally content, and I understood I was born on earth and knew the answer to every mystery - I was not told, I just knew, the light held all the answers.' Audrey Organ recalled:

> I was going upwards and had great mental awareness, a sense of great excitement. All around me were the answers to everything, no puzzles because I had been given the key to understanding everything. What was so thrilling was that the perfect, logical simplicity convinced me that only the Creator could have made it so. The same wonder as when the blood or circulation is first explained and the 'How else could it be?' sense of it all breaks through. Enlightenment is the wonder, and here I understood the universe.

Sadly, when she came back, Audrey found that 'I kept the sense of having had a wonderful experience, a revelation. Unfortunately, the magic key to understanding pure logic had been taken from me. I still see through a glass darkly.' Perhaps the difference between this mystical state of pure knowledge and that of utter bliss or absolute peace is that the latter need no validation; the feelings are sufficient in themselves and demand no proof from any other source. Something of them usually remains, a permanent reminder on which the experiencer can draw. But in the long term, unfortunately, the secrets of the universe tend to remain a mystery. We have to accept that it is perfectly possible to have such feelings of total enlightenment and then return to a situation in which we are as much in the dark as ever.

Chapter 6

Visions of Paradise

THIS is how Eleanor Cleator describes what happened to her one New Year's Eve. Within a fortnight of her thirty-fifth birthday, she was at home looking after her mother, who had Parkinson's Disease and had to have everything done for her. Also at home was her war-disabled brother.

I was feeling ill and had not been able to get my mother up that morning. At midday I crept upstairs to bed on hands and knees. By midnight I was in unbearable pain. [Later Eleanor proved to have pneumonia and pleurisy.] I do not know exactly which evening it was but I was alone in bed when I knew 'something was going to happen'. I was not afraid, and felt a great confidence. I rose out of my body and went towards the front corner of the bedroom. I do not recall any tunnel or light, I was just in a wonderful peace and wellness in a beautiful landscape setting of grass, lawns and trees and brilliant light, diffused, not coming from any central source, with a feeling of being surrounded by wonderful love, joy and peace, no illness or pain.

I was in a little bower corner, on my own. Between me and this place there was a low green trellis fence, which stopped, leaving a gap at the end. I could so easily have gone through. But I knew without anyone telling me that I could not stay there. I could see people walking around purposefully - I particularly remember seeing two nuns walking along together. I did not see anyone I knew; I would have wished to go to someone in particular had I seen him.

The next thing I remember was floating along, passing through swathes of wonderful, beautiful, translucent colours, more beautiful than any I had ever seen on earth.

I have no idea of time throughout this experience.

I remember being horizontal, above my body in bed, back in my bedroom, when I slowly 'clicked' back into my body, and eventually tried moving an arm, a leg. I had to come back to accomplish my mission of looking after [my mother]. The experience has had a lasting effect upon my life; if that was 'near death' I have no fear when my time for dying comes. I look forward to it with expectation of that wonderful joy and peace. Although it took place thirty-seven years ago it is still as vivid and real as it was at the time, and it is difficult to find words to describe the wonderful experience.

When something happens to us which is outside the range of normal human experience, as described above by Eleanor Cleator, it is ineffable - we just don't have the right words to describe it. This feeling of being lost for words is common in people who have had near-death, or indeed any mystical experiences. When they are trying to describe it, you feel they are searching for the right word, the right image; for anything in their past experience which will help them to give you a picture of what it was that they felt. Often they'll say something like, 'It wasn't quite like that, but that's the nearest I can get to it.' But when words are found, a surprisingly uniform vision of Paradise emerges. It is a picture of a heavenly countryside where there may be brilliantly coloured birds and flowers, wonderful scents, heavenly music, friends or relatives who have died, and sometimes, especially in the case of children, living friends as well. Almost a quarter of the people who wrote to us described this kind of idyllic landscape.

Mrs J. Johnston: 'I floated upwards to a beautiful vivid green field.'

Jean Giacomozzi: 'I heard music and there was a beautiful smell.'

David Whitmarsh: 'Suddenly I found myself standing in a field of beautiful yellow corn. The sky on the horizon was the deepest of sky blues that I have ever seen and I felt even more at peace in this lovely tranquil place. The brightness was strong but not overbearing and I felt comfortable and appeared to be wearing a blue gown.'

Dennis Stone: 'I awoke in another world. I stood on the top of a beautiful valley, the sun was so warm. It seemed to stretch way into the distance ... there were no shadows down the valley.'

Mary Errington: 'I went through the dark tunnel out into a beautiful bright meadow. It was so peaceful - a peace that I can only describe as heavenly - and I was floating on this meadow towards a tree that had its branches outstretched, like arms waiting to welcome me.'

David Verdegaal described 'a garden where surely beauty had found its name'.

> This was an old-fashioned, typically English garden with a lush green velvet lawn, bounded by deep curving borders brimming with flowers, each flower nestling within its family group, each group proclaiming its presence with a riot of colour and fragrance as if blessed by a morning dew. The entrance to the garden was marked by a trellis of honeysuckle so laden that you had to crouch down to pass beneath while at the other end a rustic garden gate led to the outside. It was here that my walk through was to end as I was gently led through to the other side.'

Felicity Robinson wrote to us about her mother, who had an NDE during an operation for cancer in King's College Hospital, London, during which she was afterwards told she had nearly died.

> She spoke of going down a dark tunnel and there was at the end of it the most wonderful garden, filled with flowers which were beautiful - but she didn't actually enter the garden and the brightness, as the nurse or doctor was saying, 'Mrs Robinson, Mrs Robinson.' She said she hadn't wanted to come back but she felt very sad. She never forgot the experience.

Mrs G. U. Dunn found herself 'in a lane where there were very high ornamental golden gates'.

> Inside was the most beautiful garden, no lawn, path or anything else, but flowers of every kind. Those that attracted me most were Madonna lilies, delphiniums and roses, but there were many, many more ... I pushed the gates and they gave

way to my push, but try as I might I could not get in; there was something behind me on both sides which seemed to be stopping me from going in. I was so upset at not being able to get in, but in the end I gave up trying.

Mrs Dunn, like Felicity Robinson's mother, responds just as any of us might in everyday life if we had found the place we wanted to be and then discovered that we could not stay there.

She makes a real emotional response to what seems like a real situation - and it shows that the emotional apparatus of the brain is integrated and working in a normal way. It's a high-order response, as it includes an integrated feeling of 'I', a knowledge of what 'I' want, and the ability to respond in a socially appropriate way. This is not the sort of way that a confused or disorientated brain could respond. Neither is there anything fantastic or bizarre about the gardens; it is only their loveliness which is remarkable - that and perhaps the fact that they are remarkably free from gnats, midges, spiders and all the normal irritants of country life. In fact, it's rare for any kind of animal to figure in the NDE. Only for Mrs Jean Johnstone's father (Chapter 8), who saw 'all the dogs of our life' running to greet him, did animals play a significant part in the experience.

I find it surprising that these very similar images of Paradise recur so often. Is this vision of Paradise, this heightened and idealised pastoral world, simply the vision that feelings of peace evoke? If it is a personal vision then it's odd that there are not a few more disparate accounts. There must be plenty of people for whom spiritual peace is more likely to be found on a tropical island, for example, or a windblown Scottish moor, the top of a snow-clad mountain or even in the cloisters of a monastery. Although probably few people now really think of Heaven in terms of a bowered garden reminiscent of the biblical Garden of Eden, it may be that we are more culturally influenced by this myth than we realise.

Close Encounters

I looked up and whoosh, I was in a brightness and further up were masses of people all smiling and reaching out to welcome me. I was still moving up towards them when I saw my deceased mother - not the mother I had known, but I knew she was my mother, a young mother. She was smiling at me and had her hands stretched out to me. I was so happy. I was desperate to reach her. I had nearly got to her hands when I felt myself being pulled away from her. I got angry. I felt I had a long, long, long nightdress and I was being pulled downwards. I was desolate as the people and my mum disappeared. They had looked so happy and contented. I find it hard to describe the happiness on their faces. I wanted to be with them. It was no hallucination. How can you hallucinate a mother whom you knew and loved and remembered when she died, and see an entirely young beautiful girl, and each know who the other is? I do not grieve for my mother, I know she is happy.

How old do you feel? Although for most of us psychological age - the age we feel ourselves to be - stops somewhere around thirty-five or so, if we dream of people, we see them as their physical age. It's very unusual to have this perception of them as younger than they are - at their psychological, rather than chronological age - as S. Woodham describes above.

From all accounts it looks as if the heavenly country is a place where people are usually young and beautiful and certainly well and healthy. It is as if after death the distortion and disfigurement of the body by either age or illness disappears and you are made whole. A patient of mine told me an experience she had had while suffering from meningitis which illustrates this beautifully:

I remember feeling terribly ill with a splitting headache and going unconscious. Then I was aware that Jesus or somebody like him, possibly an angel, was standing beside the bed. He led me gently through the window and across the hospital lawn, which had been transformed into a heavenly scene. As we were walking we were joined by crowds of people. They were unwrapping bandages which were round their bodies or heads, throwing away their crutches, and taking off their plaster casts. It seemed to me that they had died and were being healed after death.

The encounters in a near-death experience are usually with people who are or were known and loved. Of the 38 per cent of our sample who met someone they knew, 50 per cent met a dead relative, 9 per cent a dead friend, and 38 per cent met someone who was still alive.

Quite a lot of people (40 per cent) were aware of strangers, and 33 per cent of religious figures. One interesting example is that of W.C Ball, who met relatives he had never known.

> I could see a wall and a gate, like an entrance. Behind the wall I could see my late grandparents on my father's side and an uncle who died before I was born, but the person with whom I seemed to be able to communicate I did not recognise. He was tall with fair hair, and his features were very clear. I felt I should know him, but did not. He asked me if I really wanted to be there. It felt so good, no more pain, and so relaxed as I had never felt before. My grandmother held out her hand to draw me in, but the man told me that I had so much to give and live for. At this point I re-entered my body and sprang back up to a seated position. I was no longer in the same pain and again I was sick, bringing up more clots of blood.
>
> I was afraid at that time to tell anyone. A while later I told my mother and father. My mother identified the man as her father, who had died when she was young, and can verify that I had at no time seen a picture of my grandfather.

Gillian McKenzie also encountered her grandfather, whom she had known and loved.

> A voice at the end said, 'Gill, you know who I am,' and I thought, 'Heavens, this is God and He knows my name.' Then the voice chuckled and said, 'Gill, there is someone here you do know.' It was my grandfather, who'd died two years before. 'Grandfather,' I said, 'I'm not staying here. Hamish can't cope, I've left a pile of shirts to be ironed and he doesn't know how to do them.'

I find it intriguing that no one described distressing meetings with long-gone enemies or with relatives they did not much care for even when they were alive. Is this wish fulfilment - we long for a continuation of personal consciousness, but maybe not for everyone? Is it simply that such experiences would be unpleasant, and therefore perhaps less likely to be reported? It is difficult to believe that everyone is well prepared for death and has their relationships in good order, that they are carrying over no negative emotions that might disturb the tranquillity of Paradise. It is pleasant to suppose, though, that the occupants of an afterlife, unlike a temporal one, are universally happy and welcoming, warm and loving.

The simplest explanation is probably that you cannot easily feel hate and love at the same time, and love is usually the predominant emotion in the near-death experience. Imagine someone you dislike. Now try to imagine yourself filled with the kind of universal love that so often suffuses people in the near-death experience. In this emotional state it must be very hard to hate your enemy.

Some Odd Encounters

Not everyone meets familiar friends or relatives in the world beyond. Here are three experiences in which more unusual encounters are related.

Mrs Nita McCallum had her experience at a time when she was very ill and in excruciating pain. At the time, she says, she thought she was unique and said little about it, even though over the years her whole lifestyle was changed as a result. She wrote to me after seeing the QED television programme because her own experience was so different.

> At the time of my NDE I was a practising Roman Catholic. Had I died I would most certainly have expected that any visions I had would have related to my faith, and that if I was to see a being of light I would have related it to Jesus or Mary or an angel. As it was, when I suddenly found myself in this gentle glowing light and standing a little below the three beings above me, they appeared to me as young Indian men, and, though they were dressed alike in high-necked silver-coloured tunics with silver turbans on their heads, I felt they were young Indian princes, or rajas. Two were facing each other and the third facing me. And from a jewel in the centre of each forehead or turban three 'laser' beams emitted, meeting in the centre.
>
> My whole lifestyle was changed as a result - much reading about various religions and philosophies.

Mrs Audrey Quinn was a thirty-nine-year-old housewife, and an ex-nurse and midwife, when she had her near-death experience while critically ill after major abdominal surgery in 1980.

When I recovered consciousness, not knowing how near death I had been, I was surprised to see my husband and calmly recounted a vivid dream.

I was floating in total blackness when far ahead of me I saw a wrought-iron gate - a tall church window-shaped gate - which was open. Through the gate I saw a group of three figures, apparently male, all dressed in Arab-type flowing gowns with hoods which looked to be made from a type of chain-mail. The figures were standing on a platform, much like the Olympic type of stands, the middle one higher than the two side ones. The figures and the gate seemed to be lit from within - not quite fluorescent - but their surroundings were still totally black.

I gently floated on towards the gate, then the middle figure looked at me and slowly shook his head, giving me the impression that I wasn't to be allowed in yet, though no words were spoken.

When I awoke I felt very much at peace. I have since told people that I no longer fear death itself I've never felt the need to talk about it but have happily related the events to any inquiring person - indeed, to my own father, who has had several severe cardiac arrests and who has told me he is terrified of dying.

I have never been a particularly religious person, though brought up C of E, and I've never found any answers in religion. But since my NDE I find I have become more sympathetic to other people's problems. I have become a Samaritan, hoping to help others in some small way. I try to tell people that life is short and we must all make the best of it that we can - as someone once said, 'Life is not a dress rehearsal.'

Three figures also appeared to Mr R. J. Fletcher and to Hazel Graham. Mr Fletcher saw 'three figures standing at the end of the bed and I kept wishing they would go away so that I could go to the light, which to me was lovely and warm.' Hazel Graham:

I felt 'floaty' and then I was in a tunnel of light. At the end I seemed to be standing in front of three old Chinese men who all had long white beards, and who also wore white robes. They looked pleasant but rather puzzled. One said to me, 'You should not be here, it is not the Year of the Seventh Horse.' I remember waking up and feeling so well I got up for tea.

The doctor called in later as he said he thought I might need to be taken into hospital. He was amazed to see me up and about - and I had not even taken the pills. I did not tell him about my experience.

Hazel's encounter with the puzzled Chinese gentlemen took place when she was very ill with a 'flu-type virus, but not near death. Was it just the kind of hallucinatory episode that often accompanies a high temperature? Maybe, but most people who have such episodes recognise them as such and quickly forget them. For Hazel herself it was 'a glimpse behind the curtain', which she has remembered for twenty years.

Westerners are used to thinking in threes. Three is a significant figure in most people's minds, a recurrent number in myths and fairy stories. Wise men, little pigs, blind mice, little maids from school, ships sailing by, all occur in threes - the list is endless. Often a question of choice or polarity is involved; three is a manageable number, more interesting than the straight either/or choice of two, less confusing than four or more. So three caskets are offered to Portia, wishes are normally handed out in threes, three goddesses vied for the Golden Apple, and the offspring of fictional or fairytale kings from Lear onwards tend to be trios of princes or princesses, usually one good, one bad and one stupid. Christian tradition is dominated by the Trinity, and our image of the crucifixion is of a central cross flanked by two peripheral ones.

So perhaps it is not surprising to find that the symbolic three makes frequent appearances in the near-death experience. Betty Eadie, in her book Embraced by the Light, describes three hooded figures in brown robes, whom she believes were her 'ministering angels'. Melvin Morse quotes a six-year-old boy who had a tunnel-and-light experience after he had been hit by a car while riding his bicycle. In the light he met three men, one very tall, the other two short. The image of a dominant figure in the group of three also appears in the first two reports of odd encounters quoted earlier: only one of the three Indian princes faces Mrs McCallum; only one of the three Arab figures seen by Mrs Quinn stands on the raised Olympic-style podium.

Figures in monk-like habits or long flowing robes are a recurrent theme in near-death experiences. Ella Silver saw people in 'long garments, white, with a cord around their waist'. S. Woodham felt she herself was wearing a 'long, long, long nightdress'. Mr G. Thomas saw a figure with hair down to his shoulders and dressed in a robe with wide sleeves which reached down to the floor. D. J. R. Cook saw a person in white clothing, Alf Rose a woman in a white robe, and Hazel Graham's three old Chinese men all had long white beards and white robes.

Some of the persons encountered, for example Mrs McCallum's three young Indian princes, were dressed more exotically, but still the theme of flowing robes recurs. Audrey Quinn's three male figures were dressed in Arab-type flowing gowns with hoods apparently made from chain-mail. Michael Mizon's companion wore sandals and 'a blanket thing on with stripes on it', and David Whitmarsh himself wore a blue gown, and was with people who seemed to be dressed in the same way.

However, when people meet friends and relatives in the near-death experience they don't usually comment on their dress at all, which would suggest that it is unremarkable, and probably much the same as they always wore. The plethora of robed figures, on the other hand, were all strangers, slightly mysterious, all very much inhabitants of the 'other world', not the physical world. Even if they are not assumed to be religious figures, their clothing does seem to suggest a biblical influence. Perhaps this is another symbolic way of emphasising that in the NDE we enter a different world.

Everything Was So Beautiful

In 1986 I was rushed into Bradford Royal Infirmary and underwent emergency surgery. I spent five weeks in intensive care, then a further four months in a ward. My experience of death was wonderful. I was floating high up, no pain, great joy, and no fear. Down a tunnel with a very bright light at the end. Animals, pictures, everything was so beautiful and all the colours were shades of delicate pink, yellow, blue etc. I was overwhelmed with joy. I truly believe I was on the brink of death. I cannot have made up a story like this. I was told a long time afterwards by my relatives that I did die at the moment of entering the intensive care unit, but it was not to be. I heard my dad's voice calling me back. I was on the critical list. No hope was given to my family and now here I am with my life.

My experience has had a profound effect on my life. I thank the Lord for every new day, but if death is the wonderful experience I had, I'm not afraid of death.

As Hilda Middleton's experience shows, not only do people see, hear and smell in the NDE, but their perceptions seem to be heightened. When music is heard it is 'heavenly', colours are 'beautiful', 'vivid', 'unearthly': smells are usually described as 'beautiful', 'summery', 'flowery'.

Although many of these visions of Paradise include strong well-formed, visual images, sometimes the imagery is much less pictorial, at times almost losing its form completely. And yet it still remains intensely emotional, and still gives this very strong impression of heightened awareness. Mrs Mary Lowther:

I seemed to 'float' along a corridor towards, then into, all-enveloping brightness and light, with indefinable shades of pastel-like colours. There were what I can only describe as billions of beautiful shimmering forms, no outlines, and they were all 'cloaked' in what looked like a garment of translucent light.

Mrs Cleator's NDE at the beginning of this chapter shows how the two kinds of imagery can merge into one another.

The landscape she finds herself in at first is full of vivid detail - the bower corner, the fence with a gap in it, the people walking around. Then: 'The next thing I remember was floating along, passing through swathes of wonderful, beautiful, translucent colours, more beautiful than any I had ever seen on earth. I have no idea of time throughout this experience.' There is one very clear similarity between the images in dreams and those of the NDE. However short-sighted people are, their dreams are never blurred and indistinct - they see as clearly as if they were wearing their glasses or contact lenses. The same seems to be true in the NDE. Even people who are very short-sighted in real life seem to have no trouble recognising the relatives who greet them, or describing in vivid detail the scenes they see. When they have an out-of-body view of themselves being resuscitated or having an operation, this too is seen with clarity, even if they would normally see the world fairly dimly without their spectacles.

This is not surprising. As we have discussed, they are not seeing with their real eyes, but seeing images which have previously been seen clearly and stored in the brain. If these visual images are not already there in memory, ready to be drawn upon, there could be no visual imagery in the NDE.

Until very recently I have found no substantiated account (although some anecdotal ones) of anyone who has been congenitally blind from birth having an NDE and 'seeing' what sighted people have described during similar experiences. Then I was told about an American woman, who I will call Emily. Emily was a premature baby, and at the age of three months she was blinded by excess oxygen in her incubator. She is now forty-two. When she was twenty-two Emily was in a road accident, and lay in hospital in a coma for three days. This is her story.

> The first thing I clearly remember was being on the ceiling, looking down and seeing this body. I was really terrified by this ability to see. At first, I couldn't relate to that body, and then I realised it was me. I could hear the doctor telling the others: 'There's blood on her eardrum. Now she's probably going to be deaf as well as blind.' I was screaming at him, 'But I can hear! I can hear!' and I felt this terrible desolation because I couldn't get through to him. Then the nurse said that I'd be in a vegetative state. I tried to talk to her, but she couldn't hear me either.
>
> Then I was pulled up through the roof and I had this glorious sense of freedom. I could move wherever I wanted to. I was above the street, above the hospital, and I was ecstatic about being able to move wherever I wanted to. Then that ended suddenly. I was sucked into a tunnel, and heard a sound like monstrous fans. It was not actually that, but it's the closest way I can describe it. It was a beautiful sound. The tunnel was dark, with regular open spaces in the side, through which I could see other people travelling in other tunnels. There was one area I passed by where there was a group of drab, dull, unhappy people who were unable to move. Then I saw the distant light, and I heard these hymns. The light got brighter, and I saw Him. I saw Christ. He was incredibly beautiful.

His feet were bare. He was wearing a bright garment.
The bosom was open and you could see his chest. He had
hair down to his shoulders and a beard. There was light in and
around his head, and coming out of his head like a star.

Five people came to meet Emily: two close school friends who had
died, an old couple who had once been neighbours and her grandmother. Jesus forbade her to touch any of them, telling her that it was
not her time yet, she had to go back and live and have children. In
the light there were birds, trees and flowers. She was worried that she
was treading on the flowers and hurting them, but 'they were able to
communicate telepathically that I hadn't hurt them. I wanted to see
animals and hug them, but no animals came.'

Then Emily experienced a life review, rapid but very detailed. She
said she was able to feel her own feelings and the feelings of everyone
else. After this Christ returned. 'He embraced me. I wanted to be part
of Him. I wanted to be with Him so badly. Then I felt this violent
jolt. I started careering backwards. I heard this rushing wind, backwards. Then I felt this thud and I was back in my body with a lot of
pain.' Until this time, Emily had only been able to 'see' through touch.
She had felt a star on a Christmas tree, but she had never touched a
large figure of Christ.

Even before her experience, Emily was a Christian and a member
of a Pentecostal church. So one can assume that she might well have
been told what pictures of Christ looked like - the 'bright garment'
for example, and the beard are things she had probably heard spoken
of. But one thing we know from the experience of people who have
been blind from birth with congenital cataracts is that if the cataract
is removed and they can finally see, the world does not make sense.
They have vision, but not sight as we know it. It takes some time before they are able to integrate the jumble of impressions around them
to create any meaningful picture of the world.

Whatever it was that Emily saw made sense to her. And yet how
can she have seen anything even in her 'mind's eye' without a database of imagery to draw on? We cannot know exactly what Emily's
subjective experience would have been when she 'saw' flowers, but we
have to assume she would not have seen what a sighted person would
see. We share words with Emily, because all through her life objects
would have been described to her. But we cannot share her vision; we
can't know what pictures these shared words will have conjured up

in her imagination. In fact, we do not know how she can conjure up pictures at all, because for her, no such pictures exist. It is of interest that she reports seeing what was going on around her and then as she went through the ceiling, seeing the hospital and the streets. These are very concrete images, but again we don't know exactly what there was in her 'visual' mind. The alternative is that somehow in the NDE she did truly see. Science at present has no explanation for this, but there are some interesting parallels.

There are accounts of people who have been deaf from birth 'hearing' voices when they have mental disorders such as schizophrenia, although they have never in reality been able to hear. They describe the people they hear as 'speaking' and not 'signing', although sign language is the only method of communication they know. So perhaps we should not dismiss Emily's claim to have 'seen' in her NDE, even though we do not know what mechanism might have been involved.

The Music of the Spheres

People who have mystical experiences sometimes describe hearing 'heavenly music', and about 20 per cent of people who wrote to us heard music during their near-death experiences. Here too the music is always described as 'beautiful' or 'heavenly'. But what exactly do people mean when they talk about beautiful, heavenly music? To most of us this means harmonious music, and indeed, when people are asked to be specific they often describe it as traditional church music sung by angelic choirs. Now traditional church music is essentially concordant and rhythmic. It is only in the twentieth century that discordant, arrhythmic music has come to be widely played. I have yet to hear of an experience in which heavenly music was described as being discordant (or indeed in which discordant music was described as heavenly). 'The most wonderful thing was the music,' says Mary Lowther, 'which I can only describe as almost a tangible joy emanating from, yet part of and encompassing these forms, of which one appeared to be the source and somehow embraced all else.

M. Hilton:

I too felt this lovely feeling after an operation. I remember going into a tunnel. At the end of it was a very bright light. I heard beautiful music, something I'd never heard before: saw people standing around, all being happy with one another. Someone turned to me and said, 'She's not ready to come to us yet.' I remember coming round in a side ward and asking a nurse where the music came from. She looked at me with a funny look. But there was no music near the room. My husband said I must have been dreaming but I know I wasn't. At one time I was afraid of dying but now it doesn't bother me at all.

The music of the NDE may help us fill in another corner of the NDE puzzle. There is some evidence that a particular part of the brain, the right temporal lobe, is involved in the appreciation and synthesis of rhythmical, concordant music; if the right temporal lobe is damaged, amusia - an inability to hear music as music - sometimes develops. If we are right in assuming that the heavenly music of the NDE is essentially harmonious and concordant, it seems likely that this part of the brain may somehow be involved.

A Strong Smell of Flowers

Several people mention smells: Jean Giacomozzi mentions 'a beautiful smell', and Dawn Gillott 'the wonderful summery smell of flowers'. Mrs Holyoake too was aware of a strong flowery smell, so strong that it lingered even after her experience had ended: 'This place was amass with beautiful flowers, the perfume from them was very strong ... I got out of bed to realise all the pain I had was gone. All I had left as proof of this miracle was the perfume of the garden still lingering in my bedroom, which my husband could smell.' Mrs J. H. Collingwood described an unusual sequel to her NDE. Although she does not mention smelling flowers in her NDE, she found that afterwards she noticed a 'premonition by perfume' whenever anyone close to her was near to death, as though the smell of flowers had become associated in her mind with approaching death.

I was desperately ill in the East Sussex Hospital, Hastings three years ago with suspected cancer.

The period leading up to the operation was ten days, which were completely lost to me. I cannot even remember the preparation, or being taken down to the operating theatre. The night following the op., when I was best described as being in a semi-coma, I had an amazing and everlasting experience.

I seemed to be drifting through brightly coloured clouds, but unlike anything similar seen on earth. The nearest I can describe them is akin to the colour of old church glass windows with the sun shining through.

This seemed to go on indefinitely until I became aware of a small opaque object, like a paperweight, coming towards me. Within the glass-like disc appeared the figure of an old aunt who had passed on a couple of months previously. She looked very sad. There then appeared above her a shadow which looked like the head and shoulders of a nun. My old aunt then smiled and both images drifted away.

Two days later we heard that a close friend of my aunt had passed away at the same time as my strange experience. From then on my health steadily improved.

After this setback there were a few deaths in the family and I noticed that a few days before getting the sad news I had been aware of a strong smell of flowers around me, not noticeable to others, even though I very rarely knew that the people concerned were ill.

The Warm, Inviting Light

Feelings of warmth often seem to be encompassed in the near-death experience. Mr J. Inman describes feeling 'warm and comfortable', Mrs Holyoake, encountering Christ, could 'feel the warmth from his body'. Dawn Gillott saw 'a beautiful, warm, inviting light'. Often the warmth seems to be emanating from the light, and is felt increasingly as the person approaches the light. Many others mention the warmth too.

Maurice James: 'It was very green and pleasant and warm and filled with a golden sunlight. I could feel the warmth from where I stood at the entrance.' Mrs M. Giles: 'Then I was at ceiling level, looking down at my body. I have not read of anyone talking about the warmth which enveloped me at that stage.' Elizabeth Rogers: 'The tight iron band around my chest was getting tighter and tighter. The doctor left, warning me not to move on any account. Then everything became warm and bright and light and beautiful.' Dennis Stone: 'I stood on the top of a beautiful valley, the sun was so warm.' The father of Mr David Davies, whose NDE is described in Chapter 11, did not travel down a tunnel but was pushed on a trolley down a hospital corridor towards an operating theatre. But even in these unusual circumstances, he noticed the same phenomenon. 'It was awfully cold in the corridor,' he commented. He remembered seeing the light of the theatre at the bottom of the corridor and as he got nearer to it he could feel it getting warmer. He also recalled hearing music coming from inside the theatre.

Where does this feeling of warmth come from? One possibility is that it is connected with the release of endorphins, the brain's own pain-killing chemicals, which may play a part in the NDE (see Chapter 14). Another is that it is a real, bodily sensation which has been incorporated into the near-death experience, just as our dreams incorporate feelings of cold when the duvet slips off.

This seems less likely as many NDEs occur when blood pressure is falling and the body is more likely to be cold than warm.

We should not assume that during unconsciousness the senses are all entirely absent. We know that it is quite common for people to remember noises or fragments of conversation while they are under anaesthesia. Hearing is not the only sense that can remain in semi-consciousness. As Sue Blackmore points out, people who remember 'seeing' certain surgical procedures - seeing themselves being given injections, for example, or 'seeing' the defibrillator pads being placed on their chests when they are being resuscitated, may in fact have been feeling them. Mrs Errington, for example, describes in Chapter 3 how she 'saw' the nurse stroking her face although, she adds, she couldn't feel anything.

Mr R. J. Fletcher recounts what happened to him when he had a massive hernia operation in July 1985.

> While I was in the recovery room I felt as though I left my body and went walking towards a very bright white light which was at the end of a long tunnel. At the same time I could see three figures standing at the end of the bed and I kept wishing they would go away so that I could go to the light, which to me was lovely and warm. Just as I neared the light I felt a stab in my thigh. I am still wondering why I was sent back because I often wish I had stopped where I was. At the moment I can find no purpose for living.

The stab in the thigh which Mr Fletcher felt was almost certainly a real bodily sensation. It may be that the warmth was, too. A letter from Mrs Gogarty suggests that the reason so many people mention the sensation of warmth in their NDE may be that they are feeling warm in reality. 'I immediately awoke, my entire body covered with perspiration - even the face of my watch was awash, and the time had stopped at 3 a.m.,' she writes. 'My sister-in-law, who was asleep in the same room, rushed to my bedside and asked if I was cold as the bedroom was at that moment very cold - she could not understand how I could be so warm without a temperature.' Isabella McLeod experienced the opposite sensations in NDE, which occurred in 1959 after a post-partum haemorrhage.

> I was aware of the haemorrhage. I became very cold and was shivering uncontrollably. Then suddenly I was being propelled (I was not walking) down a tunnel which had a grey whirling mist and I could see a small bright light in the distance. I could feel a cold breeze on my face. I felt calm and peaceful. As I progressed along the tunnel the light got bigger; I appeared to reach my destination when I was enveloped in this large bright light. I was met by my grandmother, who quietly said, 'You must go back.' I was immediately back in my body and aware I was being pronounced dead. I tried very hard to move fingers, toes, anything to make the midwife aware I was alive. I felt desperate and felt I became so very tiny and crouched under one eyelid, pushing as hard as I could to try to open my eyes. I no longer fear death because of this experience.

This feeling of a breeze on the face, and the swirling mist that Isabella describes are both very understandable. Isabella had had a severe haemorrhage, and this would have made her blood pressure fall. The sensations this causes are familiar to anyone who has fainted: the feeling of being in a grey mist, the cold sweat which breaks out on the face. It looks as though both these bodily sensations were incorporated into Isabella's experience.

Notice that Isabella also describes a feeling of paralysis: she is 'propelled' down the tunnel but doesn't walk, and when she comes back to her body she has the sensation familiar in dreams of wanting desperately to run away from something but finding that your limbs are leaden, unable to move. In fact, this sensation is no dream - we feel paralysed because we are paralysed.

Mary Errington was 36 years old and the mother of three children when she had an experience, after brain surgery, which convinced her that 'something' left her body (see page 44). The story she tells is a reminder that the universal feelings of the NDE are often expressed in very different visual images. She too, was aware of a 'welcoming presence' in the light - not a figure or a 'being' but a tree with its branches outstretched like arms. (*David Hiscock/ Robert Montgomery and Partners*)

When she was five years old Audrey Organ had her tonsils removed. The next day she described the operation in graphic detail to her horrified mother (page 46). It's difficult to think of any explanation for this - except that Audrey had somehow 'watched' the surgeon at work. What is particularly interesting is that as an adult Audrey also had two near-death experiences. We know that not everyone who is near death has an NDE. Audrey's story suggests that some people may be more 'NDE prone' than others.

Derek Scull, a retired army Major, is not a fanciful man. And yet during an out-of-body experience after a major heart attack he 'saw' his wife where she could not possibly have been seen by him - unless he actually was, as he felt himself to be, floating somewhere near the ceiling of his hospital room (page 49). He himself has no doubt at all that something left his body at that time.

Until he retired, John Bowers was head of the United Nations World Literacy Programme. He was a 30 year old serving officer in the Sudan during the Second World War when he came under attack by four German Heinkel bombers. The near-death experience which followed (page 61) felt convincingly real, but for him it had a spiritual value that did not depend on any 'proof of its physical reality. It was, he says, part of his training course for life. (David Hiscock|Robert Montgomery and Partners)

Nita McCallum's near-death experience in 1972 (see page 118) is interesting because although at the time she was a devout Roman Catholic, her experience seemed to her to be quite unrelated to her faith. Like many other people, she found her NDE changed her life, widening her spiritual horizons rather than confirming any particular religious belief.
(Steve Roberts!Weston Daily Press) Visions of Paradise

The current view of dreaming is that the same psychological structures which are used in the waking state are also used in the dream. The only reason we don't 'act out' our dreams is that a special neural mechanism prevents impulses from reaching the muscles, so they are paralysed.

(See Chapter 14.) What is the significance of this to the near-death experience? Unless the person is dreaming or deeply unconscious, should one not expect the brain to respond to the very vivid 'reality' of the NDE by initiating the appropriate muscle movements? In other words, should one not expect them to act out the NDE? Isabella McLeod, crouching there beneath her eyelid trying to push open her eyes, was experiencing something very similar to this dream paralysis. And yet her account makes it very unlikely that she could have been dreaming. We know that she had haemorrhaged, and that her blood pressure had therefore fallen. People recovering from a simple faint do not report this feeling of paralysis. It is much more likely that a catastrophic fall in blood pressure had made her deeply unconscious, and that she experienced the feelings of paralysis just as she was recovering consciousness. Other people have described the same sort of paralysis that occurs in dreams. Ella Silver... 'turned my mind but not my head'.

David Whitmarsh's story, told in full in Chapter 11, is another example of the way that bodily sensations are sometimes incorporated into the NDE. While David's body was lying on the deck of his ship, after a powerful electric shock had rendered him unconscious, he was happily embarking on a journey on a blue train.

> Then it began to happen. I felt a pressure on my shoulders and a strange sensation as I began to rise. It didn't make any sense -1 felt I was being pushed down yet I was going up. I didn't want to leave my new-found friends, who were begging me to stay, and how I wanted to stay.
>
> The speed of my ascent became faster and I felt a feeling of anger mixed with regret. I didn't want to go back. Suddenly I came to and was lying face down on the deck of the frigate passageway. My colleague was pushing on my shoulder blades in the old Holger-Nielson method of resuscitation. My first emotion was one of anger: why did they bring me back? I was happy on that train. I wanted to know where we were going.

'I Heard With My Mind'

In spite of (or perhaps because of) the clarity, the intensity of the sensual experience, many people are aware that their 'real' senses are not involved. Most people report that they do not use words to communicate with others or with the being of light. Communication seems to be intuitive. 'I was hearing not with my ears but with my mind,' one person said. Another mentioned 'the person with whom I seemed to be able to communicate', although he does not say he could 'hear' him.

Others describe very similar experiences:

Alf Rose: 'Very quickly a woman in a white robe appeared in front of the lion and looked at me. She was about thirty years old, eyes set widely apart, with bobbed auburn hair. She looked quite sternly at me as an adult would if about to reprimand a child. She "spoke" to me although her lips didn't move and I could hear no voice. She told me that I should not be there and that I must go back.'

Ella Silver: 'I was aware at this point of muffled voices to my right. I still couldn't move and yet I could "see" them.'

Constance Cawthorne: 'I seemed to be in the presence of formless (but not faceless) spiritual beings who transferred to me the thought that I must go back.'

Mrs Audrey Quinn: 'I was given the impression that I wasn't to be allowed in yet, though no words were spoken.' Joan Hensley: 'I saw someone, but no one I knew. He held out his arms to me, he was smiling and called my name.

I seemed to know what he was saying but he didn't appear to talk to me. More a sort of telepathy.'

James Carney: 'I mentally asked the question, what was that? and it seemed that instantly I received a mental answer that I had passed through a stage of life.'

Audrey Organ: 'Here I was in a tunnel of glorious golden light with my dad, who had died some years earlier. We were strolling side by side but with no physical walking. We were enormously happy, conversing but without the usual verbal speech, all via the mind.'

Mrs Frances Barnshey: 'I saw no one and heard no one, but I knew I wasn't alone... I was told neutrally that this couldn't be, I had to go back.'

Sarah McAdam: 'I could hear someone calling me from behind and my mind turned to see a figure in a bright light.' However, others describe words that seem to be spoken and voices that seem to be heard in the normal way, especially when they meet friends and relatives they have known.

Dawn Gillott (Chapter 3) had a long conversation with her grandfather; so too did Gillian McKenzie (Chapter 7).

David Whitmarsh 'listened to the happy babble of the passengers'; D. A. Bak 'heard a voice that called my name'.

Anne Allcott recalls: 'A deep voice which seemed to echo in the tunnel said "Who are you to decide when you die?" ' Linda Gordon knew that 'someone was calling me towards the light, but I didn't really know who it was. The voice was very comforting.' Judith Smith was 'surrounded by voices', one of which said:' "Are you coming or staying?" and I knew that if I went I would die.' We know that when people 'hear' hallucinatory voices, the hearing area of the brain (in the temporal cortex) becomes active, and that it is probably this activity that produces the sensation of voices speaking. In some mental illnesses, too, people say they are able to read other people's minds, or that other people can read their minds. This, too, is probably due to abnormal activity in some part of the brain, though we don't yet know which part. It seems very likely that something similar happens in the NDE, and that these odd sensations and experiences arise because of activity in a particular part of the brain.

Chapter 7

'It Wasn't My Time to Go'

COMMON to most people who have near-death experiences is the realisation, at some point in the experience, that if they go any further they will never return to their bodies and so will die. With this comes the realisation that they must go back; it is not the right time for them to die. Once they understand this they find themselves back in their bodies and back with their pain.

Why do people come back? Who decides whether or not it is 'the right time' for them to go? Is it their own decision, or does it seem to be out of their hands? Are they sent back for a purpose, and if so, do they always understand what this is? Or is it simply that most human beings have a very strong will to live, and that this instinct for survival makes them fight back every inch of the way when they are on the brink of death? Of the people who answered our questionnaire, 72 per cent said that they did not simply return: a definite decision was made that they should do so. Of these, about half felt that they made the decision themselves, half that it was made for them.

Linda Gordon was one of those who felt that it was definitely her own decision to live. Her experience was during an operation for retained placenta during the birth of her first child, and she was under a general anaesthetic at the time.

> I remember seeming to float through a long tunnel, which was dark from my end but became lighter. I know someone was calling me towards the light, but I didn't really know who it was.

The voice was very comforting, I wasn't afraid, but more unsure of what to do.

Then I was thinking of my family, to whom I am very close, but suddenly I felt I wanted to go into the light. I was in no pain, my body felt warm and comfortable - I wanted to go into the light, to get away from my husband, who was very cruel to me, and continually ill-treated me - I really wanted to be free of him so much. I was aware that I was not breathing, but it wasn't uncomfortable, I felt I didn't need to. I was about to let myself be drawn deeper into the tunnel but then I remembered I'd just had a child, and suddenly I panicked, I wanted to go back so I could look after her. I didn't want my husband (ex-now) bringing her up. I was just so worried that I'd left it too late and wouldn't be able to get back, so I fought like mad. Just at this point I felt I couldn't breathe. It felt like someone was trying to smother me; at this point I was terrified. Then I heard a voice (it turned out to be the doctor in intensive care) say 'She's coming out of it.' Then he spoke to me and explained that I was on a ventilator and told me to relax and not to fight the machine. It turned out I had had a cardiac arrest. They explained to me later that I nearly didn't pull through.

What I didn't tell them was that I had had a big part in the fact that I pulled through - it was mainly my decision whether I lived or died.

Many other people too were quite sure that it was their own decision to return. Some simply did not want to die just yet; others were moved by more prosaic considerations, like Gillian McKenzie, who was anxious about leaving her husband to deal with a pile of unironed shirts. Henry Foster (Chapter 4) had 'no sensation of being called or beckoned, the presence was simply waiting for me. Something inward told me "not yet" and the light began to recede.' His head of department was on the point of administering first aid when 'I breathed very deeply and said, "It's all right, I'm coming back." I cannot remember saying anything but I believe that this indicates that I had made the decision not to go, and not any other person or presence.' James Carney: 'The peace and happiness was overwhelming, but I knew that if I stayed longer I would not return. I then thought of my wife and young child and knew I had to return.'

Judith Smith:

At the end of the tunnel there was a very bright luminous light and a landscape beyond, very beautiful. As we approached the light, one of the voices said, 'Are you coming or staying?' and I knew that if I went I would die. I thought about it -certainly there was no fear - but I said, 'No, I haven't finished my life yet.' Instantly I was whisked back (I can only describe it as being like when you blow up a balloon and let the air out) and I was in the recovery room and a nurse was saying, 'She's not coming round, she's not coming round - oh, it's OK, she's all right.'

Maurice James:

Several times I went beyond the end of the kaleidoscope tunnel and was able to see the world beyond. It was as though I was at the entrance and was able to have a good look but also to be able to go in or stay was my decision. I had the sense that I still had work to do and could go in a minute - a similar feeling to those one had as a child and one had to make a decision about whether to go out to play or stay and finish one's homework.

Sheila Berry heard 'a voice in my head' which said that she had to go back. 'I can still remember someone taking my hand and I had a feeling of great peace and a oneness with what I can only describe as the universe. I can remember returning to the weight of my body H. N. Smith, whose experience is described in Chapter 11, sensed that the people around him were waiting for him to make up his mind.

At this point I got so angry that 'they' were doing this to me and that I had to make a decision. I made myself go back up to the top of the slides and then I felt a tremendous pain in my chest. I came to surrounded by doctors and nurses and subsequently found out that I had suffered a cardiac arrest and had been clinically dead for approximately three minutes.

Mrs A. Burns:

I knew instinctively that in just a moment I would come face to face with my 'maker', as I thought of him, rather than God. At that point I seemed to panic and I fought against the feeling thinking, 'No, I'm not ready.' I have no recollection of how I came back or what happened.

The next moment I had snatched the mask off my face.

Gillian McKenzie's experience occurred during the birth of her first child, in 1968, when she was thirty-four. She was just about to be taken into the operating theatre for an emergency operation and was in considerable pain.

I was facing the doors of the operating theatre and I was aware that they were getting further and further away. Then I was coming out of the top of my head - it was as if my body was being rolled off me like a rubber glove, and I was coming out of my head. I was immediately in pitch darkness. To the right (I was still thinking quite logically) above me was a small pinprick of light and I was 'flying' towards it. At the same time I thought, my God, I'm dead. I was quite angry -1 thought, it's not fair, I'm not even in the operating theatre yet and it's not going to be very easy for James (I was sure my baby was going to be a boy and I'd already chosen his name) if I'm dead. And anyway, I don't want to die. I felt very annoyed about it.

I got closer and closer to the light which was getting bigger and bigger. As I approached it I could see it showed up the walls of a tunnel. I flew towards it and emerged into it. I was surrounded by it. I can't tell you how brilliant it was, there's no way to describe it. It wasn't only the light - it was a feeling, I don't know what words to use - a feeling of exhilaration, of joy, of warmth. I wasn't afraid. It's nothing I've ever felt either before or since.

I became aware of what I can only describe as a 'being' of light and I heard a voice say, 'Gill.' I thought, heavens, it's God; surely I can't come before God straight away, surely there should be a sort of reception place or something. And the voice said, 'Gill, you know who I am.' And I said, 'Yes, I do, but I can't stay.' And the voice sort of chuckled and said: 'Well, here is someone you know,' and it was another being of light. I didn't see anybody, I just knew it was there. And then I heard another voice and I knew immediately it was my grandfather. We had had a very close relationship when I was a child, and he had died only two years before. I was so thrilled to be speaking to him again. And I said, 'Grandpa, I can't stay here. I've got to get back. I've just had a son and Hamish has just got a new job and he won't be able to cope with a new baby. I know there's a pile of ironing waiting to be done and Hamish can't iron his shirts.' And Grandpa laughed and said, 'Gill, it doesn't matter a damn. You'll have to put up a better case than that.' So I said, 'Grandpa, I'm only thirty-four, I've got so much more to do with my life. I haven't had my money's worth. I want to go back.'

Gill then had a long conversation with her grandfather in which she recounted all the things that had happened to her in her life which were of value to her, and which she felt could somehow be used to help other people. She then found herself in the operating theatre looking down on her body on the operating table.

I was very anxious to find Hamish and tell him I was coming back. So I went into the corridor and saw him sitting on a seat. I saw the doctor go out and speak to him, and tell him we had a son but that there were complications with me. Then Hamish went down the corridor to call my mother on the phone, and it was as if I could hear both sides of the conversation. She said, 'When you see her keep talking to her, and in the meantime, pray.' The next thing I knew I was back in the ward, but still on the ceiling, and Grandpa was still with me. Hamish was sitting beside the bed. I didn't know how to get through to him to tell him I was all right. Then I saw an old-fashioned phone box. I thought, if I press button B I will get my money back, but I will have to stay with Grandpa. So I pressed button A and I heard Hamish saying 'Hello, hello,' - and then I came round. Hamish said, 'We've got a son.' And I said, 'Yes, I know all about that.' One more thing happened which was very peculiar. My mother told me later that after Hamish had telephoned her, she had phoned her godmother, my great aunt, and told her she was worried about me. And my great aunt had said, 'You don't have to worry about that, Gladys.

Harry (Harry was my grandfather's name) is looking after her.'

Some of the elements of Gill's experience can be explained quite logically. Because she was kept in hospital unexpectedly after going in for a routine check-up she was concerned about Hamish - she had wanted to go home and cook him his lunch before coming into hospital, for example, but was not allowed to do this. She had spent some time trying to telephone him when she knew she was to have an emergency Caesarean, but had not been able to get through. So it is not surprising that Hamish's welfare was much on her mind, or that telephones figured so prominently in her experience. Yet she saw her husband going down the corridor and phoning her mother, and could 'hear both sides of the conversation' - and her family later confirmed that what she had seen and heard had taken place. As she herself says: 'I've put all the logical arguments to myself, that it was due to hallucinations or drugs, that I'd been trying to telephone Hamish beforehand. But whatever the medical or psychological explanations, I don't really believe them. The experience was of such great value to me and even nineteen years afterwards it is still very real. Why did it happen to me?'

Just as often though, people have little or no say in whether they go or stay. Avon Pailthorpe, for one, found a great sense of freedom in realising that the decision wasn't hers to make at all.

Around me, as the tunnel began to lighten, there were presences. They were not people, and I didn't see anything, but I was aware of their minds. They were debating whether I should go back. This was what made me so safe; I knew that I had absolutely no responsibility to make any decision... I also knew I could not influence what decision they made, but that whatever it should be it would be right. There was total wisdom and goodness in them ...It was as if there were many minds gathered on each side into one, and these two debated the decision about me. I didn't know the outcome, but I was intensely interested and peaceful.

Mrs M. Hilton saw 'people standing around, all being happy with one another. Someone turned to me and said, "She's not ready to come to us yet." ' P. Fearn described the experience of a colleague.

After a while, one of these people said to him, well, Fred (they knew his name), it's time for you to go back now.

> Fred said he did not want to, as he was quite happy there with them. The same person chuckled and said, I bet you do, but Fred, what you do not know is that we are not ready for you yet, it's not your turn, and you are before your time, so you cannot stay. The next thing Fred remembers was being aware that he was back in hospital again.

Anne Allcott and Ella Silver were among several people who felt that the decision to return was imposed upon them against their will. They wanted to stay, but were forced to return.

Anne Allcott, who describes her experience fully in Chapter 3, remembers:

> I thought, 'please let me die quickly.' I felt so ill and had much too much pain. A deep voice which seemed to echo in the tunnel said 'Who are you to decide when you die?' and I turned and floated away from the light. I then had this looking-down-from-the-ceiling feeling, knowing it was my body people were working on. They appeared to be lifting an eyelid. Then a male voice said, 'She will make it now,' or similar words, and I realised I was to live.

Ella Silver:

> I was aware at this point of muffled voices to my right. I still couldn't move and yet I could 'see' them ... I 'knew' they were discussing me... although I couldn't hear what they were saying. They stood close together and seemed to be looking down at something in their hands. One suddenly looked towards me. I didn't know him but he seemed to have great presence and authority. His face was very serious. He returned to the discussion and then in a beautiful voice, very loud, he said, 'She must go back.' Oh, the terrible feeling. I felt resentment. I didn't want to go back. I didn't

feel they rejected me, because I knew they loved me. It just wasn't for me to decide.

Although relatives are usually seen as welcoming, beckoning presences, encouraging their newly arrived kin to 'come over', it is often a relative who acts as the person's conscience, reminding him of his obligations in his earthly life, or giving the message that it's not yet time to go. Isabella McLeod, for example, was met by her grandmother, who quietly said, 'You must go back.' 'I was immediately back in my body and aware I was being pronounced dead.'

Elizabeth Rogers:

> I saw a group of people between me and the light. I knew them. My brother, who had died a few years before, was gesticulating delightedly as I approached. Their faces were so happy and welcoming. Then somehow my mother became detached from the group. She shook her head and waved her hand (rather like a windscreen wiper) and I stopped, and I heard the doctor say, 'She's coming round,' and I was in my bed and the doctor and my husband were there. My first words to the doctor were, 'Why did you, bring me back?'

Mrs J. Johnston saw her father, 'all in white with his arms outstretched towards me ... I floated towards him. But as I got near he waved his arms and gestured for me to go back.' Dawn Gillott's grandfather was worried about her son, who needed his mother. 'I told Grampi I didn't want to go back, I wanted to stay with him. But Grampi insisted I go back for my children's sake.'

The following lovely account was sent to us by Mrs Jean George. Mrs George was exhausted from caring for her father and sick husband. Her husband was very scared of being ill and had told her that if he died he would take her with him.

> On the day of the funeral *(her husband's)* I felt very ill. I spent that night with friends. It was then that I had this travelling through a dark tunnel. There seemed to be people with me but I couldn't see their faces; they seemed to get out of the tunnel before me and I went on to this lovely land, green grass, blue sky, beautiful stream, so quiet and peaceful.

I seemed to wander and I started down this hill by the stream, and as I began to wonder what to do, my mother's voice told me to go back. 'You haven't got Dad and Tom to worry about now, you must go up the hill, go back, that's the way.' I came to and my friend was beside me. She had worried in the night as I had looked so ill when I went to bed and was relieved to see me wake up. I somehow feel my husband did want me but my mother knew that, had I died, my children would have been left with no one and she loved my children.

It's now four years since my husband's death but I can still see that beautiful land, and yet I knew I didn't want to stay there. But if my mother's voice hadn't told me to come back I feel I would have stayed there.

For Mrs George, the meeting with her mother helped to resolve a personal conflict, allowing her to go back to care for her children without feeling that she was being disloyal to her husband. It is interesting to compare this with the account sent to us by Jean Giacomozzi, who suffered severe haemorrhaging after a hysterectomy. Jean seemed to feel the same pull between life and death, her dead father calling her at one end of the tunnel, her real-life lover calling her back at the other end.

I recall floating in a very bright tunnel, everything seemed so calm and peaceful. At the end of the tunnel my father, who had died three years previously, was holding out his hand and calling me to come.

As I said, the feeling of calmness was indescribable. I heard music and there was a beautiful smell. I stopped floating a few feet before I reached my father and then I heard someone calling me. I turned and saw his face at the other end of the tunnel. It was Fabio.

Some people are sent back by the being of light, like Mrs M. T. Gogarty.

I could look into this light without hurting my eyes and then I drifted towards it. I was so happy but then the shadow of what looked like a man suddenly appeared in this light and waved at me to go back. I went back, but again I felt compelled to go towards this lovely light, and again I was waved back.

My own opinion is that although I was trying to leave this world, it was not yet my time to do so. However, death holds no fear for me now - it is simply the beginning of a new life.

Mr G. Thomas told us: 'I wanted to stay with him and stay in this wonderful glow, but slowly he waved towards me in such a way as if to indicate, go away, go back, but when he did this I felt, oh no, I don't want to leave, please don't send me away, let me be with you forever.'

Unfinished Business

Often people feel they have been sent back to accomplish some specific task, or a piece of unfinished business. In most cases they believe they have been sent back to look after children who still need them, or that they have to fulfil other family responsibilities. Eleanor Cleator felt she was sent back to complete the task of looking after her mother, who had Parkinson's Disease.

Sarah McAdam: 'I then looked down on my body and remembered my new son, Jamie. I then saw him in his incubator on the first floor of the hospital and I said, "No, I can't come yet, as I have to look after my son." I knew that if I turned my body towards the light I would go and "die", but I went back to my body.' Mrs Margaret Dinkeldein: 'I felt a very intense pull back from the threshold to this other "place", mainly because of my strong feelings of responsibility to the baby and the rest of my family.'

It's not surprising that people are reluctant to leave beloved children or partners, or abandon family responsibilities. But here again, as so often when we're looking at the NDE, we have to ask ourselves how it is that people manage to think so logically and coherently at a time when one would have expected logical thought to be impossible.

In a few cases, however, people believe they have been sent back because there is something left undone in their lives, some task they have to complete before it is time for them to go. What this is is not always made clear, and often remains a puzzle after the experience. Mr H. T. Mill:

All I knew was that I was under orders to go back and complete an unspecified task. I had no idea what that task was, but I knew that some time something would happen and I would know what was required of me ... With regard to the special task I was sent back to do, at the age of eighty-two years I still do not know for sure what it is ...However, in 1974 [thirty years after his NDE] in Australia I witnessed a very special atmospheric phenomenon which I have been researching for the past twenty years... I believe that that is the task I was ordered to complete.

M. Drury:

When I insisted that I must return and gave my reasons, they assured me that all I had to do would be done from where I was. At one point they told me to look down at myself. I was warned of the disabilities I would have to overcome as well as the pain I would have to endure, which would be worse than I had ever experienced. I said I still wished to return. They assured me that they would give me as much support as possible but the recovery was up to me and that I would have to live with what I achieved. Furthermore, I was also given new tasks which I would have to do and told that I could not return if I gave up.

The whole time my spirit was away from my body was totally calm and peaceful. Although it sounds as though I was arguing with these other people (spirits), I was not and neither were they. We were all very calm and talked very peacefully.

What are we to make of these feelings of destiny, of a mission to be carried out or a task to be completed? It is very seldom that people are told exactly what the task is - indeed, like Mr Mill, they may still be searching for it years later. One explanation is that the feelings arise largely because people are trying to explain what is a very puzzling experience to themselves, investing it with meaning and value. An enormous, a momentous thing has happened: you have lived when you might so easily have died. Is it surprising that you should ask why, and try to find an answer? For some people the answer is easy. If you have a family or dependent relatives then it must seem obvious that this is why you have been sent back. But what if you have no family duties to fulfil, if your life or death seems to have no particular significance to other people? In these circumstances you might well tend to believe that you must have been sent back for some other purpose, even if this isn't immediately apparent. It's perhaps relevant that all three of the people quoted above were young adults at the time of their experience, and none had family dependent on them.

The comments made by Mr R. J. Fletcher, who was sent back by three figures (Chapter 6), illustrate this point very clearly. It is obviously hard for him to accept that he cheated death either through chance or medical expertise. He feels there must have been a reason, even though he has no idea what it is: 'I am still wondering why I was sent back because I often wish I had stopped where I was. At the moment I can find no purpose for living.' The strength of this feeling that such a powerful experience must be for some purpose is also apparent in the story told to me by Mrs Doreen Shingles about her husband's experience in Chapter 5. It occurred shortly before he died, when he was very ill with cancer. He knew this, but, says his wife, never accepted that he would die. He too believed that he had been sent back because his work was not finished, and yet he died only a few days later. In this case at any rate one wonders whether it might not have been Mr Shingles' own strong will to live that brought him back.

Allan Pring, an ex-RAF pilot, had an NDE while undergoing surgery at Manchester Royal Infirmary. It was an exceptionally full experience, which began, unusually, with a life review (see Chapter 8). The knowledge that he had to return was, he says, 'the worst moment of my life'. Recalling this experience is still emotionally upsetting for him, bringing tears which are 'a mixture of terrible sadness and extreme happiness'.

> I found myself 'floating' along in a dark tunnel, peacefully and calmly but wide awake and aware. Eventually I emerged from the tunnel as its end widened out and I found myself in a place that is impossible to describe. It was a landscape without form, composed only of light and colour. I was met by a figure of light, and it was what can only be described as a 'Jesus' figure. But I 'knew' that the appearance of the figure was to make me feel comfortable in this new place. We did not speak to one another because words were not

necessary. The figure led the way for me to follow. I just cannot describe the place or my feelings and emotions. I experienced absolute happiness, utter bliss, complete love, perfect peace, and total understanding.

I knew that I was dead. I knew that my body no longer existed; I knew that as an individual I no longer existed; I knew that I was in a place where I would stay and be happy and learn. It was already obvious to me that what I had considered to be ultimate knowledge was only the beginning.

And then, in a moment of utter despair, I realised that I could not go on. I stopped and my companion ahead of me turned to look at me. No words were spoken but my predicament was completely understood. I loved my wife more dearly than life itself and I could not leave her like this. I knew that we would never meet again because as individuals we would cease to exist. The concept is so very sad and it is utterly inadequate to say that it does not matter. I had to be able to tell her that there is no death and that it is possible to gain complete understanding. The journey back was desperate. Leaving was the worst experience of my existence and it will affect me for as long as I live. I have no regrets.

It is very easy to accept without question the assumption that the NDE experiencer makes, that he is on some kind of journey. And yet, why should he feel this? The reason is never made explicit. True, he floats down a tunnel away from darkness into light, but why should he assume that this is a journey away from this life into another? The only way one can explain this is to accept that at some level these people believe they are dying and our culture, our spiritual beliefs and therefore our psychological make-up embody the feeling that death is a journey. This gives quite a satisfactory scientific explanation. Or is there something within us - a departing soul, perhaps - which really does leave and set out on this journey?

Without a Backward Glance

In very many near-death experiences the ties to earth seem difficult to loosen. Time and again, people say that it's the knowledge that they are needed by their family that seems to draw them back. And yet this is not usually a particularly emotional feeling, more a sense of duty. Very few say that at the time they felt any grief or sadness at leaving their family - their own inner sense of joy seems so overwhelming. It is as if the experience transcends personal feelings and is quite separate from them. In fact, in an 'earthly' sense, there is an absence of emotion. The people who described these feelings to us were all people with families they loved, and all of them later expressed a sense of disbelief and even guilt that they were apparently quite ready to leave without a thought or backward glance. Ella Silver says: 'I never once thought of my husband or my children, who were quite young then.

It all seemed terribly personal, nothing to do with anyone else... Later, I was riddled with guilt because I had not considered my family, and I told my husband about it when he came in that night.'

Elizabeth Rogers: 'I love my husband dearly and it now seems very strange that there was no "pull", no regrets at leaving, nothing only pure joy and peace.' Jenny McMillan:

> I realised that I must be dying and the odd thing was that I didn't mind in the least. I remember being very interested in the experience in a very unemotional academic way and feeling that it was quite an adventure - no regrets at all. While I was there, I was very surprised at myself for feeling like this. My husband and two-year-old son were everything to me and I was shocked and amazed at myself for not minding the thought of leaving them, yet I was overwhelmed by a feeling of peace such as I had certainly not known in all my adult life. I knew how devastated they would be at my death but even this did not really move me. I felt extraordinarily comfortable, relaxed and free of any cares at all...
>
> I have always remained mystified and slightly guilty about my lack of reluctance at leaving my family. My other son had died earlier that year aged three months, but at the time I was 'up there' I had no conscious feeling of going to join him that might have explained a willingness to die. In fact, he, like everyone else, was further from my thoughts then than probably at any moment in the three months before or the year after the experience. Once back with my feet on the ground, my first thought was to retrieve my surviving son from my mother and get my family together and to make sure that nothing separated us again, but the fact remains that for that short time I had not minded at all.

Standing at the Barrier

Entry to Paradise is not automatic in the near-death experience. Many people are left standing at the entrance, but prevented from going in by some kind of barrier, a point of no return, beyond which they know they cannot go. About a quarter of the people in our questionnaire mentioned this. Sometimes the barrier is physical - a gate, or a fence; sometimes it is psychological - the person simply knows that he can go no further. For some the light itself is the barrier, and often there is the feeling that once they enter the light they cannot come back.

Eleanor Cleator was in 'a little bower corner, on my own. Between me and this place there was a low green trellis fence, which stopped, leaving a gap at the end. I could so easily have gone through. But I knew without anyone telling me that I could not stay there.'

Mrs G. Dunn: 'I pushed the gates and they gave way to my push, but try as I might I could not get in. Something behind me on both sides seemed to be stopping me from going in. I was so upset at not being able to get in, but in the end I gave up trying.'

Eleanor Cleator realised that though there was a gap in the fence which she could so easily have gone through, she knew instinctively that she could not stay. And however hard Mrs G. W. Dunn pushed the ornamental gates of her garden, 'something' stopped her from going in. This barrier is mentioned in many other accounts, too.

Mr H. N. Smith: 'As I was going down the slides I could see a barrier at the bottom. It was like a shiny black leather bench. I knew that if I went over the barrier I would be dead.'

Mrs Audrey Quinn: 'I was floating in total blackness when far ahead of me I saw a wrought-iron gate - a tall church window-shaped gate - which was open ... I gently floated on towards the gate then the middle figure looked at me and slowly shook his head, giving me the impression that I wasn't to be allowed in yet, though no words were spoken.'

Elizabeth Rogers: 'I knew I was going right into the growing heart of that light, but then I saw a group of people between me and the light.'

Mr Cook: 'I found myself beside a door which began to open, shedding a white light... I consciously recall a great desire to pass through the door. I knew that if I did there would be no return.'

Joan Hensley: 'There was a light or glow at the end of a tunnel, a beautiful gold like the sun rising. I felt it was warm and pleasant. It made me feel very secure and loved. I saw someone, but no one I knew. He held out his arms to me. He was smiling and called my name. I seemed to know what he was saying but he didn't appear to talk to me. It was more a sort of telepathy. I felt very comfortable and secure... I knew I only had to touch his hands and I would join him.

There was definitely some threshold I had to cross. At the time I thought it was betwixt Heaven and Earth. I felt reluctant to go.'

And if they do go beyond the barrier, what then? Well, that of course is the billion-dollar question. If the whole experience is psychological, then why hasn't someone crossed the barrier and come back to tell the tale? Is it that we are psychologically incapable of creating an image of our own death? After all, no one has ever reported that they died in dreams. When you dream that you are falling off a cliff, you wake up the moment before you hit the rocks and even if you do hit the rocks you do not die. Perhaps death is so far beyond our experience or imagination that there are no images even comparable locked within the brain. Or perhaps we have to assume that there is a real separation of body and spirit and the experience does in some way mark a real transition between life and death.

Chapter 8

The Life Review

O N 10th June 1791 Mr. Midshipman Francis Beaufort went to Portsmouth, to join his ship, the Aquilon, a frigate of 32 guns. Perhaps unwisely for someone who intended to make his career at sea, Francis had never learned to swim, and soon after joining his ship the small rowing boat he was in capsized as he was trying to tie up alongside the ship. He was rescued by the first lieutenant, who spotted him struggling in the water, but not before he had nearly drowned. As his biographer, Nicholas Courtney, recounts:

"...of the actual moment of drowning, however, he had perfect recall, even years later.

'From the moment that all exertion had ceased, a calm feeling of the most perfect tranquillity superseded the previous tumultuous sensations - it might be called apathy, certainly resignation, for drowning no longer appeared to be an evil - I no longer thought of being rescued, nor was I in any bodily pain. On the contrary, my sensations were now of a rather pleasurable ease, partaking of that dull but contented sort of feeling which precedes the sleep produced by fatigue. Though the senses were thus deadened, not so the mind; its activity seemed to be invigorated in a ratio which defies all description.' Francis had total recall of those exact thoughts. It really was true that 'every past incident of my life seemed to glance across my recollection in retrograde succession; not, however in mere outline, as here stated, but the picture filled up with every minute and collateral feature; in short, the whole period of my*

*existence seemed to be placed before me in a kind of panoramic view,
and each act of it seemed to be accompanied by a consciousness of right
or wrong, or by some reflection on its cause or its consequences; indeed
many trifling events which had been long forgotten then crowded into
my imagination.'*

What fascinated Francis was that although he had been
'religiously brought up,' all his thoughts were confined to the
past and nothing to the future. He was amazed that he saw
so much during the space of what cannot have been more
than two minutes between suffocation and rescue."

Midshipman (later Admiral) Beaufort described his experience
over two hundred years ago, long before the first account of near
death experiences was published in the West. And yet the parallels
between Admiral Beaufort's account and later well documented experiences are inescapable.
(Reference: Gale Force 10. The Life and Legacy of Admiral Beaufort. Nicholas Courtney. Headline 2003)
In 1979 Allan Pring was a fifty-four-year-old ex-RAF pilot who
had worked as an air-traffic controller for twenty-four years. He was
very fit, played squash, cycled and ran. The operation he was to undergo was a minor one, and he says that as far as he knows nothing
untoward occurred during or after it. But he believes that during the
operation he died.

In 1979 I had no knowledge whatsoever of NDEs. I did not
believe in life after death, I was not religious; I did not believe in God but I did believe that there was a scientific explanation for every mystery, though it could well take quite
a few million years for man to figure it all out. Basically
my views have not changed a great deal, except that now I
believe that it is impossible to die, which is not necessarily
good news. The events of 1979 are as fresh and vivid in my
memory as if they happened yesterday.
On Monday 6 August the preparation for surgery was routine and I lost consciousness within seconds of being injected
with an anaesthetic. All perfectly normal. But the manner
in which I regained consciousness was anything but normal.
Instead of slowly coming round in a drowsy and somewhat

befuddled state in a hospital ward I awoke as if from a deep and refreshing sleep and was instantly and acutely aware of my situation. Without any anxiety or distress I knew that I was dead, or rather that I had gone through the process of dying and was now in a different state of reality. The place that I was in cannot be described because it was a state of nothingness. There was nothing to see because there was no light; there was nothing to feel because there was no substance. Although I no longer considered that I had a physical body, nevertheless I felt as if I were floating in a vast empty space, very relaxed and waiting. Then I experienced the review of my life which extended from early childhood and included many occurrences that I had completely forgotten. My life passed before me in a momentary flash but it was entire, even my thoughts were included. Some of the contents caused me to be ashamed but there were one or two I had forgotten about of which I felt quite pleased. All in all, I knew that I could have lived a much better life but it could have been a lot worse. Be that as it may, I knew that it was all over now and there was no going back. There was one most peculiar feature of this life review and it is very difficult to describe, let alone explain. Although it took but a moment to complete, literally a flash, there was still time to stop and wonder over separate incidents. This was the first instance of distortion of time that I experienced but it was the beginning of my belief that the answers to many of the questions that are posed by NDEs lie in a better understanding of the nature of time and what we term reality.

After the life review I spent some time resting and considering the implications of what had happened. I did not feel that I had been judged except by myself. There was no denying the facts because they were all there, including my innermost thoughts, emotions and motives. I knew that my life was over and whatever came next would be a direct consequence of not only what I had done in my life, but what I had thought and what had been my true feeling at the time.

Then I moved to a different place. It is very difficult to describe but I knew that I no longer had a physical existence. I was not conscious of having a body and the only senses that I was aware of were sight and sound, but even these were very different. I felt that everything existed inside my non-existent head. Nevertheless I had no doubt that everything that I was experiencing was real. I was in a room, without windows or doors, but having four corners in each of which 'sat' a 'person'. 'They' began to question me in a friendly way, rather like being de-briefed after a wartime operational flight. At first the questions were simple to answer but the next questions followed on logically and became progressively more difficult. However, I knew the answers. Eventually the questions were becoming impossible to answer; they concerned existence, the meaning and purpose of life and the universe itself. I could not possibly know the answers but I did! The questions came faster and faster and I knew with the most intense feeling of joy that no matter what 'they' asked me I would know the answer. The peculiar feeling that I had experienced for so many years now made sense. [Allan Pring's childhood out-of-body experiences are discussed later in the chapter.]

My 'examiners' were happy for me and we 'talked' for a while before they indicated that it was time for me to leave.

Allan Pring's account of a life review was the fullest and most detailed we were given. It illustrates every facet of what is regarded as the 'classical' life review, in which the person is shown his or her whole life in a panoramic fashion. Although actions which have been carried out are often seen as shabby and self-interested, the person does not feel judged; guilt is made more tolerable by the supportive quality of the surrounding light of love. Often the person experiences himself the emotional or physical pain that he has caused to others. Usually he is left with a feeling that he has learned from this and a determination to change and do better.

Many NDE researchers believe that the life review is a common feature of the near-death experience. Greyson, Moody, Ring, and Noyes and Kletti (who made a special study of life reviews) all found that between a quarter and a third of all the people they studied had this kind of experience. But other workers have found them to be less common. Dr Sue Blackmore has never come across a classic case of life review, and Michael Sabom found only two amongst 116 people who had had an NDE. It is an acknowledged piece folklore that when you are drowning your past life flashes before your eyes, and it is intriguing that Noyes and Kletti report that nearly half of the life reviews they found had occurred in people whose near-death experience had been during a near drowning. One of the few accounts of life reviews which we were given, recounted by Mrs P. Morris, also occurred during a near-drowning incident.

> I was on holiday in a small holiday camp with its own swimming pool. A friend asked me to go in with her. I was not a strong swimmer, but this girl didn't tell me she couldn't swim. She jumped in the deep end, went down and called for help. I tried to save her, but she pulled me down with her. What happened next was remarkable. All my past life and incidents passed through my mind in a flash, things I had forgotten, right back to about two years of age, when I was given a rag doll. Then I entered this dark long tunnel, which had this bright fantastic light at the end. It took me a good while to float to the top but I made it and entered this wonderful garden, full of flowers, grass, shrubs, but it had no sky or birds and was completely empty. But the peace of it all and the brilliant light, much greater than sunlight and darker yellow, more of a gold. I wanted to stay, it was so peaceful. The next thing I remember was a man over me. He had pulled me out of the water and was working to bring me round.

However, not every drowning NDE includes a life review. We received one letter from someone who was nearly drowned during a murderous attack. While he was in the bath, his head was pushed down and held underwater. He describes how it felt to breathe in cold water - surprisingly, rather like taking in a breath of cold Alpine air, with no feeling of choking. He then left his body, went down a tunnel, had a discussion with the being of light, and then he returned in an out-of-body experience to see himself being carried by his assailant from the bathroom into the sitting room, where he was laid on the sofa. But he had no life review.

In our experience a full life review such as Allan Pring describes occurs only rarely. Although 15 per cent of the people we questioned said that scenes or memories from the past came back to them during the experience, most of these were simply fragments of memory, sometimes quite random memories. Only about half said the memories that came back to them were 'significant'. They were more often in the form of pictures rather than verbal memories. This fascinating account, sent to us by M. D. Drury, is one of the most detailed we were given.

My experience happened in October 1983. I was relaxing in my armchair with a glass of wine, and my mood was very relaxed and happy when my husband, with no warning, attacked me from behind with a 7lb lump hammer. This attack left me with a depressed fracture of the skull plus other fractures and bruises.

In Casualty .. . nobody considered for one moment that I would live. I was informed much later that my breathing and heart did stop. During this time I - my spirit I presume - was high above Casualty in another large white room with people who were also in white. These people sat around me and I seemed to know them, but I can no longer recall who they were. They wanted me to stop fighting and stay with them; I had achieved what I was sent to do. They recalled many of the good things I had done through my life and informed me of the comfort I had given to many of the patients who had died whilst in my care. They also mentioned the wrong things I had done in my life.

When I insisted that I must return and gave my reasons they assured me that all I had to do would be done from where I was. At one point they told me to look down at myself. I was warned of the disabilities I would have to overcome as well as the pain I would have to endure, which would be worse than I had ever experienced. I said I still wished to return. They assured me that they would give me as much support as possible but the recovery was up to me and that I would have to live with what I achieved. Furthermore, I was also given new tasks which I would have to do and told that I could not return if I gave up.

The whole time my spirit was away from my body was totally calm and peaceful. Although it sounds as though I was arguing with these other people (spirits), I was not and neither were they. We were all very calm and talked very peacefully. One man did most of the talking. All I can re-member of his face were his relaxing eyes and that he was older than myself (I am thirty-two).

The length of time I was in the spirit world has no rela-tion to Earth time. I was with the spirits for ages and there was never any rush whereas it is clear that I could only have died for minutes in Earth time. There is so much rush on Earth and so little time.

When I regained consciousness four days later I knew exactly what had happened to me, though nobody had told me at the police's request, as naturally they wished to ques-tion me. The neurologist and surgeon say I am a walking miracle because due to the amount of brain damage I sus-tained I should be a cabbage, which I was initially. But due to my spiritual warnings of what to expect plus their help and guidance, I now have only a slight paralysis down my right side, which is hardly noticeable, plus epilepsy, which is controlled by medication. I have always told my friends when they have felt pity for me because of my disabilities, which were very marked to begin with, and the way my entire life had been shattered initially, 'Yes, I have lost a lot, but due to this experience I have gained so much more.'

It is interesting to note Ms Drury's comparison of Earth time with spirit time - this is quite different from the experience in dreams, in which dream time and 'real' time have been found to approximate very closely. What is also interesting in this account is Ms Drury's comment that when she recovered consciousness she knew exactly what had happened to her, even though the police had asked peo-ple not to talk to her about the attack. When someone has a severe head injury memory is always lost for events around the time of the injury - in fact, the extent of memory loss is a good indication of the severity of the injury. When you recover, the period of un-consciousness remains a total blank. The memory circuits just do not work. So how is it that Ms Drury, unconscious for four days and suffering from a severe head injury, could remember either the assault or this very detailed near-death experience? Had she 'seen' the assault while she was out of her body? Even if we accept this as a possibility, we still have to explain how she retained the memory in her unconscious state.

When memories are played back during the experience, they are not necessarily particularly significant memories. They seem just as likely to be random moments plucked haphazardly from memory, trivial events or people or places - 'the man on the bus, the lady in the shop' referred to by Ms N. Baker in her account of her NDE in Chapter 4. Her report again shows very well the stretching-out of subjective time that seems to be a hallmark of this part of the experience.

'All the Dogs of Our Life'

Shortly before his death in 1951, Jean Johnstone's father told her of a wonderful dream he had had. Or was it a dream?

> He was dying on his feet - we all knew it... I heard him go down to the kitchen very early one morning, and put on the kettle. I joined him, and he said, 'I have had a very vivid dream, more than a dream, it seemed. I was walking in the foothills of the Himalayas' - he had served thirty-five years in Government service in India - 'in the dawning, when suddenly all the dogs of our life, including the dog of my boyhood, came running to meet me, jumping and wagging their tails as they did to welcome me. I felt younger and stronger every minute, and the light grew behind the mountains, brighter and brighter. I was so happy. Then, there was a hand on my shoulder and a voice: "You must go back, it's not time," and I woke up. I wish I had not had to come back.' He asked me not to tell anyone - 'They'll think I'm finally in my dotage.' He died not long afterwards.

Animals, even beloved pets, make very rare appearances in NDEs. And yet there must be many people who are more devoted to their dogs than to some of their relatives. The enchanting vision of 'all the dogs of our life' running delightedly to greet Mr Johnstone seems a very close parallel to the happy smiling faces of friends which welcome most people who have an NDE. The light behind the mountain getting stronger every minute, the intense happiness, the feeling that 'it's not time' all make this experience seem to be, as Mr Johnstone felt, more than a dream. What is also interesting is Mr Johnstone's feeling of growing 'younger and stronger every minute'. In dreams we tend to see ourselves (and other people) as we are. But in the NDE, as we have seen, it is quite common for people to see themselves and others as their psychological age - the age they feel themselves to be - rather than their actual, chronological age.

It is as though in leaving the physical body everything is made symbolically whole - parents or grandparents are sometimes seen as youthful too, and some people report seeing crippled or bandaged figures throwing away their crutches, unwinding their bandages and becoming healed again.

An even more dramatic shedding of the years during a life review is graphically described by Mrs J. Langschield who had an NDE during childbirth. 'Instances of my past life were relived briefly, passing rapidly along, backwards,' she recalls. 'I actually felt my body diminishing in size ...

Whilst being drawn down the long tunnel towards the bright light... I regressed to the very moment of my birth.'

Glimpses of the Future

Perhaps even more interesting are the 'previews' which some people are given about what will happen to them if they return. Often (as in the case of Ms Drury) people are given glimpses of both the past and of the future. D. A. Bak of Leicester had such a preview during an experience which occurred under anaesthetic.

> I found myself looking down at my anaesthetised body, and in this condition I heard a voice that called my name, and while above my body I turned towards the voice and found myself facing another person who spoke to me and extended a hand to me, which I could feel, and held in this out-of-body experience, and this person then told me that I had to go with him as he had something very important to show me. I was aware of moving through a golden light, and there met a group of other beings, who explained to me the reason for this experience, and proceeded to show me the major events in the future of my life, which at that time I could never see happening. But all the events revealed at that time happened and fell into place.

Like so many features of the NDE, these windows on to the past and the future do not seem to be specific to the near-death situation (Mr Bak's life was not in danger) and they can also occur in isolation without any of the other phenomena of the NDE. A German friend had the experience while he was very ill and in intensive care of seeing scenes from his childhood which were intensely real - far more real, he says, than any dream or hallucination. It is perhaps to be expected that anyone who is facing death is going to spend some time contemplating their life, asking themselves whether it has all been worthwhile; whether, given a second chance, they would play things the same way again. The life review seems to give an absolution, something which may be psychologically very necessary at the end of a life. Noyes and Kletti found that people who thought they were going to die (whether or not they were clinically near to death) were more likely to have life reviews than those who did not.

Kenneth Ring suggests that people who suddenly find themselves near death (in an accident or during a heart-attack, or, classically, in a near drowning, for example), are more likely to experience a life review than people who have a near-death experience during a long drawn-out illness, when they have more time to contemplate death and what it means to them. We too found that the few full experiences we were told about did occur in a 'sudden-death' situation, and also that it was very rare for anyone whose NDE occurred when they were not actually dying to experience any of the features of a life review.

People who are given these glimpses of the future often find that they subsequently experience various psychic phenomena such as feelings of deja vu, almost as though they have been shown a speeded-up video of their future life, and later recognise and remember odd frames from it. Allan Pring, whose life review is described at the beginning of this chapter, also had an out-of-body experience as a child. He himself feels that there may be some connection between the two, and that his NDE activated memories of this earlier experience.

> From time to time, perhaps once or twice a year over a period of many years, I would have a most peculiar feeling, deliciously pleasant but lasting only a moment. Most people have experienced the feeling of deja vu, and everyone knows what it is like to have a name on the tip of the tongue but not quite be able to recall it. The fleeting feeling that I would have was like a combination of the two. But the oddity was that I felt that if I could only think in a slightly different way, or somehow see in a different way, then I would gain or remember this tremendous knowledge. In fact, I used to

describe the feeling to my wife by saying that I felt in some magical way that I would know everything that there was to know...

I believe that the feeling of 'having forgotten' or not being able to quite remember stems from the fact that as a child I was desperately ill for some years. When I was eight years old there was an occasion when my parents were summoned to see me for the last time. I was at death's door but I have the clearest recollection of the scene, though I was supposedly deeply unconscious. My bed in the ward was surrounded by screens and my mother and father stood at the foot of the bed while the matron of the hospital stood at the right-hand side. My parents were in tears but selfishly I was quite unconcerned as I observed the scene, looking down on it all, including my own body, from a point at the head of the bed, higher than the screens, from where I was able to see the whole of the ward.

[When, in 1979, I had my near-death experience] it was as if all the information stored in a massive computer had been instantly downloaded into my brain. It was a truly awful and shattering experience. Even now the memory reduces me to tears ... I consider it possible that this [his childhood experience] left some kind of trigger in my brain that was to be activated in 1979.

Sometimes previews of the future are associated with a feeling of choice, as though, although the experiencer is being shown the future, he does not have to accept it.

In 1965 Mr D. Cook was a seventeen-year-old living in Rhodesia. One day, while riding his motorcycle down a hill which curved to the right, he was in a head-on collision with a station wagon which pulled out of a side road on his left. He describes what happened then.

Nothing happened for a long time, no sound or other [feeling perceptible to any] of the five senses. Then I was travelling in darkness in an unknown direction but at tremendous speed in a straight line. It seemed a long journey. There was no wind resistance, no pain. Then I perceived a dim light which became pure white light. It should have hurt my eyes it was so bright, but it did not. Then darkness.

My next recollection was as if I were 'standing' in darkness. To my right a door silhouette began to open, shedding the white light. I became aware of a voice and a person in white clothing for an instant, but heard 'his' voice. I do not know what was 'said' but recollect a sense of absorbing, welcoming, and consciously recall a great desire to pass through the door. I knew that if I did there would be no return. I remember protesting that I had not lived my life yet and I wanted to have children.

I was given a chance to go through a door to my left and was urged to choose the right door, to which I was drifting all the time. I was initially six or eight feet from the right and left doors as it was at this point that I saw myself. I saw that T (i.e. my head) was obscured by the head and shoulders of a man. 'I' was lying on my back, and although I could not 'see' my own face, I recognised my clothing. I could see the heads and necks of about eight people peering over me, scuffling, kicking up dust. Someone said, 'Leave him, he's dead.' I shouted from about fifteen feet above the ground, 'No! I am not! Get back from me, I am trying to breathe.'

It was then I knew I had chosen the left door, although it had been an enormous task to pull back from the threshold of the right door. At that point in time I knew that, depending on my actions during my life, I might not again be given the choice of the two doors, although I knew my life would be full of choices which would be hard. I knew it would be a hard life but a long one.

I recall the man saying, 'Give him air, move back,' and remember seeing myself cough. I had no sensory faculties of pain, and neither did my body. T descended and arose twice, as if I had not made up my mind which direction to go. But the callous comment ['Leave him, he's dead,'] had really made me angry.

Later Mr Cook discovered that the man he had seen bending over him, obscuring his view of his own body, was a doctor whose surgery was opposite the crash site. He went to thank him and was told that he had in fact choked on a mixture of blood and petrol and had stopped breathing.

Mr Cook was not simply given the choice between dying (the right door) and living (the left). He was given a glimpse of his future, which indicated that if he chose to live, his life wouldn't be particularly easy, and that only through his future actions would he earn the right to make this choice again.

And yet, knowing this, why did he decide to return when the pull towards the right-hand door was so strong? As so often seems to happen, the decision to return is an emotional one, sparked off by some intensely personal motive - in Mr Cook's case his anger with the person who suggested leaving him for dead, coupled with his desire to have children.

These glimpses of the future often involve an awareness that when the person returns, there is work to be done. Sometimes, as in the case of David Verdegaal, described below, this is a specific task; others, as we have seen, simply know they are being sent back to achieve something, but they may not know then (or indeed ever) what it is they have to do. If one regards this sense of 'unfinished business' as being essentially the same as a limited life preview, then the preview seems to be quite common - certainly much more common than the experience of a life review. Of the people we questioned about their NDEs, 13 per cent said they saw scenes from the future; for 22 per cent of these the glimpses were of the world's future, 48 per cent were personal and 29 per cent experienced both.

David Verdegaal's experience as he lay in a coma for two weeks is a beautiful example of a preview which contained specific instructions about a job to be done: 'While in the coma I was told many things, one being that I was meant to write a book recounting my life. Although I felt this was a definite instruction, I dismissed the idea as an improbable one as I was no author and the opportunity was not likely to occur. Feeling on safe ground, I submitted to the request if the situation in the future ever made it possible.' Although David emerged from the coma both blind and paralysed, he gradually regained his faculties until, three years later and still only partially sighted, 'there was no excuse for not starting on the work. I joined my local training centre, where I was introduced to computers. Now I could neither write nor spell, the computer became my saviour as the work could be polished up later. Since then I have plodded on at a snail's pace, at the same time regaining my memory and coming to terms with the past.'

David's NDE (which is described in full in Chapter 14) fascinated me because I could find no satisfactory explanation for how such an ordered memory could have been recalled with such clarity from such a damaged and disordered brain. But although David's experience was so extraordinary, it was not unique. Shortly after I had heard from David, I had the following letter from Mrs Carol Mizon about her son, Michael, who is now twenty-two.

Michael was expelled from school at fourteen years of age for being disruptive etc. His educational abilities are very poor and remedial treatment was tried without much success. He is of no particular religious persuasion, although the family are mostly C of E (non-practising).

In July 1990, when Michael was eighteen, he suffered serious brain injury in a car accident and was in a coma for three months. During February 1991, as his condition improved and he was able to talk, he started to talk about a 'journey' he went on while he was 'asleep'. He also said that he wanted to write poetry and words. He said that the words came into his head at great speed and asked me to take them down for him (he has great difficulty controlling a pen due to the brain damage).

This is Michael's story.

The first thing I remember is being in what looked like the cockpit of a plane. The person next to me was slumped over dead. [Michael's mother adds that no one else was killed or seriously injured in the crash.] This dead person opened his hand and a dove appeared. The dove rose up slowly from the hand. I am not sure whether I became the dove or followed the dove. The next thing I remember is being in a dark space with all of the universe whooshing by me. Gradually things changed and got lighter and I found myself walking along a beach. I looked down and was aware that I had a companion. I could see his sandals walking at my side. He had a blanket thing on with stripes on it and a hand covered his face. I sensed no good or bad feelings about this person, if anything he seemed indifferent. He did not speak to me at this point, but beckoned me to follow him.

We both walked along the beach until we came across these huge wooden doors about as high as three houses. I managed to open one of the doors and we went in. What I saw was the inside of a huge church that went on in the distance as far as the eye could see. My way was shortly blocked by two large trestles, each with a book resting on them. My companion flicked through the book to my left and I saw the whole of my life very quickly. He then turned to the right and flicked through the pages of this book, but there was nothing on them. He then spoke to me and said, 'This will be your life if you go back,' and the empty book suddenly became full. He then said to me, 'Do you want to go back?' The part of me that was human did not want to go back. The part of me that wasn't did. The part that wasn't seemed to override the part that was, and I felt that I did not really have a choice, I must go back.

We walked back along the beach and my companion spoke to me again. I felt these words were important but I have forgotten them.

The next thing I knew was hearing what sounded like the crack of a whip, and also the feeling that I was travelling along the wavy line of the whip as it cracked.

Now, nearly four years later, Michael's memories of the experience are fading - in contrast to those of most experiencers, which remain very vivid. But what is truly surprising is that he had any memory at all. Here is a boy who had suffered such severe brain damage that he had been in a coma for three months. And yet the first thing he did when he recovered consciousness and was able to talk was to describe his 'journey', an experience so vivid and important for him that its memory remained clear. The clarity and coherence of the experience in a severely damaged brain is very hard to explain, something Mrs Mizon herself commented on: "What I find interesting is that Michael's day-to-day memory was very bad at the time he wrote the early poems, but his memories of the events he wrote about seemed crystal-clear, almost photographic, and remained so for some months. One other thing. Michael says that as things happen in his life he knows they are going to happen just before they do, sometimes seconds before, and he will verbally trip over himself trying to tell me. Michael also says that he is not frightened of dying. He is not sure what will happen to him, but in his own words, he has been to the 'halfway house'."

Michael's mother now has almost sixty of the poems he dictated to her after his accident. Two of these are reproduced here. These poems are interesting in themselves, as they seem to reflect elements of his experience. But it's even more interesting that he wrote them at all. Remember, this is an eighteen-year-old lad whose educational abilities were poor.

I asked his mother whether she thought he would have had the ability, or more importantly the inclination, to write poetry before his accident. His mother thought not; his sister and a family friend who knew Michael well agreed with her.

I'm sure there's more
More thought, more fact
But there may be a crack
In this door of mine.
But I am sure I can pass through it,
What's on the other side?
Some kind of light
That pulls me in.

It's funny, I see Heaven but I'm not dead no more
I live again, yet I survived death as you know it.
Bleep! Bleep! I'm still alive,
People at my bed, I'm no longer dead
In this hospital bed.
I'm still alive and I will thrive
To live another duck and dive.

These glimpses of the future seem especially significant when they are given to people like Michael Mizon, David Verdegaal and Ms M. D. Drury who have been badly injured and for whom the future is inevitably going to be difficult. It is as if these people are being prepared for what is in store for them, by being given a choice about whether they return and accept it, or a sense of purpose to make their future life worth living, however difficult it may be, or an assurance that they will be helped to endure whatever they have to face. Their experiences give a wonderful feeling of compassion, a sense of order, that seems to stem from some higher destiny than from a dying, damaged brain.

For a moment let's take these experiences at face value. If we do this, then they seem to show a deterministic world in which events are preordained. It even seems as though some of these events are designed to help personal development. But within these experiences there is a contradiction between a future which seems to be determined and the existence of free choice. The idea of predetermination is a difficult one for most of us to accept; we like to think that we can make choices, bring about change and so exercise some sort of control over our lives. It may make more sense to look on these events as some kind of preparation. These people are being made aware that they will have to face pain and frustration in the future and shown that if they decide to come back they have no choice but to accept it.

The fascinating thing is that there are aspects of the near-death experience which only start to make sense if you take them literally. Let's accept that 'something' does leave the body and have experiences outside the body. The memory of these experiences would therefore have to be stored outside the brain, too. And because they were stored independently of the brain, memories acquired in this state could not be lost when the brain was damaged. A theory of this kind would explain how memory is retained in spite of brain damage. But it still gets us no further in understanding where and how such memories could be stored, or how they could be accessed.

'At Last I Knew the Reason Why'

Most life reviews are on a very personal level, but sometimes people are shown glimpses of the past or of the future on a more cosmic scale. Mr Maurice James was shown a vision of the past, an impersonal past and yet a past of which he seemed always to have been a part, and which seemed to contain within it the seeds of the future.

Maurice James was in hospital waiting for a coronary bypass. From his room in the ward he could see Peterborough cathedral. He was also able to see small Ws' of swans flying across the sky. But before the operation he suffered a coronary thrombosis, followed by a cardiac arrest, and was rushed to the Intensive Care Unit, where he remained unconscious for about twenty hours.

> When in the ICU I several times felt myself become weightless and float up into the sky and join the swans in their family group. I was conscious of being a very junior member of the group. The amazing thing was, though, that sometimes the cathedral was not built. It was as if the fens were in a

primeval state... I felt as if I could not only fly forever but also see forever in a backward way, never into the future. I could see men in mediaeval dress in their tiny sailing craft punting across the great meres, and then I was able to see the cathedral being built, rising up out of the muddy ooze. The landscape below me rolled very quickly like a speed-ed-up film, very like the 'bird's- eye' films one sees on TV but with no sound and with a feeling of power but peace. On some of the 'flights' I could feel and sense the wind and freedom on my skin, and the peacefulness, but also a great knowledge, as if at last I knew now the reason why. I really not only felt immortal, I felt as if I had existed forever, my being and 'soul' had been this way before.

Chapter 9

Transformation

EVERYONE who has written about or studied the near-death experience describes its powerful effect on people's lives. Some researchers have even said that unless an NDE 'transforms' the person in some way it isn't a 'real' NDE.

Certainly, from the letters we have received, it looks as though people who have had a near-death experience rarely come through it quite unchanged. Seventy-two per cent of the 350 people in our sample felt they had been changed by their experience: 42 per cent said they felt they were more spiritual; 48 per cent became convinced of survival after death; 22 per cent that they were a 'better' person for the experience; 40 per cent that they were more socially conscious. But by far the most common change reported (in 82 per cent of people who felt they had changed after an NDE) was in attitudes towards death. However they felt before the experience, most say that after it they have no fear of death, though they may still feel apprehensive about dying. Over and over again people expressed this conviction. This lack of fear of death is not necessarily linked to a conviction that there is an afterlife - it is felt even by people who don't have any strong belief in a life after death.

Mrs M. Lowther: 'So death can come at any time and holds no fear for me as a result of what I consider to be a privileged experience.'

Mrs M. Hilton: 'At one time I was afraid of dying, but now it doesn't bother me at all.'

Ms Linda Gordon: 'I'm certainly not afraid of dying. I'm pleased, in a way, I was given a preview.'

H. N. Smith: 'During the whole of this experience I was not afraid and the feeling that remains with me is one of peace and certainty that there is no need to fear death.'

Eleanor Cleator: 'The experience has had a lasting effect upon my life; if that was "near-death", I have no fear when my time for dying comes. I look forward to it with expectation of that wonderful joy and peace.'

Mrs Holyoake: 'I shall never be afraid of death because there is another form of life.'

Judith Smith: 'There may well be "life after life" or it could be the way the brain shuts down; either way, death is something to look forward to, when it comes.'

Pauline Hill: 'I have never really feared death since. It opens up marvellous possibilities! If this life were all we had, I should think it most illogical and rather a poor deal for many. As it is, my experience suggests there may be something much more meaningful hereafter. I hope so.' Often people feel that their experience is something they can use to reassure others about death. Indeed, for many this was the main reason they gave for talking about it at all.

Mrs C. Proctor: 'This incident changed my life. It made me realise that the moment of passing from life to death is wonderful, although one is unable at the time to tell people around one, and that is a sadness. I have spoken of what happened to me in the belief that it might help the grieving relatives left behind wondering and unknowing.'

Audrey Quinn: 'When I awoke I felt very much at peace. I have since told people that I no longer fear death itself - I've never felt the need to talk about it but have happily related the events to any inquiring person - indeed, my own father, who has had several severe cardiac arrests and who has told me he is terrified of dying.'

Jean Giacomozzi: When people tell me they are afraid to die I always come trotting out with this experience even if they do think I am nuts. I feel compelled to do it... I don't know what I think about it all, after all these years, except I still think it happened. I truly don't think I feel bad about my own death now. My husband never really believed there was a life after death, and watching him die, I saw an expression of puzzlement which I had never seen before on his face. I hope he found out the great mystery. I certainly know he didn't think I was beside him. No, he was 'somewhere else'.

'I Feel I've Changed'

Some people said they felt the experience had made them more caring and more sympathetic towards other people's needs. Mrs Audrey Quinn, for example, felt she had become more sympathetic to other people's problems. She became a Samaritan after her experience.

Sarah McAdam: 'Since this experience sixteen years ago I have always felt "different". I always want to help people. I cannot stand all the evil, war and fighting going on as it is so opposite to the place we all go to and to what I now feel inside.'

Audrey Organ: 'Whether this was the influence that made me return to nursing I don't know. I was certainly a far better nurse than I had been in my youth.'

For some the changes have been very practical. Henry Foster, the college lecturer whose account is given in Chapter 4, had his near-death experience at a time when he had been overworking and was under a great deal of stress. He says:

> As a consequence of this experience I have become very aware of my own limitations. Also, although I have never been afraid of death, now I believe that death is in fact a beautiful experience and at the end of my life, which I hope has been a useful one, I shall not be afraid to die. One lesson I have learned is to make sure that my colleagues never overwork themselves, and as a result we are a very happy and close-knit team.

Almost everyone who has had an NDE finds they have a different perspective on life, and at least one correspondent, Jane Dyson, found this made it hard to be patient with other people's preoccupations and priorities.

> Since recovering from my injuries I have found it very difficult to relate to people apart from my daughters and grandchildren. The rest irritate me so much I could shout at them. They all seem so concerned with such trivial matters, which to me are not important. I have almost a feeling of disdain, which I know is unfair, but there it is always at the back of my mind, that I went to the end of the tunnel and with my own effort was able to turn back.

So people often *feel* they've changed, but have they really? Finding objective evidence of such change is often a different matter. A story told to us by Mr P. Fearn is particularly interesting because it gives us a third-person view of just such a situation.

A colleague of Mr Fearn's had returned to work after an accident. He had spent a long time in intensive care, most of the time unconscious and very ill. Mr Fearn noticed something different about him:

> He seemed to be a changed man. Nothing that I could at first put my finger on, but eventually, after a few weeks, I spotted the difference. His bustling, heavy-handed approach had gone, and in its place was a gentleness, quiet, and calmness that had never been there before.
>
> It was months later that he eventually opened up to talk about his experience. 'Peter,' he said, 'what would you say if I told you that I died in the hospital, went to Heaven and was then ordered back?' He could remember floating between floor and ceiling. He then seemed to move off into a misty area and eventually arrived somewhere that was again misty but lighter in colour, like sun shining through a field fog. He did not remember coming down to Earth, or wherever it was, but suddenly he was talking and laughing with a group of people who seemed to know him, but whom he could not identify, as he could not see their faces clearly. After a while, one of these people said to him, well, Fred (they knew his name), it's time for you to go back now. Fred said he did not want to, as he was quite happy there with them. The same person chuckled and said, I bet you do, but Fred, what you do not know is that we are not ready for you yet, it's not your turn, and you are before your time, so you cannot stay. The next thing Fred remembers was being aware that he was back in hospital again.
>
> A story like this, coming from a man whose character I knew very well, was one that I had to believe. It was so way out that for a man to even speak about it amazed me.

But transformation, or at any rate permanent transformation, is by no means universal. James Carney, for example, said that after his experience he 'was filled with the feeling of compassion and concern for other human beings. This feeling was alien to me and I am afraid to say that in my world of having to take care of myself and survive it did not last long.' And Mrs A. Burns said, rather wistfully, that she didn't think the experience had transformed her at all.

> Sadly, I don't think the experience has changed me very much. I think I would consider myself more on the atheist side of beliefs rather than the Christian, although I was brought up in the usual middle-class way of Sunday School, church on special occasions. I have never been in church except at Christmas or Easter since I was confirmed at the age of seventeen. I have always felt more in touch with nature and the seasons and closer to any higher being on a walk rather than in a church.

Faith and the NDE

'I always did believe in God but only because it was bred into me,' says Mrs Anne Thomson. 'But since that experience I have a lot of faith towards God and towards life beyond our lives on Earth. I firmly believed he made me well and helped me through all my time of rearing three children alone in the years that followed.'

Most people who have had near-death experiences have a strong conviction that some important part of them - consciousness, soul, call it what you will - can exist quite independently of their body. When you hold this conviction, it is easy to believe, in fact it follows quite naturally, that there is a continuation of some sort of existence after death.

For a few people the NDE is confirmation of a religious faith they already have. But for many, perhaps most, it is a spiritual awakening that may have very little to do with religion in the narrowest sense, and nothing to do with dogma. It seems to broaden religious faith rather than simply confirm it, leading to a recognition that many paths lead to the same truth. It certainly tends to confirm belief in some form of afterlife. But there is very seldom any sense of exclusivity in the experiences: when the presence of some higher 'being' is felt, this is only seldom defined as, for example, a Catholic or a Jewish God. And Christian icons such as Jesus and Mary are notably absent except in very rare cases. The experiences have a universal quality. If this were a purely psychological experience, one would expect it to be much more culturally influenced than it seems to be.

I found it interesting that, although most people's natural tendency is to try to interpret a new experience in the light of their existing belief system, experiencers tend not to do this with the NDE. They are much more likely to try to modify their belief system if the experience does not seem to fit into it. One correspondent, for example, said that he found none of the religious tenets of his own Judaeo-Christian tradition relevant to his experience. He did, however, have a Hindu doctor friend who was also a Brahmin. During their talks together he found that the Hindu belief system of life and reincarnation seemed much closer to his experience.

Mrs Nita McCallum was a practising Roman Catholic. At the time of her experience she says she was very ill and in excruciating pain. She herself was surprised that her experience did not seem to be related to her religion.

> Had I died I would most certainly have expected that any visions I had would have related to my faith, and that if I was to see a being of light I would have related it to Jesus or Mary or an angel. As it was, when I suddenly found myself in this gentle glowing light and standing a little below the three beings above me, they appeared to me as young Indian men, and though they were dressed alike in high-necked silver-coloured tunics with silver turbans on their heads, I felt they were young Indian princes, or rajas ...
>
> My whole lifestyle was changed as a result - much reading about various religions and philosophies.

Other people echoed this view, or expressed something very similar. Mrs Joan Hensley:

> Certainly my life changed. I am less frightened of dying personally, and I do believe there is life after death. But it hasn't particularly made me more 'religious'; what I do feel is that there are so many religions in the world, why should our God be the only one or indeed the correct one? I feel my experience proved there is a God - before that I don't think I really believed in anything, just accepted what my parents believed in.

Frances Barnshey told us: 'I've always believed in life after death, though I no longer belong to any form of organised religion, preferring to find my own path, but if I needed anything to confirm my belief in another plane of existence, that experience certainly did. I feel so grateful to have had it.'

Mrs Langschield is a retired state registered nurse whose NDE occurred during a difficult childbirth in 1954.

> I was driven and drawn back into another sphere and dimension which had been there all along ... It was as if I were going home, so familiar was it to me. As if returning to where I had originally come from ... The absolute peace, the oneness, the completeness, was the most striking ... The knowledge of that positive experience has never entirely left me, never faded or diminished over the past years... Now I understood something more about God being the Omega and Alpha of the whole of existence ... that phenomenon experienced was God ...
>
> [The experience] has left me with a striking awareness of our very transitory existence here, through life itself; also that that other afterworld is far more real that this one ever is. It has coloured my whole existence ever since.

Since then Mrs Langschield says she has had no fear of death (though she is still apprehensive about dying). She has visited Lourdes several times because she feels 'it is the one place on earth that holds a certain portion of that "oneness"'.

Should we be surprised at the fact that the NDE produces change? Perhaps this isn't a particularly startling claim. Any intense emotional experience, whether it is positive or negative, changes people in some way. Anyone who has lost a day's work on the word processor knows how effectively even such a trivial experience modifies behaviour, how obsessional they become about backing up their discs - for a while. And most people, when they feel they have had a real stroke of undeserved luck, tend to be nicer to those around them for a few days, perhaps in an unconscious 'pay-back' attitude. Such fairly minor events usually produce only temporary change. The more profound the experience, the more permanent one might expect such a change to be. And any experience that is capable of producing permanent change is, for that reason alone, worth taking very seriously.

Richard Hands was one of the few people who specifically states that the experience he had as a child held no particular spiritual significance for him. He says:

I don't pretend to understand why these things happen to so many people, but as an atheist I cannot accept any talk about a soul. Rather, I view it as a function of the chemical changes that occur in the brain on death, producing such images, similar to the life flashing before your eyes occurrence that happens to people in life-or-death situations, now attributed to the brain undergoing a rapid memory search to find a way of coping with the situation in hand.

If we look at Mr Hands' experience (see Chapter 12) it is clear that it was neither particularly positive nor emotionally overpowering. There is no reason to expect it to have influenced his adult commitment to the view that the brain is all. Compare this with the account given by Mr J. Inman at the beginning of Chapter 5. Their experiences were similar in that neither was strongly visual, and both men say they are not religious, and did not attach religious significance to them. Mr Inman saw nothing, but describes a 'state', a feeling of complete release ... a sensation of serenity, timelessness'.

For him it was such an emotional experience that it had the power to cause a radical shift in his belief in an afterlife:

> My own belief - and I am not a religious person (I did not believe in an afterlife before this happened) - is that we leave this life as easily as passing from one room to another, into a state - a period of waiting, and that state, be it the soul, electricity or whatever energy, then passes into another receptacle, perhaps shortly after conception to be born again.
>
> Before my experience I had wondered, like most, about death, and, like most, was afraid of the unknown. I now count myself among the privileged in that I now know that there is no pain, there is nothing other than the ending of one chapter and the turning of the page.

The experience of the transforming light is for many the most profound emotional experience they have ever encountered. The feeling is one of being overwhelmed by universal love, of being accepted in totality by some loving being. The memory of these wide positive feelings, the loving acceptance of your own grubby behaviour, seems to enable people to see themselves in a very different perspective, and in some way to feel and behave as a different person.

There are other psychological reasons for change, too. Survivors of disasters in which others have died are marked by the experience. They may feel guilty - 'Why me?' - and wonder why they have been singled out for survival. The fact that they have survived is so momentous that it may be hard for them to believe that it could have been just random chance, the luck of the draw. One way of making sense of this is to feel that their own escape was in some way their destiny, that it has personal significance.

If even the thought of death is something we find awesome, to come near to death and then escape it must be one of the most profound human experiences, with or without an NDE. It must in some way alter your perspective on life, and so it is not really surprising to find that it is capable of producing permanent change. Anyone who has ever been in a situation where death seems imminent or inevitable, but who then survives, feels to some extent reborn. It is as though you have been given a second chance, that you are somehow 'special' to be alive when you might so easily have died.

'The Nowness of Life'

So often we come to value something only when we realise how easily it might be lost. Most of us spend most of our time planning our future or thinking about our past, so that all too often the present slips by us almost unobserved. But in the face of death we realise how tenuous, how unpredictable are our links with the future. All we really have is the present, and it is only 'now' that will form our past. One of the glories of the near-death experience is that it does not simply change people's attitudes towards death; often it helps them to celebrate life more freely as well.

Gillian McKenzie: 'It was the most valuable experience I've ever had in my life. If that is what it's like to die I have no fear of dying. But I feel that it showed me more about life than death. It made me think of all the things that were of value in life. I became very aware, I noticed things far more - the leaves on the trees, the clouds in the sky. I became more alert to the world around me. I became more aware of people - some people in particular, whom I always refer to as kindred spirits, even though I hardly know them.'

Avon Pailthorpe: 'After the accident I was very ill in hospital. However, the memory of the accident is not horrific to me, because this experience was so reassuring. It was also in a way exciting, and helped me to feel positive and strong to continue living, because there was a reason why I couldn't die.'

Hilda Middleton: 'The effect of my experience has had a profound effect on my life. I thank the Lord for every new day, but if death is the wonderful experience I had, I'm not afraid of death.'

Ms N. Baker: 'I believe I died for a short time. I am not a particularly religious person, but this experience has totally changed my life. After nearly three years I am unimaginably lucky only to suffer from slipped discs. I know there is some form of life after death and it is a truly wonderful "Heaven".

I love life and live it to the full. I'm just happy to be allowed to live on this Earth for this comparatively short time.'

Elizabeth Rogers: 'I now feel every day is a new gift to me. Material things are not nearly as important as they used to be and I now look forward with peace and joy to the day of my death. Before that [her NDE] I was not afraid of death really, but I didn't like the thought of it. But now I am looking forward to dying, to death. It has absolutely no fears for me. Recently someone asked me what I would say if I was told I had to die now. My answer was, "I'd say, 'This is a lovely now.' " '

The sadness is that we seem to find it so hard to live our lives positively until they come under threat. Any one of us could enrich our own lives if we too could learn to say, 'This is a lovely now.' No one has expressed this truth - that by accepting death our attitude towards life can be transformed - more movingly or with greater clarity than the playwright Dennis Potter, in his final interview with Melvyn Bragg in March 1994, a few weeks after he learned that he had terminal cancer, and a few weeks before he died.

> However predictable tomorrow is ... there's the element of the unpredictable, of the you don't know. The only thing you know for sure is the present tense, and that nowness becomes so vivid to me that, almost in a perverse sort of way, I'm almost serene. You know, I can celebrate life.
>
> Below my window in Ross... the blossom is out in full now ... and looking at it, instead of saying, 'Oh, that's nice blossom,' ... I see it is the whitest, frothiest, blossomest blossom that there ever could be... Things are both more trivial than they ever were, and more important than they ever were, and the difference between the trivial and the

important doesn't seem to matter. But the nowness of everything is absolutely wondrous ... The fact is, if you see the present tense, boy, do you see it! And boy, can you celebrate it.'

Chapter 10

Psychic Powers

ALMOST everyone who has studied near-death experiences has found that at least some of the people they have talked to feel that since their experience they have become more sensitive or intuitive. Forty-seven per cent of our sample reported some kind of psychic ability after their NDE. At its least spectacular, this is described as a form of heightened awareness. Sheila Freeman describes what happened to her when she had a cardiac arrest during an operation.

One of the worst moments in my life had an unexpected ending, which I suppose was to completely change my attitude to life ... Eventually I blacked out, 1 felt myself grow light and weightless, the pain just stopped. It seemed like a miracle ... I felt myself drift up and up, towards a brilliant white light. I seemed to hear my name spoken in a beautiful voice. I felt totally, wonderfully happy, quite unafraid - eager to reach the light, which I somehow knew was the perfect place, Heaven, I suppose. But it was the emotion I felt that was so memorable; uplifted, transported, supremely at peace ...

Since that traumatic time, I have no fear of death, although the 'dying' is not so easily dismissed. I believe there is something wonderful beyond the veil, awaiting all of us. A very important aftermath was that it has left me with a sort of heightened awareness. Everything creative, like art, music, literature, also people, animals and nature seem almost too beautiful, touching or vulnerable - I get such a deep emotional response, sometimes it seems almost unbearable.

Several people say that they acquired the ability to heal after an NDE. Often they regard this as a gift given to enable them to pay off a debt - a life for a life, perhaps. 'I have been given the ability of healing and am grateful to be able to help in this small way,' one woman said. And another, Constance Cawthorne, who became a healer and teacher after her NDE, says she feels she has been given support in the form of 'healing power' which she channels 'to help people become more aware of their potentialities and strengths.' Many others report various psychic experiences - they may have deja vu feelings, or be able to tell what is going to happen in the future. Among these is Mrs Margaret Dinkeldein ,a registered nurse whose near-death experience in 1979, while giving birth to her third child, appears in Chapter 4:

I am not a particularly religious person, but at various times in my life - particularly during adolescence and at times of extreme stress -1 have had extraordinary 'psychic' episodes that have come completely uninvited. In no way do I dwell on spiritualism or try to encourage it in myself.

I am basically a fairly down-to-earth sort of person, a mother of four children, with plenty of friends and outside interests.

AN UNWELCOME GIFT

Many people have ambivalent feelings towards the psychic abilities they seem to have acquired as a result of having an NDE. Often they regard them as an unsolicited and not entirely welcome gift.

Audrey Organ: 'Some places affect me. I am uneasy. I have never dabbled in any form of spiritualism, I feel one shouldn't pry. My doctor once told me he believed I was psychic and scared me witless.' Gillian McKenzie: 'The other thing I was aware of which worried me a bit, was that sometimes I know things in advance. I know when people are going to telephone me, or I'll know when they are in trouble and I'll phone them. Sometimes it's just before, sometimes days in advance. That used to worry me, but I've got used to it now and take it as a matter of course.'

Mr B. Boardman: Since the accident I have become very aware of psychic things and on several occasions have had strong premonitions [of things] that have eventually happened. These are generally of bad news, I suppose good news is no news, as they say. I do not claim to be, nor wish to be, clairvoyant; in fact this ability is quite distressing at times, as my predictions seem to be totally irreversible. I'm sure the psychic ability existed before the accident, which merely made me more aware of things.

Psychic ability can be especially disturbing when, as often seems to happen, premonitions concern death. As recounted in Chapter 6, Mrs J. H. Collingwood found that after her NDE she noticed that when there was a death in the family 'a few days before getting the sad news I had been aware of a strong smell of flowers around me, not noticeable to others', even though she very rarely knew that the people concerned were ill.

Foretelling the Future

For several people, the precognitive ability they acquired was bound up with a 'life preview' they were given during their experience. Mr D. Cook's near-death experience after a motorcycle accident is described in Chapter 8. Since the accident Mr Cook says he has experienced various psycho- logical phenomena, such as waking up at the exact time of his son's birth, and later, his mother's death. From time to time he has deja vu feelings. He has also found that he can anticipate major future occurrences in his life. He explains this: 'It is almost as if, during the near-death experience, I saw a speeded-up video of my future life in order to select it or the other. It seems that the odd video frame has been remembered. Similarly I can foresee some people's destiny, but not everyone's, just people who seem to have a say in my own.'

Other people also described similar glimpses of the future which they were shown in their experience. Mr D. A. Bak of Leicester gave a very full description of his preview in an NDE under anaesthetic in Chapter 8. He subsequently found that the major events in his own future shown to him by the beings he encountered did happen.

The time involved was from the early 1950s to 1969. The last thing that was said to me [by the beings] in this experience was that contact would be made again in 1969.

In 1969 I was again in the position of needing an anaesthetic, but chose to have a local one in view of what happened all those years before, and so I thought that I had broken contact. No one to whom I tried to explain the experience would believe it would happen. However, a few weeks later I reluctantly met a very sensitive and highly aware person, who had no knowledge of what had happened to me in the 1950s, but gave me details of the event, and then brought through the entity that I had met in the experience referred to above, and then proceeded to give me details of the next phase of my life, which again did not make sense to me at the time. But as my life progressed, it all fell into place with amazing accuracy. The details given to me then and also up to the present time, I have kept records of, and the persons who were described to me at the time I had no knowledge of, but when I became aware of the event the description was very accurate.

In Chapter 8 I described the case of Michael Mizon, who was injured in an accident and lay in a coma for three months. When he recovered he described to his mother the 'journey' he had been on, which included a life review and preview. Now, reports his mother, 'Michael says that as things happen in his life he knows they are going to happen just before they do, sometimes seconds before, and he will verbally trip over himself trying to tell me.' I asked her if she could give me any specific examples of this, and her reply illustrates very clearly how difficult it is to decide how reliable these feelings really are:

As to the question of Michael's ability to know things before they happen, this has been a more difficult task. It is difficult to separate fact from fantasy. A friend recently had a minor car accident and Michael said that he knew of this. Going back to 1992, at the time Michael was writing his most interesting poems, he did make a prediction that did indeed come true. These were his words and the outcome: 'I am going to have another accident, but I will survive it, and there will not be much improvement in my life until after this accident.' Michael had an accident in August 1993. He had had a few drinks and was found in a local car park by police.

They are not sure whether he fell over or was hit by a hit- and-run driver. The result was a broken leg and minor bruising, which kept him confined to the rehab unit for a month.

After this there was definitely a marked improvement in his understanding of the problems he faces, and other improvements in behaviour were noticed. This may be just coincidence, or him generally coming to terms with the effects of his accident, but his life has improved since.

The sudden flash of recognition that says 'I've been here before' or 'I've done this before' is something most of us have experienced at some time or another and will recognise. It's quite common, too, to feel a premonition that something is going to happen. How often have you felt the phone was about to ring just before it actually does, or picked up a ringing phone and said to the friend on the end, 'I was just going to ring you.' Whether this is telepathy or simply coincidence, it is so common that we take it for granted - and if the feeling proves unfounded, we quickly forget it. Even when a premonition of disaster on a grand scale (an earthquake or aeroplane crash, for example) comes true, it is difficult to evaluate. We don't know, for example, how many such predictions *don't* come true. It may be that those that do form such a tiny proportion that we have simply to put them down to coincidence.

The 64,000-dollar question for scientists has always been, why do people who have precognitive powers not become immensely rich on the horses, the dogs, or even the stock exchange? The answer usually given is that people who believe they have these gifts often have the feeling that they must not be misused. Dannion Brinkley is the American author of *Saved by the Light*, a detailed account of a near-death experience he had after being struck by lightning. He too found he had paranormal abilities after the experience, and in the following passage from the book he describes how he feels about using them:

> When I first discovered these paranormal abilities I used them in ways that I now consider to be dishonest. I was a tough one to beat at cards, since I knew what the other players were holding in their hands ... And at one time I correctly predicted the winning team in football games 156 times in a row ... I soon felt guilty about using these powers in such a

way. I felt that they had a certain God- given aspect to them that made them holy. I abruptly stopped gambling and began looking for positive ways to use my psychic powers.

One of the only people we have found who said that they were able to make this kind of prediction is Mr Dennis Stone of Coventry. Mr Stone's NDE, which he had during an attack of meningitis as a child, is described in Chapter 12. Here he describes how he felt about the psychic precognitive ability he developed after his recovery.

The second part of my tale begins shortly after arriving home again. In August 1938 my first premonition of impending disaster occurred. I saw a vision of the Second World War. I found myself standing about a hundred yards or so from my home, watching Coventry burning and hearing the bombs whistling down and bullets spanging off brickwork. I looked down the London road and watched a bomb set fire to a fuel dump close to the local cemetery.

All this I told my family and I became agitated because they did not believe me. That is until it actually happened in precise detail - with one exception: it was not quite in the precise spot on that fateful night. I was ducking the machine-gun bullets from German planes, which, I might add, killed nine of my neighbours close to me.

I also found I had developed an acute sense of hearing when the wind was in the right quarter. This enabled me to hear German bombers when they crossed our coast and approached Birmingham or Coventry long before the sirens alerted us. Some ten minutes or so. I was never wrong. I knew when they changed direction, also, to fool the defences.

Many things happened during those war years which must surely have killed me, yet the shield remained in place and protected me. I began to think I could not be killed and took far too many chances, I fear.

As an adult Dennis continued to feel that he was under some sort of' protective shield', and continued to have visions which were forebodings of events, both good and bad, to come.

One Friday night I suddenly saw a greyhound racing track and could clearly see the first two dogs out of six in the race past the post. Number 1 and number 6, in that order. The time came into my mind, 3.02 p.m. The next morning my two brothers-in-law called round and suggested an afternoon at the dogs in Birmingham. I told them of this vision and asked them to put five shillings on a forecast with the Tote as I could not go - I had promised to take my girlfriend shopping. At exactly 3.02 Chris and I were walking in Birmingham city centre when I stopped and saw the vision again and I knew it had taken place. On arriving home my jubilant relatives presented me with my winnings. They too had bet numbers 1 and 6, having known of my visions before this.

Eventually, however, Dennis began to feel that the advantages of precognition failed to outweigh the disadvantages. One day, while staying home from work with a cold, he had another, much more terrifying vision of a house being blown up.

I knew it was about to happen, but I knew not which one or what to do. I only knew lives were at risk. My first thoughts were of an unexploded bomb, perhaps, or gas. As a coopted member of the Royal Warwickshire Bomb Disposal Unit, I thought I had cleared the street of delayed action bombs since it was my lot to locate and report any. If I phoned the police they would think me mad without evidence, so I ran up and down the street, hoping to detect a gas leak. No luck! I had just returned home when the end house in my street blew up. The occupants were a wife and baby. Their lives were spared because... an inner wall protected them.

This was the final straw for me in the wretchedness of being unable to help in any way. So I did the only thing possible. I prayed that God would take away this gift of second sight. In time it has subsided, though I still get the sense of impending danger in advance.

The following story was told to me by another patient who had had a near-death experience during an attack of meningitis. In it she had seen two close relatives, both of whom were still alive. One had bandages around his stomach, the other, a young nephew, was dressed in a green T-shirt and cut-off jeans and had a bandaged head. About a year after her recovery the first relative died of cancer of the stomach. A little later her nephew died of head injuries sustained in a motorcycle accident. She said she couldn't bring herself to ask what he was wearing at the time.

Such experiences are both disturbing and, when they happen to you, overwhelmingly convincing. But there is another possibility that needs to be considered. If you were to ask ten people at random whether they had ever had any experiences that could be regarded as psychic - strong deja vu feelings, premonitions, an occasional apparently telepathic communication with someone close to them - probably at least half would tell you that they had. The belief that one has healing powers is also quite common.

So it may well be that people who have psychic experiences or acquire healing abilities after an NDE might in fact have had them prior to the experience but perhaps have been unaware or taken no particular notice of them. This is certainly so in the case of some of the people who wrote to us. Mrs Margaret Dinkeldein, for example, mentions that even before she had her NDE she experienced psychic episodes, particularly during adolescence and at times of stress.

Another explanation is that either the experience itself or any associated brain injury might release the power to be psychic or a healer or a visionary. There are many reports of people who have developed such gifts after a head injury. One of the most well known is that of a Dutchman who fell off a ladder and sustained a serious head injury. When he finally recovered consciousness in hospital, he found that he could read the thoughts of the doctors and nurses around him.

Intrigued by these stories, in 1984 I carried out a study with some colleagues to see if we could find any connection between head injury and the appearance of psychic gifts. Our hypothesis was that there was a special area of the brain, the right temporal lobe, which gave the tag of meaning to the world. If this tag was misapplied, then we would feel that we knew things, or that things were about to happen, although this had no basis in reality.

We tested a group of seventeen mediums and a group of control subjects, and found that there was more evidence of brain damage in the mediums. Some of them had indeed noticed their gifts for the first time immediately after a head injury. We also found that it was the right side of the brain that was damaged more often than the left, and the right temporal lobe.

An account of this experiment was published in Psychic News, and several people who read it wrote to tell me that they too had developed psychic gifts following a head injury. There does seem to be strong evidence that such injuries, probably because they alter brain function, do lead to the emergence of psychic powers. This could explain why psychic gifts are so often reported by people who have had NDEs, since some of them will undoubtedly have sustained some degree of brain damage. But if psychic powers are simply the result of brain damage, they would be of little interest. In our experiment we did not test the accuracy of the psychic powers claimed, and this is clearly a fruitful area waiting for someone to carry out further experiments. If it could be shown that these were indeed genuine, then it's difficult to see how we can simply write them off as perceptions of an altered brain function. A much wider explanation of consciousness would be needed to explain such a very different universe.

Chapter 11

Looking For a Pattern

ONE of the features of the near-death experience which has fascinated many people is that it seems to follow such a consistent pattern. They argue that when so many people experience the same phenomena, they must be getting a 'real' glimpse of what it is like to die and what we can expect to find in the next world.

But does such consistency really exist? There are certainly strong similarities in many experiences, and frequently recurring themes, and in the story so far we have been emphasising these. But it is not the whole story. Here are four cases which give a picture of a quite different world - in fact four quite different worlds.

Knocking on the Door

One of the interesting differences between dreams and near- death experiences is that although dreams often incorporate fragments of everyday experiences and show a clear relationship with the person's waking life, the world of the near-death experience usually seems to be a quite separate one. Different people enter what seems to be the same world. However, in this account given to us by David Davies of an experience described to him by his father, it is easy to see how real events have been incorporated into the NDE.

Mr Davies's father had worked as a miner until he was forced to take early retirement. In 1981, after having had several strokes, he was admitted to the Royal Gwent Hospital in Newport and remained unconscious for about seventy-two hours. When he regained consciousness, his speech was unaffected. His son says:

I clearly recall the first conversation I had with him. He told me how, on the previous evening, he'd been taken to the operating theatre. He remembered having difficulty in getting on to the theatre trolley - it had taken three or four porters to lift him from his bed. He recalled travelling down the hospital corridor towards the theatre. 'It was awfully cold in the corridor,' he commented. He remembered seeing the light of the theatre at the bottom of the corridor and as he got nearer to it he could feel it getting warmer and he recalled hearing music coming from inside the theatre.

When eventually he entered the theatre it was very large and bright and was occupied by one doctor, whom he described as being a big man with a beard, who was wearing an ill-fitting white doctor's coat. He went on to describe the short conversation that he had with the doctor.

The doctor asked him why he was in the theatre and my father's reply was that he had just been brought there by the porters. The doctor then told my father that he 'was not ready for him yet', and that he would have to be taken back to the ward. My father apparently complained at that prospect because he did not relish the thought of the long cold corridors again. The doctor insisted that he wasn't ready for my father and subsequently arranged for him to be taken back to the ward. My father finally recalls the cold corridors once again, when he was returned to the ward, and then waking in his bed.

Quite honestly, I was convinced that what my father had recalled was quite true, because his recollection had been so clear. In fact, I spoke personally to the ward doctor concerning my father's 'pending' operation and about which day he had been taken to the theatre. The doctor informed me that my father hadn't been moved from his bed since his admission and that his condition didn't require any surgery.

My father still recalls the conversation we had about his journey to the theatre. I don't consider myself or my father to be particularly religious people, but I have been convinced since that time that my father at the very least 'knocked on the door', as they say in this part of the world, and that something or someone wasn't ready for him.

Was this a dream? If so, why should it incorporate so many elements of the NDE - the tunnel (corridor) with the bright light at the end; the increasing warmth as he approached it; the music; the god-like presence of the bearded doctor insisting that he should return, and Mr Davies's own reluctance to do so? Was it an NDE? If so, it is unusual in that the imagery is taken so directly from Mr Davies's immediate surroundings. This would make it more like an out-of-body experience, because we have seen that the OBE, whether it occurs on its own or as part of a full near-death experience, is dictated by the surroundings. And yet Mr Davies does not describe leaving his body: he remains on the trolley and is wheeled to the operating theatre. Mr Davies himself is convinced that his father was 'knocking on the door', and I think he was probably right.

Sliding Through Nothingness

Here is another experience in which the imagery is quite unlike that in any of the other accounts we were given. Mr H. N. Smith, who described it to us, had had a cardiac arrest and was told afterwards that he had been clinically dead for approximately three minutes. This is his story.

> Following a heart-attack I was admitted to the Coronary Care Unit. After various tests and sedation I was settled down for the night, and went to sleep. The next thing I was aware of was sliding horizontally down five parallel long children's slides. These were surrounded by an absolute nothingness. As I was going down the slides I could see a barrier at the bottom. It was like a shiny black leather bench. I knew that if I went over the barrier I would be dead. At the barrier there was a young man waiting to help me. He was swarthy-skinned, muscular, with dark curly hair and he was smiling. He was holding his arms out to help. There was an intense white light all around, so bright that I could not see any colours. Also in the background all around were figures clothed in monk-like habits. Men, women, boys and girls, none of whom I recognised. They were not frightening in any way, but I sensed they were waiting for me to make up my mind.
>
> At this point I got so angry that 'they' were doing this to me and that I had to make a decision. I made myself go

back up to the top of the slides and then I felt a tremendous pain in my chest. I came to surrounded by doctors and nurses and subsequently found out that I had suffered a cardiac arrest and had been clinically dead for approximately three minutes.

During the whole of this experience I was not afraid and the feeling that remains with me is one of peace and certainty that there is no need to fear death.

Although it seems so atypical at first glance, Mr Smith's story bears all the hallmarks of an 'ordinary' NDE. The feeling of peace, the lack of fear, the light, the barrier, the moment of decision: all these are there. The feeling of being surrounded by 'absolute nothingness' that Mr Smith describes is in essence very little different from the feeling of being surrounded by blackness that others have experienced in the tunnel.

I'd have no hesitation about describing this as a near-death experience, even though the imagery is so different from the Garden of Eden pastoral idyll that recurs so often. It is another pointer to the near-death world being a psychological world without any reality in physical space.

Journey on the Blue Train

At the time of his experience in 1961, David Whitmarsh was seventeen, and serving aboard a Royal Navy frigate. Part of his duties was testing power points with a portable fan-blower. David describes how he plugged this into a socket above a hatch around which were hung safety chains. He leaned against these, the cool chains resting in the small of his back. Unfortunately, the fan had been connected incorrectly: the earth wire swapped with the 450-volt live supply. When David switched on the fan, his bare leg resting against the machinery, he became a live circuit between the fan and the steel chains.

The powerful throbbing of the ship's turbines seemed to force the electricity through my body. I heard myself screaming as all I could see was a mass of flashes like flames licking around my body and heard a terrible roar. Eventually the flashing stopped and silence ensued. I seemed to be floating in a beautiful velvet-like darkness, feeling completely at peace away from the frightening flashes. I seemed to be going through a tunnel angled slightly downwards when suddenly I found myself standing in a field of beautiful yellow corn. The sky on the horizon was the deepest of sky blues I have ever seen and I felt even more at peace in this lovely tranquil place. The brightness was strong but not overbearing and I felt comfortable and appeared to be wearing a blue gown.

Suddenly, on the distant horizon I saw something that appeared to be a train, in fact a blue train. At first I thought that there was no sound but the beauty of the scene had been so intense that I hadn't noticed gentle music in the background plus the quiet rumble of the blue train.

For some unexplained reason I appeared to get closer to the train, which stopped in front of where I was standing. I could see people in the carriages beckoning to me and telling me to climb aboard. It was difficult to make out their features, which seemed to be shrouded in a grey mist. Then, again almost as if by magic, I was in the train compartment with the faceless passengers, who, I noticed, seemed to be dressed in the same way as I was.

I felt a complete sensation of happiness and contentment as I listened to the happy babble of the passengers. It was almost like being a child again going on holiday with all your friends.

Then it began to happen. I felt a pressure on my shoulders and a strange sensation as I began to rise. It didn't make any sense -1 felt I was being pushed down yet I was going up. I didn't want to leave my new-found friends, who were begging me to stay, and how I wanted to stay. The speed of my ascent became faster and I felt a feeling of anger mixed with regret. I didn't want to go back.

Suddenly I came to and was lying face down on the deck of the frigate passageway. My colleague was pushing on my shoulder blades in the old Holger-Nielson method of resuscitation. My first emotion was one of anger: why did they bring me back? I was happy on that train. I wanted to know where we were going.

To this day I still remember those events as if it were only yesterday, and strange to say I seem to have no fear of the end of my life. In fact I am looking forward to that trip on the blue train and maybe next time I will reach my destination.

One of the features in this account which differs from many NDEs is that David Whitmarsh meets no barrier. When people on the train beckoned to him he was actually able to go aboard. Nothing seemed to be holding him back or preventing him from boarding. One feels that David was well on his way when resuscitation intervened. It's also interesting to see how the resuscitation procedures (the pressure on his shoulder blades) are incorporated into the experience. This account and the previous one have another odd feature in common - both experiencers travelled downwards.

Adventure in the Red Fort

Finally, another story with a military flavour, which was told to us by Mr H. T. Mill. Here it is in his own words.

The events of my story occurred in the Red Fort, Delhi, during the hot-weather season in 1935. I was twenty-three years old, a private soldier in the 9th Light Tank Company, and it was my first year of service in India. I might add that I was perfectly fit, unworried and with no family history of mental disorders or other troubles.

I had just completed a two-hour stint of guard duty, roaming the tank park on the look-out for intending malefactors, and keeping a watchful eye for the orderly officer making his rounds. It was midnight, fourteen hours since our guard had come on duty that morning. The day had been hot, and now in the supposed cool of the evening the sun's stored heat in walls, stonework and the hard earth was radiating uncomfortably, making people perspire profusely, including me. Thus, when I had completed my two hours of patrol duty, I was glad to lay on a hard wooden bench in the guard room to rest for the next four hours before taking the 4 to 6 a.m. turn of duty. For this rest period sentries were permitted to sleep - if they could - provided they did not remove their webbing equipment and arms. In my case, besides my webbing harness I had on a 0.45 Webley pistol in a stiff leather holster and ammunition in an equally stiff leather pouch. I suppose I soon fell asleep because I obviously went into a torpor from which I did not recover for six hours.

During that comatose state I had a weird vision. I was able to see myself lying on my back in a wide dark cavern, with my feet pointing towards a large rock in the distance. I could see the rock quite clearly because there was a brilliant white light spilling out from the rear and to the right of the rock. I found I was one of a great number of other bodies being drawn in a current towards the gap beside the rock. At first the power of the current was slight but it increased with contraction as the distance to the rock shortened, and although I could not clearly see any of the bodies I was nevertheless aware that the whole floor was covered with them, all human, and that they were writhing and wailing and like me their feet were pointed towards the gap to the right of the rock. I was not wailing; indeed I was quite interested in my situation and was looking forward to seeing what was behind the rock. I had the feeling I should see God, and the closer I came to the gap the more certain I was that God was on the other side. And then, by exerting pressure against the current of bodies, I arrested my forward motion. Bodies swept by and the wailing became more pronounced - almost as a protest against my hesitation. Perhaps I relaxed again, because I realised that I was still drifting towards the gap.

I did not put up much resistance and was about to give up altogether when a voice in the gap called out to me, 'Go back, your time is not now. You have a job to do and it is not completed. Go back.' I knew the message was directed at me. The voice seemed not to be the voice of God, but the voice of an angel - perhaps. At the time I wondered if it was the voice of Jesus Christ, but I had no way of knowing. All I knew was that I was under orders to go back and complete an unspecified task. I had no idea what that task was, but I knew that some time something would happen and I would know what was required of me. With that I exerted more pressure against the tide of wailing humans and gradually I overcame the current, until... I looked around me to see that I was lying on the hard wooden bench in the guard room.

It is worth recording what happened to Mr Mill next, if only to show the difficulties institutions (such as the Army or even perhaps the medical profession) have with people who return unexpectedly and inconveniently from the dead.

> I sat up. The guard commander looked at me in astonishment and let out a string of obscenities. The other two guards rushed in to see what had caused the outburst. All three looked at me aghast. 'You're supposed to be dead!' one of them cried. 'Bloody dead!' And all three railed at me.
>
> 'Look,' said the lance corporal guard commander, opening the guard commander's report book. 'See? It is written here in ink. You're reported dead. You're bloody dead.' And, as an afterthought: 'You're on a charge.' The next four hours were very strained. Sentry duties were completely disrupted. I was not permitted to stand guard, but had to consider myself a medical case.

Eventually a way was found to bring the incident to an orderly conclusion compatible with Army discipline.

> Our lance corporal guard commander arrived at a decision. He would report directly to the company sergeant-major and abide by his advice. What actually happened was that the page with the offending report in the guard commander's report book was removed and the incident scrubbed and I was not put on a charge. I was also told by the sergeant-major that I should forget the incident altogether.
>
> Perhaps the reader knows the old Army song: 'There is no promotion this side of the ocean, so cheer up my lads, bless 'em all.' That was true for the Army in 1935. All promotion and appointments were made in England, so there really was no promotion until Duff Cooper changed the system in 1936. However, in the meantime our commanding officer made an exception in my case by promoting me to Provisional Acting Unpaid Lance Corporal. A rank of convenience.

These travellers to another realm seem to have taken a different route and reached a different destination from most people who undergo an NDE. How do we explain the fact that the imagery in all four of these cases is so different from the usual imagery of the near-death experience? Perhaps we can learn more by looking for consistency rather than focusing on the differences. If we analyse these experiences, they all contain features of a more 'typical' NDE.

It's as though the same underlying pattern is indeed there, but it is being interpreted in a different way to show a different world.

	1	2	3	4
Light/brightness		•	•	•
Tunnel		•		
Music	•			
Colours			•	
Presence		•		•
Barrier		•		
Decision		•		
Peace/bliss		•	•	
Sent back	•		•	•
Task to do on return				•
No fear of death		•	•	

It looks very much as though the 'realm' to which people travel is something created entirely by their minds, and will be different for everyone. The common ground is in the light which is seen, the feelings of peace or joy evoked, the ambivalence about dying - the knowledge that even though you may want to go, if it is not your time, then you have to return.

CULTURAL PATTERNS AND THE NDE

Near-death experiences seem to know no boundaries. They happen to young and old, to people from all walks of life, to those whose life has a spiritual dimension and to those who profess no faith at all. And perhaps most significantly, there are many, many examples of people who have had near-death experiences at a time when they did not even know that such a phenomenon existed.

However, if the NDE is truly a universal human experience, it should occur universally, in all cultures

Although most accounts of and most research on near-death experiences has been in the West, there have been enough reports of NDEs in other parts of the world to enable us to make some comparisons and to find out to what extent they are culture-bound.

Indian Experiences

Satwant Pasricha, an Indian psychologist from Bangalore, and Ian Stevenson, an American psychiatrist from the University of Virginia, have begun to broaden the picture by looking at the near-death experience in India. They found some interesting cultural differences, but plenty of similarities too.

CASE 1: *A Case of Mistaken Identity (Pasricha and Stevenson, 1986)*

> Two persons caught me and took me with them. I felt tired after walking some distance; they started to drag me. My feet became useless. Then there was a man sitting up. He looked dreadful and was all black. He was not wearing any clothes. He said in a rage, 'I asked you to bring Vasudev the gardener. Our garden is drying up. You have brought Vasudev the student.'

Vasudev was brought back by the same two men who had taken him. He further reported that his namesake the gardener did in fact die the following day. He also identified the black man - who, he said, had a club and used foul language as Yamraj, the Hindu god of the dead. Pasricha and Stevenson add that Vasudev's mother, a pious woman, had regularly read him the scriptures so that even as a young boy, before his NDE, he was quite familiar with Yamraj.

CASE 2: *Administrative Errors (Pasricha and Stevenson, 1986)*

> Four black messengers came and held me. I asked, 'Where are you taking me?' They took me and seated me near the god. My body had become small. There was an old lady sitting there. She had a pen in her hand, and the clerks had a heap of books in front of them... One of the clerks said, 'We don't need Chhajju Bania. We asked for Chhajju Kumhar. Push

him back and bring the other man. He (meaning Chhajju Bania) has some life remaining.' I asked the clerks to give me some work to do, but not to send me back. Yamraj was there sitting on a high chair with a white beard and wearing yellow clothes. He asked me, 'What do you want?' I told him that I wanted to stay there. He asked me to extend my hand. I don't remember whether he gave me something or not. Then I was pushed down.

Stevenson and Pasricha were told that Chhajju Kumhar died at about the same time as Chhajju Bania was revived. He told them that the experience had changed his behaviour, particularly in making him more honest.

CASE 3: *Missing Paperwork (Pasricha and Stevenson, 1986)*

A third case concerned Durga Jatav, who had been ill for several weeks with typhoid. At one point his family thought he had died, but he revived, and told his family that he had been taken to another place by ten people. He had tried to escape, but they had then cut off his legs at the knees. 'He was taken to a place where there were tables and chairs and forty or fifty people sitting. He recognised no one. They looked at his 'papers', saw that his name was not on their list, and said, 'Why have you brought him here? Take him back.' To this Durga had replied, 'How can I go back? I don't have feet.' He was then shown several pairs of legs, he recognised his own, and they were somehow reattached. He was then sent back with the instructions not to 'stretch' (bend?) his knees 'so that they could mend'.

When Pasricha and Stevenson interviewed Durga in 1979 (thirty years after his experience) he was still apparently following the instructions to keep his knees in a fixed position. They were shown fissures in the skin on the front of his knees which had apparently appeared after his experience. Durga claimed never to have heard of such experiences before he had his NDE. He said afterwards that it 'seemed like a dream', which was perhaps fortunate for him, in view of the nature of the experience. Nevertheless, he told Pasricha and Stevenson that it had strengthened his faith in God.

At first glance these Indian experiences seem to have more in common with each other than they do with most Western experiences.

None of the Indian subjects had an out-of-body experience and viewed his own physical body. Neither did they describe going down a tunnel. Instead, the subject is taken by 'messengers', and as a result of some bureaucratic bungling, usually a case of mistaken identity, is finally brought or pushed back. Although Indian subjects sometimes meet relatives or friends, they apparently do not play any significant role or influence the decision to return. Yamraj, the king of the dead, is a well-known figure in Hindu mythology; so too are his messengers and the man with the book, Chitragupta. Stigmata, such as those which appeared on Durga's knees, seem to be a phenomenon only of the Indian NDE.

Nevertheless, we can recognise plenty of parallels. Chitragupta's book can be seen as the equivalent of the Western 'life review'; it contains a record of all a person's actions during his life. On this he or she is judged and assigned to either Heaven or Hell until it is time for his or her next incarnation. The notion that if it is not your time to go you have to return is common to both cultures; so too is the very fact that after a return from the dead (a momentous event in anyone's book) an explanation of some kind must be sought.

Notably absent in all the Indian accounts are the positive feelings so often reported by Western subjects. This may well be because, as Pasricha and Stevenson themselves say, the subjects were not systematically asked for details about the content of the experience. Even so, these feelings are usually the first things to be reported by Western subjects, and seem to them to be the most significant. Certainly, if it is true that they have a chemical basis, and are the result of endorphins released by the brain, as suggested in Chapter 14, then I would expect them to be a feature of any NDE, wherever and however it occurs. However, it's possible that there is a cultural difference here too; that we in the West attach great importance to feelings of personal bliss and peace and so are very likely to report and emphasise them.

Comparison of Indian and American NDEs (Pasricha and Stevenson, 1986)

	Indians (16)	Americans (78)
	%	%
Saw being of light or religious figure	75	53
Met dead acquaintances	25	15
Return through own volition	6	20

Saw physical body		65
Life review		27
Sent back by loved one		14
Taken by messenger	75	
Met man with a book	50	
Sent back - administrative error	62	
Some other person due to die	44	
Brought back by messengers	81	
Stigmata after NDE	25	

Chinese Experiences

In 1976 there was a large earthquake in Tangshan, China. Eleven years later, two Chinese doctors, Feng Zhi-ying and Lin Jian-xun, interviewed eighty-one survivors. All were patients in a paraplegic convalescent hospital and had been nearly crushed to death when their homes had been destroyed. Most were partially or completely paralysed. They found that thirty-two (42 per cent) of these had had near-death experiences. This is a surprisingly high proportion; most Western researchers have estimated that only about 10 per cent of people who have been near death have near-death experiences. However, we have to remember that this is not a random sample: it is unusual in that all the people interviewed were survivors of one particular disaster, and all remained together eleven years after the event.

The main differences between the findings of Dr Feng and Dr Lin and the experiences reported by our sample were that significantly fewer of the Chinese earthquake victims reported feelings of peace or joy, or experienced the tunnel or the light. More of the Chinese had life reviews. There seem, in fact, to be more similarities between the Chinese experiences and those from the Indian subcontinent than between either of these and experiences reported in the West, which suggests strongly that culture plays an important part in the form that experiences take.

	Chinese	UK sample
% %		
Feeling of peace or euphoria	52	77
Life review	51	17
Thought acceleration	51	38
Time acceleration	43	22
Out-of-body experience	43	65

Seeing deceased or religious figures	28	39*/33
Sudden understanding	28	34
Unearthly realm of existence	26	24
Being judged or held accountable	22	
Visions of the future	17	13
Feeling of cosmic unity	16	
Tunnel	16	51
Point of no return	15	24
Unnaturally brilliant light	15	72
Extrasensory perception	14	33
Meaningful sounds	12	24+
Feeling of joy	10	31
Unusual scents	1	

*deceased

+ music

In 1992, while in Hong Kong, I had the chance to do a radio broadcast (which was translated into Cantonese) about the NDE. During the broadcast I asked people who had had such experiences to write to me. There was no response. I wondered at the time whether this was because near-death experiences were not acceptable in the Chinese culture (as was the case in the West until twenty years or so ago), and so not something that could easily be spoken of. Six months later, back in the UK, a letter was forwarded to me from Hong Kong. It was from a young man who had 235 the following experience as a child during a bad attack of typhoid fever.

> I stayed in hospital for over eight months. In the initial period of my hospitalisation I was dead for three times. In one occasion the doctor had signed the death certificate and asked my parents to prepare the funeral and I was sent to a mortuary. During the unconscious period, there was a person wearing a white coat with a pair of wings, [who] picked up my spirit from my body and [we] ascended together. Before my ascension I saw a doctor, nurses and other staffs surrounding and turning my body. I shouted to them that I would come back and asked them not to destroy my body. They couldn't hear me and I ascended gradually and left them. I came to a place where I had never been there, and there was beautiful sunrise, a big golden plain with

sunflowers and other plants, a cock singing a morning song and there was music from distant that was the hymns of a choir. That tranquil and peaceful feeling that I couldn't find again in my late years.

Not sure how long it had lapsed, the angel accompanying me told me the Lord would see me. He led me to a temple and it was very dark inside. Looking around, I saw a head with white beam shining at its back. The face was not well seen but a firm, powerful and solemn voice said to me: 'Boy, it is not the place you should be here at this moment, you have to go back to your world.' I replied immediately: 'Lord, I'm now here, how can I return to my world?' He pointed at once to a speckle of light which just liked a star in Heaven and He said to me: 'You can go back to your world by following the light.' Soon after that, the white beams over His head disappeared and he could not be seen again. Yet his voice remained in my heart forever. I followed His instruction, not sure how long it took and how many roads I passed. I finally came back to my world back to a bed in a hospital. My body was very weak, very thin, and I couldn't walk.

Now, this is a very 'Western' type of experience. Although this man was not a Christian when he had the experience, he became one later. We don't know whether his was a conversion brought about by the experience or whether he had already come under some Christian influence. There is certainly a distinctly Christian flavour in the imagery he describes. We also know that he spent the first ten years of his life out of Hong Kong, and had this experience within a few months of his return. So it seems very likely that there were other cultural influences in his life apart from his Chinese heritage.

It is interesting too to see the similarities between this and other childhood experiences. It shows the very literal interpretation of Heaven that is characteristic of many childhood NDEs: the winged angel, the presence of the Lord, even the notion of Heaven as a distinct place and a distant one at that. Whatever unearthly realm is visited in NDEs, Heaven is usually proximate and the journey time minimal, as if we retain some sense that the kingdom of Heaven is within. It's also highly unusual for the return journey to present such problems; nearly always the person simply finds himself back in the world he thought he had left behind.

The Tibetan Book of the Dead

The stages of the near-death experience bear a remarkable similarity to teachings in the Tibetan Book of the Dead concerning what happens during dying and after death. Sogyal Rinpoche, in his book The Tibetan Book of Living and Dying, discusses the relationship between the NDE and the Tibetan *bardos*, which are the states of living, of dying and of 'becoming' the state you enter after death.

It is the transition from the *bardo* of dying to the *bardo* of becoming which carries many parallels with the NDE. As dissolution or death dawns, you enter a black experience which has many features of the tunnel. You then move into an area of light, 'a great expanse of light beyond birth or death'. After death individuals stay around the place of death and can witness what is happening in much the same way as happens in the out-of-body experience of the NDE. They can see living relatives but are unable to communicate with them.

The body tends to become idealised, as we have seen happens in some NDEs. They can move where they wish and gain perfect knowledge. Wonderful visions are seen and transcendental music heard, and in some accounts of the *bardo* there is a judgement scene very reminiscent of the 'life review' of the NDE. Sogyal Rinpoche's comment seems equally applicable to the NDE: 'Ultimately all judgements take place within our own mind. We are the judge and the judged.'

Crossing the Atlantic

When we compare the accounts of experiences we have collected in the UK and published accounts of American near death experiences, similarities between them are much more apparent than differences. But there are some interesting differences. The life review, for example, seems to be more common in reported American experiences. American workers such as Greyson, Moody, Ring, and Noyes and Kletti (who made a special study of life reviews) all found that between a quarter and a third of the people they questioned had these experiences. In our own study, although about 14 per cent of the people we questioned said that scenes or memories from the past came back to them during the experience, only a handful had had the 'classic' life review, in which every event, every thought in your life is reviewed, and judged, and in which you 'feel' yourself the wrongs you have done to others.

Two American accounts of near-death experiences have recently been published in book form: Betty Eadie's *Embraced by the Light* and

Dannion Brinkley's *Saved by the Light*. Both are very fantastic, vivid, full of detail and of extraordinary events. They seem to have a much more complex 'storyline'. They are more authoritarian: life reviews and previews are common, people come back having been told what is to happen to them, what they are to do with the rest of their lives. It seems to be a more controlling experience.

In each case there is a spirit world full of very concrete visual images. Betty Eadie, for example, visited many other worlds in her experience, all the creations of God. She met people who had been her friends before she came to Earth. She met spiritual beings who were weaving cloth 'like a mixture of spun glass and spun sugar' to make spiritual clothes for those coming into the spirit world from Earth. She was taken into a room similar to a library but without any books. It was a 'library of the mind' in it, by simply reflecting on a topic, all knowledge on that topic came to her. She met warring angels: 'giant men, very muscularly built', whose purpose is to battle for us against Satan and his angels. She met angels whose purpose was to answer prayers, who 'flew from person to person, from prayer to prayer'.

Dannion Brinkley was struck on the head by lightning and resuscitated after a cardiac arrest. He too journeyed through a tunnel to a spiritual realm where love permeated everything. He relived his whole life, experiencing all the considerable grief and pain he had caused others, saw himself as worthless, but felt the burden of his guilt lifted from him through the love of the being of light. He travelled to a 'city of cathedrals made entirely of a crystalline substance that glowed with a light that shone powerfully from within.' Dannion met thirteen beings of light who filled him with knowledge. 'In the presence of these beings of light I would become knowledge and know everything that was important to know. I could ask any question and know the answer.' The knowledge he was given came in boxes which opened to reveal a tiny television picture to give him glimpses of future world events. And his experience has left him with profound psychic abilities, so that he can read minds and predict the future with amazing accuracy.

As the book was published in 1994 it is difficult to comment on predictions reported in it about events which happened before this date, events such as the Chernobyl nuclear disaster and the Gulf War. The dates of these events 1986 and 1990 and many other pre-publication happenings came into Dannion's head with pinpoint accuracy as he saw them on his spiritual tele-screen. But, as tends to be the way with prophecies, those events due to take place after 1994 are foretold with less precision: a world in 'horrible turmoil by the turn of the century', two horrendous earthquakes in America 'by the end of the century', Armageddon somewhere around 2004. Dannion is also able to hedge his bets; he was told that 'the years between 1994 and 1996 are critical ones'. He himself had the power to change the direction of events and avoid Armageddon. He was told how to do this, and understood that this was his mission the reason he had been shown these visions of the future and then allowed to return.

Not everyone can feel easy about a God who behaves somewhat like Nostradamus, about crystal palaces, or angels who flit from prayer to prayer like a butterfly from flower to flower. But if we pare away the more extravagant aspects of these two experiences we are left with a great deal that rings true the tunnel, the light, the feelings of joy and tranquillity.

Evangelical Christianity is more common and more acceptable in the States - some churches have their own TV channel for example. This evangelism seems to be reflected in these accounts. When Betty Eadie met the being of light, there was 'No questioning who he was. I knew that he was my Savior, and friend, and God. He was Jesus Christ.' In each case the whole experience is directed towards giving a meaning and purpose to life. Each returned with an evangelical sense that he or she had to carry out the mission.

Even so, Dannion felt that what he was experiencing was not related to any specific religion, it was 'a monument to the glory of God'. Betty Eadie, too, felt that she was experiencing a universal truth to which each religion carved its own path. And for both love was the core of the experience.

Betty Eadie returned with a simple 'message' that 'We are to love one another. We are to be kind, tolerant, to give generous service.' All these are elements which have been expressed over and over again by people on this side of the Atlantic. Once again we seem to be looking at a universal experience coloured by the culture in which it takes place.

So is there consistency in the NDE? A surprising amount, in my view. There are certainly cultural differences, just as there are personal influences and probably environmental influences too. I would find it strange if these differences weren't apparent. Much more interesting are the similarities.

Everywhere we find the concept that between life and death there is a symbolic divide, a border to be crossed which forms a point of no return. Some features (the tunnel, the feelings of peace and joy), seem to figure more often in Western experiences. Others (the life review) seem to be more predominant in America and China than in either the UK or the Indian sample. Cultural differences undoubtedly exist, but on the whole they seem little greater than the individual differences due to personality, circumstances and religious beliefs which are found amongst the people in any one culture.

The common ground between cultures and between individuals is that the NDE seems to be an 'awakening' experience, often arousing a sense of spirituality and a stimulus for personal development.

Chapter 12

Children and the Light

ALF Rose had this experience many years ago when he was ill with pneumonia as a young child of four or five.

Suddenly I was out of my body and floating near the top of the window in my bedroom. I could see myself in bed and my mother kneeling at the side of the bed. She was crying and looked very distressed. I gazed at this scene for a little while and remember that I didn't feel any emotion at all and was completely indifferent to what I saw. Without any warning at all I was travelling very swiftly through a dense forest. After what seemed a short space of time I found myself on the edge of a clearing, very brightly lit with bushes and trees surrounding it.

Somehow I seemed to know that I had reached a significant stage and waited. Suddenly a lion appeared from the bushes on the opposite side of the glade. It was large, crouched on the ground and looked very hostile, gazing very fixedly at me and flicking its tail rapidly from side to side. I didn't feel the slightest bit afraid and just waited to see what would happen. Very quickly a woman in a white robe appeared in front of the lion and looked at me. She was about thirty years old, eyes set widely apart, with bobbed auburn hair. She looked quite sternly at me as an adult would if about to reprimand a child. She 'spoke' to me although her lips didn't move and I could hear no voice. She told me that I should not be there and that I must go back. Without any conscious effort on my part I suddenly found myself back in bed again, opening my eyes and telling my mother that I was hungry.

Later, my mother told me that she was sure I had died, but that when I asked for food she knew I was going to recover and that everything would be all right. I told her about the lady in white. She reassured me and explained that my lady in white was my guardian angel and that she had looked after me.

Was this a dream or a 'real' experience? Although it happened seventy years ago I still vividly remember all the details, and am sure I would recognise my lady in white. For me this was a true real experience, I am fully satisfied about that. I believe I had died or was on the point of death and was told to return. Why? I don't know. I haven't led a particularly significant or important life. I do know that I have no fear of death.

We found Alf's a most fascinating and extraordinary story. The young Alf could not possibly have had any conception of what death meant, let alone his own death. And yet on his journey into the forest he experienced many of the phenomena of an NDE. He met a barrier (the 'significant stage' at which he had to wait); he found himself in a clearing with a 'brilliant light' and met a 'being' who made him aware that he should not be there, and who told him he had to go back. His lack of emotion at the sight of his distressed mother exactly parallels what adults have told us about their lack of concern for the families they are leaving behind them.

And the lion? Well, to me it would be even more surprising if a four-year-old peopled his NDE with long-lost friends or relatives. The imagery is very much the imagery of a child. Alf's lion confirms my feeling that while some elements of the NDE are universal and independent of the experiencer, the visual imagery is largely a product of the individual and is very personal. The interesting thing is that Alf had absolutely no fear of the lion, for all its evident hostility and despite the feeling of reality which coloured the whole experience.

'CHILDREN DON'T HAVE NEAR-DEATH EXPERIENCES'

This was the reaction of a colleague when Dr Melvin Morse, an American paediatrician, described what he'd been told by a thirteen-year-old girl whom he had resuscitated after she had nearly drowned.

When Dr Morse talked to the girl, Katie, at her follow-up examination, she seemed to 'remember' clearly details of the medical personnel who helped resuscitate her and of the procedures she had undergone. She described being taken by a 'guardian angel' through a tunnel to Heaven, where she met Jesus and the Heavenly Father. She also saw her grandfather, who was dead, and two young boys she said were 'souls waiting to be born'. At one point she had been in her own home, watching her family, who had been astounded when she was later able to describe to them accurately what they had been wearing, even what they had been doing at the time.

So impressed was Dr Morse with Katie's story that he decided to investigate a group of children who had suffered cardiac arrest or recovered from deep comas. This was the first time anyone had made a systematic study to see whether children who had nearly died had had the same kind of experiences as adults so often reported.

Dr Morse found that of the eleven children he interviewed, seven had memories of the time they were unconscious. Six remembered being out of their physical body, five had memories of entering darkness, four of being in a tunnel, and three of deciding to return to their body.

In fact it is quite clear that children do have near-death experiences. About 14 per cent of the people who wrote to us were describing experiences they had had as children. And childhood experiences are particularly interesting because they are much more likely to be 'clean'. The notion that people see what they expect to see has always coloured attitudes towards adult NDEs. In recent years the numerous books, media articles and television programmes on the subject mean that no one can easily have escaped the knowledge of what might happen to them when they are near death, and the form such an experience might take. But it's reasonable to suppose that young children are largely free of such expectations. Indeed, it is just because of this that it was generally assumed, until Dr Morse published his findings, that they were unlikely to have near-death experiences at all.

At three years old, Amie Greensted is the youngest child I have come across who has had a near-death experience. By the time Amie's mother wrote to me I needed no convincing that people who described NDEs were not just making it up. Even if I couldn't explain just what was happening to them, I had no doubts at all that they were giving me absolutely truthful accounts of what they had experienced. If I had had any remaining doubts, Amie's story would probably have dispersed them. I had to agree with her mother there is no way Amie could have made up the story she tells.

Amie has a rare medical condition called reflex anoxic seizure (reflex cardiac standstill), in which the heart slows and may actually stop for a short time. Amie is not literally 'near death', because the condition isn't dangerous. It occurs because an over-active nerve (the vagus nerve) makes the heart slow down, but it very quickly starts to beat again. Nevertheless, for a short time (up to a minute) Amie is unconscious, not breathing and has no heartbeat. Her mother says:

> Amie tells me about when she 'goes', as she calls it, and how she floats out to the ceiling and watches her body and us. She has told me exactly what has happened and what I did, said etc. whilst she was 'gone' on many occasions. She tells me that she 'clicks' back into the body. She is 100 per cent right in everything that has happened. Amie is very honest and there is no way a child of her age could make up such things. Amie has never been told about OBEs or NDEs, but she has such incredible detail that I am totally convinced.

Amie has described seeing a warm, bright light 'like the sun'. She says that although the light is warm and nice and she has touched it, she knows she mustn't go into it, she must go back to Mummy. She even tells her mother how it feels when she goes back into her body 'head first it's not very nice'.

Mrs Mabel Cowe was almost exactly the same age as Amie when she nearly drowned while playing by a river nearly fifty years ago. What happened had no special significance for her at the time, and it was only many years later, when she read an article on NDEs, that she realised that other people had had similar experiences.

> It was such a good feeling to see more than one person relate exactly the same experience and get it precise. They are

telling the truth. I am fifty now and when I was a small child of three or four years old I had an NDE. There was a river very close to our house and whilst playing I slipped in and was washed away. I screamed frantically and was rescued by workmen nearby. I had put up a plucky fight but unfortunately got some water on my lungs and became very ill with pneumonia. There were no drugs for pneumonia then and I was at death's door. I remember clearly in the middle of the night my father looking down at me and I said to him, 'I have just been flying at great speed through a tunnel with a light at the end.' He told me I had been seeing my own bedside lamp, which was a small paraffin lamp (we had no electricity). I loved my dad and accepted his explanation and never spoke of it again.

Young children who have these experiences are usually puzzled by them. They know something interesting has happened to them (if it wasn't interesting, they wouldn't remember it, as so many of them do, many, many years later). They accept it, but they don't understand it. Neither do they think of it as being religious or mystical these are concepts they haven't yet formed. And yet, time and again, they describe the sensations and experiences adults describe.

Richard Hands is a scientific journalist who describes himself as an atheist and Something of a sceptic where strange phenomena are concerned'. When he was nine, he was taken ill with appendicitis while on holiday. After the operation there were complications. His condition was serious and a second operation was necessary.

Only two images can I still recall. The first is of looking down on a body on the operating table, being fussed over by green-clad surgeons and nurses. I couldn't actually see the face someone was in the way - but I assume it was mine. This image is particularly vivid, and despite its goriness is not associated with any pain or distress, even in recall.

The second image is of a blackness with a pinpoint of light far off in the distance. I feel drawn towards the light, but there is a terror and a feeling that I do not wish it to pull me towards it. My mother is with me in this scene, trying to pull me back from the light. There is also a wind rushing past, towards the light. Again this image is startlingly clear, unlike many other things I remember from that time.

As we have seen, Richard is adamant that for him, the NDE he had when he was nine had no spiritual or religious significance (in fact, he was one of very few adults in our sample to hold this view). In fact I think at the time he had his experience his feelings were probably very similar to those of many other young children. They experience fragments of the NDE, perhaps feeling that they are out of their bodies, or experiencing sensations of moving through darkness, or of light. None of this means much to them. They don't understand it, and they don't attach any particular meaning to it. But they do remember it. Often it is only later, when they read about similar experiences, that they realise what it was that happened to them. And then inevitably they will interpret it through their adult eyes, in the light of their personal belief, or lack of it.

Many other people have given us a very similar picture of the way something that has mystified them since childhood suddenly falls into place when they learn something about the near-death experience later in life. Mrs Dunn, for example, says of her experience: 'Thank God I didn't realise the significance of it at the time, but as I got older I understood. I never told anybody about this, but I still remember it - I can see it as if it only happened yesterday and I am now over eighty years old.'

Mrs Pelling to had an NDE in childhood which remained extraordinarily vivid. When, years later, she saw a television programme about the phenomenon which she found 'so completely real, having experienced some of those exact same feelings as young as I was then, and knowing so very little of life and all its experiences.'

Mrs S. A. P. Thirlwall, too, was puzzled by the experience she had as an eight-year-old child while having seven teeth extracted under dental anaesthesia.

> I started zooming down this really black tunnel at what seemed like 100 mph. Then I saw this enormous brilliant light at the end which seemed to take on the shape of an angel. When I reached the light I heard a voice saying, 'Go back, go back' and seeming to will me to make the return journey. I then came back along this tunnel, but very slowly.
>
> I couldn't get the experience out of my mind and told my mother. She laughed and thought I'd made up the whole

thing. Then years later I read about the entertainer Ronnie Dukes. He'd had the same experience suffering a heart-attack. I showed this article to my mother and it left her stunned as she knew then an eight-year-old couldn't have made it up. I'll never forget what happened. I can see it all so clearly now all these years later.

Slightly older children are more likely to put a religious interpretation on their experience. Usually they have a more simplistic view of religion than adults and tend to think in more concrete terms. In adult near-death experiences, the 'Jesus figure' is found only when there is a basis of Christian faith. People who have no particular faith do not usually see anything quite as specific as 'Jesus' or 'angels'. They are more likely to see a less easily identifiable 'being', or to be aware that they are in the presence of God or a God-like figure.

We found that accounts of childhood experiences were much more likely than adult ones to include descriptions of a very concrete Heaven, peopled by angels, Jesus figures and golden gates. 'There was a big window and I saw Jesus with two child angels either side floating down to me,' one woman remembered. J. Cassidy also saw angels when, fifty years ago as a child of five or six, he was very ill with double pneumonia.

> I saw the doctor put the sheet over my body as I too was rising over my own body. I clearly saw angels around the window, then I sort of drifted back into my body. The next thing I remember was a neighbour bringing me grapes.Later I was told by my mother that my father pulled back the sheet and forced brandy through my teeth.
>
> You don't talk about these things as folks will think you some kind of nut. Only my close family knows about this. I will never forget this experience as long as 1 live.

Dennis Stone was thirteen when he had his experience in 1938, during an attack of meningitis.

> My mother waited outside my cubicle whilst the doctor treated me. Mother saw at once something had happened and indeed it had. Dr Galpine declared me to be dead and tried to comfort my mother at the ward door. At this time I awoke

in another world. I stood on the top of a beautiful valley, the sun was so warm. It seemed to stretch way into the distance. Suddenly I felt a powerful presence close to me. A voice spoke to me saying, 'Don't be afraid, everything will be all right' - a wonderful deep vibrant voice I could not locate - and, looking further, I noticed that I was fully clothed but did not cast a shadow. This puzzled me, for there were no shadows down the valley. I then knew I was in the presence of God, though I could not see him. He then covered me with an invisible force field, which felt so warm and safe. I remember thinking what happened to the terrible pain that I had been in, for it had gone and I felt so well. Then I reawoke in the hospital bed with Dr Galpine bending over me. Mother told me that he had suddenly turned back to the bed and could not believe I was alive and conscious.

At thirteen, Dennis was old enough to put a religious slant on his NDE. He was in the presence of God. But God also covers him with an 'invisible force field'. There are shades of Star Wars about this; it is very much the concept of a thirteen-year-old boy.

Elizabeth Kubler Ross, who has worked extensively with dying children and their families, tells in On Children and Death of a mother whose four-year-old daughter woke her one morning in a state of extreme excitement, almost euphoria, saying, 'Mom, Mom, Jesus told me I'm going to Heaven... and it's all beautiful and gold and silver and shining, and Jesus and God are there.' She went on to describe this 'beautiful golden Heaven, with wonderful things, and gold angels and diamonds and jewels'. She insisted that it was not a dream but 'really, really real'. Within seven hours the child was murdered, by intentional drowning.

Was that simply an astonishing coincidence or something more? The mother could find no explanation. Theirs was not a particularly religious household. When the children had asked about Heaven, their mother had always told them she did not know what happened when we died. But the children did go to Sunday School, though not regularly, and this does sound like a Sunday School interpretation of Heaven, the kind of Heaven that a four-year-old could comprehend. The quality of the child's reaction - her euphoria and insistence on the realness - certainly suggest that she had had an experience which she'd interpreted in the light of the only data available to her.

I find this very puzzling. Children undoubtedly have NDEs, but on the other hand, children do not expect to die. On the contrary, they seem to believe they are here forever. As anyone will tell you who has ever tried to persuade a teenager to give up smoking on the grounds that he will then almost certainly live a little longer, thoughts about their own mortality sit very lightly upon adolescent shoulders.

The younger the child, the odder it is that he or she should have any conceptual awareness of death. Many of the people who told us about childhood experiences were no more than seven or eight at the time they had them. The ability to think in abstract terms (and one's own death is a fairly abstract concept) does not usually develop until later in childhood. And yet, without the conceptual awareness, why should they have the experience at all - unless it has some sort of independent reality? Mrs G. U. Dunn is now eighty-five and lives in an old people's home - though as she says, she is 'still with it'. The visual impression of her NDE was obviously very strong - powerful enough for her to review it through adult eyes and identify the flowers in the garden, because it doesn't seem likely that a seven-year-old girl would have been able to identify the flowers she saw (or indeed would have bothered to do so).

> When I was seven years old, I had measles and was very ill, at home in bed. How long I lay there I don't know, but what I do know (and every word of this is true) is that I was in a lane where there were very high ornamental golden gates. Inside was the most beautiful garden, no lawn, path or anything else, but flowers of every kind. Those that attracted me most were Madonna lilies, delphiniums and roses, but there were many, many more. I thought how I would love to go in. I pushed the gates and they gave way to my push, but try as I might I could not get in; there was something behind me on both sides which seemed to be stopping me from going in. I was so upset at not being able to get in, but in the end I gave up trying. I opened my eyes and saw my mother and father kneeling either side of my bed, crying like babies. Mother looked at me and almost shouted, 'Look, Charlie!'

It's hard to believe that young children think they are dying, however ill they feel. And yet very often they too seem to be aware of the 'point of no return' that adults describe. Even at three years old, for example, Amie Greensted had the feeling that she must not go into the light, she must go back to her mother.

It's very striking, too, that even when they see their parents grieving for them they don't feel the distress that a young child normally feels when seeing a parent cry. Pauline Hill was only seven, 'maybe younger', when she had the experience she still vividly remembers during a bout of pneumonia. Her observation that she felt 'happy for herself, even though she was a bit sad for her parents, shows exactly that combination of overriding personal joy and emotional detachment from others that adults so often describe.

> I recall being in my parents' bed, in their bedroom with a fire in the grate and round the bed a nurse, a doctor and my parents. I was in great pain and very hot and distressed. The next second I was high above, looking down, and all the pain was gone. I floated over the bed and looked at myself and my parents and felt a bit sad for them, but happy for myself that I could leave my body behind, and as I turned to the top corner of the room to float away in a sort of golden haze, my mother's voice said my name: 'Pauline, oh Pauline,' and the next second I was back in my body with all the pain. Afterwards I looked back on the experience with some surprise, but daren't relate it to anyone for fear of ridicule. However, it was so real to me, and still is.
>
> I have never really feared death since. It opens up marvellous possibilities! If this life were all we had, I should think it most illogical and rather a poor deal for many. As it is, my experience suggests there may be something much more meaningful hereafter. I hope so.

Alf Rose, whose story opens this chapter, describes the same feeling: 'I could see myself in bed and my mother kneeling at the side of the bed. She was crying and looked very distressed. I gazed at this scene for a little while and remember that I didn't feel any emotion at all and was completely indifferent to what I saw.'

Despite this feeling of detachment, just as parents often make the decision to return because they don't want to leave their children, a very similar feeling draws children back into their bodies and away from oblivion. Mrs M. Giles: 'I wanted to stay where I was but Mother

was crying.' Dora Parker: '1 had to go back, my lovely nanna wanted me.'

Children and the Light

I remember still, with total clarity, the feeling of utter overwhelming peace and tranquillity. I was looking down on myself
in the bed, my mother sitting beside it, and my father standing by the window. I knew he was crying. I seemed to 'float'
along a corridor towards, then into, all- enveloping brightness and light, with indefinable shades of pastel-like colours.
There were what I can only describe as billions of beautiful
shimmering forms, no outlines, and they were all 'cloaked' in
what looked like a garment of translucent light.

The most wonderful thing was the music, which I can only
describe as almost a tangible joy emanating from, yet part
of and encompassing these forms, of which one appeared
to be the source and somehow embraced all else. Another
impression was the vastness, no horizon, no 'cutoff points;
infinity, I suppose is the best description.

I longed to be able to tell my parents not to grieve, that if
they could only know how joyously happy I was they would
rejoice instead. For that is the dominant feeling, the memory
and knowledge of ultimate, total peace. So death can come
at any time and holds no fear for me as a result of what I
consider to be a privileged experience.

That was Mary Lowther's memory of what happened to her when,
as an eleven-year-old, she suffered a burst appendix which resulted
in acute peritonitis. Although she was very ill, it doesn't seem likely that a child of that age, however ill he or she was feeling, would
expect to die. What she describes so vividly are not images, but the
overwhelming feelings evoked - of joy, of peace, of being enveloped
in the light.

This isn't anything an eleven-year-old would expect; it isn't even
anything you would expect an eleven-year-old to experience.

It isn't simply that children, too, see the light, though that in itself
is interesting. It is how they experience it that seems most significant
to me. They often attribute the same qualities to the light that so many
adults have described. This is Mrs M. Giles's account of how, as a child
of seven, she was admitted to hospital with third-degree burns.

Feeling quite poorly, I seemed to lose my fight for life. I was not aware of leaving my body, except for a sort of 'ping'. That is the only way I can describe it. Then I was at ceiling level, looking down at my body. I have not read of anyone talking about the warmth which enveloped me at that stage. I was not frightened and felt most loved and pure. Everything was bright all around, and although I saw no one it seemed as if I was known and welcome in that bright place.

As I looked down my mother was waiting to visit me and she was on the other side of the door to the ward entrance. I wanted to stay where I was but Mother was crying, and then I was back in my body and so was the pain.

I have a saying which is this: until you have been to heaven and back you've not been 'humanised'. When you talk to people who have had this experience they have a certain quality about them. No, I'm not being big-headed, just observant. And like me, they are not afraid of death.

Mrs H. Pelling was a child of six desperately ill in hospital after an operation for peritonitis. For her, too, the light was 'brilliant', the feelings of warmth and comfort all-enveloping.

My recollections are of being up in the corner of the ceiling at the end of the ward, completely encompassed in this most brilliant light with an ecstatic feeling of warmth and comfort, looking down at myself in bed, with the vicar and ward sister kneeling at my bedside in prayer giving me the last rites (so I was told years later). I can still see it all as clearly now, all these years later. I remember the doctor saying to my mother on later visits, 'It was a miracle, she had the will to live.'

The OBE is a very common feature of childhood experiences - it features in almost all the accounts we were given. Children seem to find it easier than adults to slip in and out of their bodies. One explanation for this might be that children are not attached as firmly to their bodies' boundaries as adults are. The brain is still setting up its coordinates. It hasn't yet acquired a fixed idea of where it is.

Fifty years later Dora Parker remembers very clearly the out-of-body experience she had during an attack of 'flu when she was seven years old. Although she was ill, it is unlikely that she was near death, and yet the light that she saw gives it very much the feel of an NDE. Mrs Parker's mother had her own explanation for what evidently became part of the family mythology.

My nanna gave me broth surely laced with whisky, though she says not, but my mother said it certainly must have been. I had my two-year-old sister in bed with me - it was the done thing then so Jenny would catch the 'flu, and then it would be over. I can remember I wanted to be alone. I left my body and felt relief that I was free. I looked down on my sleeping sister. I heard a noise and my nanna coming upstairs. I touched her hair. It was long and flowing; she must have been combing it. Nanna only combed her hair or let it down when she was nervous or upset (I learned that later). I continued to float and the light at the bottom of the stairs was brilliant (we only had gas). I was inquisitive, I needed to see why the light was so bright. I got to the curtain (we had a curtain at the bottom of the stairs) and I heard my nanna scream and scream. My body started to shake. I was tangled in the curtain. I had to go back - my lovely nanna wanted me - so I floated back and as she let my head on the pillow I came into my body feet-first. This was a family story kept alive by Nanna and Mother.

Notice Dora's grandmother's reaction. It clearly never crossed her mind that Dora was asleep; she was heard to 'scream and scream'. Other people too have mentioned this terrified reaction to the sight of a body that seems 'empty' of the person meant to be inside it.

E. A. Hearn-Cooper is now eighty-nine. It was during the 'flu epidemic of 1918 that the episode occurred which he describes here.

My whole family went down with it [the 'flu]. How my mother kept going I know not, for she too was ill. We all became so weak, lying in our beds, unable to move, just able to drink a little of the water my mother struggled around to give us. Within a few days we were like skeletons.

In the boys' bedroom there were two beds, a double near the window where my two young brothers slept, and a single bed for me. We three were lying there, unable to move. Yet

I felt myself rise up, float into the highest part of the room and look down upon myself lying there 'asleep' on my bed, across to my brothers asleep in theirs. I felt marvellous, no pain, free from all ills, just floating there.

But I realised that I had a 'cord' linking me with my body below me, and whilst I felt very happy floating there, I somehow knew that if I moved too violently I would break the 'cord' and I would never be able to return to my body. I decided to return, and did.

What I experienced was the act of dying, when your soul, the real you, is about to depart from your body. But in my case I was granted a further spell on Earth. I wished to return.

Last year, at the age of eighty-eight, I had a similar experience in hospital, where I had been taken with a severe heart-attack: looking down on the nurses and doctor bending over me, and, as I consider I have something else to contribute to life here, I returned.

We have to remember that many of the accounts we were given were adult memories of childhood experiences. However hard they try not to, it must be difficult for adults to remember and report something that happened long ago without looking at it through adult eyes and perhaps attributing more to it than they actually experienced at the time. Even so, I think we can pick up some useful clues about the NDE by looking at these childhood accounts.

To begin with, there seem to be far more similarities than differences between childhood and adult experiences. The same features are seen, and they seem to occur with more or less the same frequency. In all age groups, out-of-body and tunnel-and-light experiences are very common. I would have expected that fewer children than adults would report life reviews during their NDE because they have, after all, less of a past to review, and fewer conflicts to resolve. In fact, there was very little difference - full life reviews are rare in both children and adults, and about the same proportion of each (15 per cent) said that some memories from the past came back to them during their NDE.

There are some differences, but many of these probably arise because a child's intellectual and perceptual world is simpler than that of an adult. Children are more likely to see living people, to see strangers

Allen Pring, an air traffic controller and ex-RAF pilot, was not - and is not - a religious man. But his near-death experience (which was one of the few to include a life review) was emotionally so powerful that the knowledge that he had to return was, he says, the worst moment of his life (pages 155, 163). What he feels his experience showed him was that it is impossible to die, and that existence is possible in a non-physical reality beyond the limitations of time and space. (Photograph by John Clay)

In 1989, when he was 42 and on a sales trip to Austria for his family firm, David Verdegaal suffered a massive heart attack, followed by a stroke. For at least 30 minutes he was clinically dead, and for two weeks he lay in a coma, from which he emerged both blind and paralysed. The story of his experience during that time is one of the most remarkable we were told (pages 179, 298). David is a Christian and regards what happened to him as an experience from God. He describes his 'walk back to life' as a walk forward, with each step taken in the faith that God was from now on in charge of his life and nothing could harm him.

Michael Mizon lay in a coma for three months after a car accident when he was 18 - severely brain damaged and completely unconscious. And yet on recovering consciousness he appeared to have an almost photographic memory of an incredible journey he had been on while he was 'asleep', though his day-to-day memory at the time was very poor. He also asked his mother to take down the words of poems, which came into his head at great speed, and which seemed to relate to this journey (page 180). Michael has told his mother that he now often feels that he knows when things are about to happen in his life. These feelings of precognition quite often seem to develop after a near-death experience.

Now aged 74, Alf Rose can still remember clearly the experience he had during an illness in the early 1920s. What he describes has all the hallmarks of a near-death experience, seen through the eyes of a child - Alf was only five years old at the time (pages 243/244). Alf believes he was at the point of death and was told to return. He does not know why his life was spared, but he does know that, in common with most people who have had near-death experiences, he now has no fear of death.

and to see identifiable religious figures such as angels or Jesus. The younger they are, the less likely they are to see their experience as spiritual or mystical, or to feel that it made them more religious.

Few of the younger children saw scenes from the future or experienced a gate or border. The younger the child, the more emotionally neutral the experience seems to be - young children are less likely to have the feelings of peace or love than either older children or adults. Older children are more likely to feel fear in their NDEs than either young children or adults.

Most of the children's experiences occurred during illnesses such as pneumonia, influenza or meningitis - illnesses marked by a high temperature. But even though hallucinations, with random, complex and often bizarre visual imagery, often accompany a high fever, few children describe experiences which have these hallucinatory qualities. If anything, their experiences are less elaborate, less bizarre, than many adult ones.

Children, too, often feel a tug towards their parents; they too are sent back, and sometimes make the decision to return themselves. It is very difficult to explain why a three-year-old child should have such strong feelings that she is not allowed to go on and must return.

Secondly, it looks very much as though NDEs occur in children of all ages, or certainly as soon as the child has speech and can describe what is happening to him and his internal world. This is really very significant, because if it is true it means that the NDE does not depend on the maturation and development of the brain. Given this, do we have any reason to suppose that it cannot happen to children even younger than the three-and four-year-olds who can tell us about it? Could it be that these experiences are not just the weavings of the mind machine but reflect some fundamental features of experience to which the dying brain, at any age, has access? One of the strangest stories we received was from Mrs Florence Nilsson. This is what she told us.

> I was born in 1947, at home, with no midwife or doctor in attendance, except a sister-in-law who was helping my mother. My mother was forty-five when I was born, and she was crippled with rheumatoid arthritis. I don't know if this had any significance in the birth. However, I was born and apparently did not breathe. It was then that I had this out-of-body experience. I know it may sound absurd that a

newborn infant could remember an event when so young, but I know to this day that what I experienced actually did happen to me. The event has had such a profound effect on me that I have always had this fear of dying, which is an awful affliction to have to bear because logically we all know that to die is the only thing in life that is certain.

When I was born I remember floating on to the ceiling (it was a nice experience) and then looking down at my body. I can't remember details like wallpaper or anything but I remember looking down seeing my mother in bed with me and my sister-in-law. After floating on the ceiling somehow, I don't know how, I found myself in this dark place, climbing frantically up these walls. I had to get past these horrific, horrible, decrepit dead people who were moaning and trying to grab me with their arms (this is the part that still frightens me). Then I remember going at great speed down a dark tunnel (the horrid decrepit people were not there) heading towards a light. Just as I reached the light, however, for some reason I came away from it and that is all I remember.

I was told in later years that when I was born they thought I was dead. Apparently the doctor arrived to find me blue-black all over. He dipped me in cold water in the bath and after a couple of tries I breathed life and cried.

This must have been when I came away from the light in the tunnel. I know this happened, even though I can't explain how I can remember an event that happened when I was born, when generally our memory can only go back to about age two or three. And can you suggest any way I could rid myself of the burden that I carry round every day, namely fear of death?

It is difficult to believe that this can be a literal memory. It's possible that it might have been a childhood nightmare (which are often so vivid and so terrifying that they are remembered long afterwards). But its reality in one sense is beyond question. Mrs Nilsson has a pathological dread of dying and something must have happened to her to cause this. If she has no memory of what this was, it's conceivable that when she was told what happened at her birth she may have assumed that this was the cause. Memory traces of an earlier nightmare might have reinforced this belief. Or one can accept that she did indeed have such an experience, however and whenever it occurred.

Comparison of Childhood and Adult NDEs

	3-9 %	10-15 %	16+ %
OBE	61	61	65
Saw scenes from past	15	21	12
Detached or emotionally uninvolved	50	76	57
Felt love	24	33	40
Felt joy	34	33	40
Felt peace/calm	67	90	83
Felt fear	14	20	14
Darkness	33	33	38
Light	90	66	71
Tunnel	80	60	50
Saw landscape	20	25	25
Saw colours	33	43	35
Heard music	24	25	19
Experienced gate/border	10	33	25
Aware of people known	41	51	37
People were living	55	43	36
People were strangers	50	61	40
Saw religious figure	44	39	33
ESP/sense of things going on elsewhere	33	50	33
Saw scenes from future	9	25	13
Decision to return	52	70	75
Personal decision	50	33	54
Wanted to return	50	60	59
More religious afterwards	50	75	90

Chapter 13

The Road to Hell

PEOPLE who have had a near-death experience are almost unanimous in their belief in an afterlife. But are they any more likely to hold this belief than people who have not had the experience? If we are to draw any conclusions we need to know the level of belief in survival after death in the population as a whole.

In 1982 Gallup conducted a poll on a sample population of 1,500 American adults over eighteen to look at this very question. Of their sample, 67 per cent said they did believe in an afterlife; 27 per cent did not. These answers correlated quite strongly with the level of religious belief in the sample as a whole: 70 per cent had some religious belief; 20 per cent did not. Gallup also found that levels of belief varied widely amongst different sections of the population. For example, only 32 per cent of doctors and 16 per cent of scientists thought there was an afterlife.

However, it does seem that most of us are pretty selective in our beliefs. For many people, belief in an afterlife is synonymous with belief in a Heaven. Gallup found that 77 per cent believed in a Heaven, and 64 per cent thought their chances of getting there were good (only 4 per cent rated them as 'poor'). Not every section of the population questioned was quite so sanguine about its chances. Twenty- four per cent of doctors and only 8 per cent of scientists believed in the existence of Heaven. But when it comes to the possibility of Hell, levels of belief drop considerably, right across the board. Far fewer people - just over half of the whole sample - believed in Hell, and only 15 per cent of the doctors and 4 per cent of the scientists did so. It seems that a belief in Heaven is considerably easier (or more comfortable) to sustain than a belief in Hell.

Even so, belief in Hell seems to be quite widespread. And if over half the population do still believe it exists, it might be expected that at least some of them would have hellish near-death experiences. And yet these appear to be rare. Only two or three of the people who wrote to us described their experiences as 'hellish'. Some investigators (Moody, Ring and Sabom) have found no hellish experiences amongst the people they have questioned. Others (Margot Grey, Bruce Greyson and Maurice Rawlings) have collected a few accounts of journeys to hell and back. Greyson estimated that only about 1 per cent of NDE subjects had hellish experiences; Margot Grey found slightly more, about 12 per cent.

Why do glimpses of Heaven seem so much easier to come by in the near-death experience than glimpses of Hell? Is it because, where life after death is concerned, we are all past masters at giving ourselves the benefit of the doubt? Gallup survey certainly found that most people, even if they believed in Hell, rated their personal chance of ending up there as 'small'.

Or is it because even if we think there is a Hell we don't like to dwell on it much? The stereotypical vision of Heaven - pastoral landscapes, gentle clouds and figures in flowing robes - is much more frequently depicted, more comfortable to think about and therefore possibly much more likely to be fixed in memory than archetypal visions of Hell.

Some researchers have suggested that the reason so few hellish experiences have been described is because they are quickly forgotten; subjects need to be interviewed very shortly after the experience if it is to be remembered. But we did not find this. What we did find was that those who had these bad experiences were strongly affected by them, and much more reluctant to talk about them than people who had had positive experiences. People who had had 'good' experiences are usually happy, even eager, to talk about them and willing to have them published. Those who had had negative experiences did not, on the whole, want to relive them by writing them down. 'I had a hell-type experience twenty years ago,' said one woman, 'and it has haunted me ever since.' She refused to give us any more details. When negative experiences do occur, they seem to be just as powerful, and just as memorable, as the good ones.

It is possible that a few people manage to suppress negative experiences so that they simply do not remember them. One man had a psychiatric breakdown after his negative NDE. When we talked to him it was almost a year after the operation during which he had had the experience. He said he had kept a 'voluntary silence' during this time because of its horrifying nature. But what he also said was that his hellish experiences 'alternated with positive stories and experiences of bliss and joy'. This seems a good indication that the 'Hell' he experienced was a transient state of mind, alternating with a more 'heavenly' (but equally transient) one.

Margot Grey interviewed five people who had had hellish experiences. It is worth quoting one of these - a woman working in a nursing home who was overcome by the heat from the Aga cookers - because it provides an interesting parallel to a story that was recounted to us.

> I rushed outside the back door feeling faint and sick. I remember going down three or four steps. I don't remember falling, but the next thing that happened was that I had this experience. I found myself in a place surrounded by mist. I felt I was in Hell. There was a big pit with vapour coming out and there were arms and hands coming out trying to grab mine ... I was terrified that these hands were going to claw hold of me and pull me into the pit with them.

One of the most fascinating and detailed letters we received was from a man who suffered two cardiac arrests after a coronary thrombosis, and had several experiences during this time. Most were positive, but he also had an experience of 'Hell'.

> It was really like all the images I had ever had of Hell. I was being barbecued. I was wrapped in tinfoil, basted and roasted. Occasionally I was basted by people (devils) sticking their basting syringe with great needles into my flesh and injecting my flesh with the red-hot fat. I was also rolled from side to side with the long forks that the 'devils' used to make sure that I was being well and truly roasted. I wanted to call out but no sound would come, it felt as if my brain or consciousness was buried deep within me and was too deeply embedded for either them to hear or for me even to make it work. I was overcome with the feeling of utter doom and helplessness.

This writer explores various possible rational explanations for what he experienced, partly to his own satisfaction, though he says he does have some nagging doubts. But, he says, 'Hell has an easy explanation - I was wrapped in a tinfoil blanket, an electric heat cage was put over me and during that time I was turned several times and innumerable injections were given.' A similar explanation could equally well apply to Margot Grey's story of the cook overcome with heat from the Agas.

However, it doesn't explain why people who have other equally unpleasant bodily sensations do not incorporate them into their experience: one would expect many more unpleasant experiences if this often happened. Is there something special about heat? It does look quite possible that in the NDE, as in life, we tend to create our own Heaven or Hell. Look again at the experience of Mr Mill (described in Chapter 11) at the Red Fort in Delhi, when he was in a stupor which was possibly heat-induced. He does not describe his experience as 'hellish'. On the contrary, for him it was very positive. And yet reading his account, it does contain one or two features which to the objective onlooker might seem distinctly reminiscent of Hell. He found himself one of a 'great number of other bodies ...the whole floor was covered with them, all human, and they were writhing and wailing ... bodies swept by and the wailing became more pronounced.' If he had not told us otherwise, we might have assumed that Mr Mill had had an archetypal experience of Hell.

Another explanation could be that the same experience can be interpreted in different ways. Some of the accounts we have received suggest that this may well be so. One can imagine that with a slightly different mental 'set' Mr Mill could have believed he was approaching Hell and might not have subsequently regarded this as such a positive experience.

Another case concerned a sixth form celebration that ended in disaster. Simon and his friends were, in his words, 'well tanked up' at an end-of-term party after the hard slog of their A Level exams. The car Simon was in skidded on black ice and was wrecked. Simon hit his head but managed to pull the other occupants clear before collapsing and falling on to his back. He vomited and choked, and had to be resuscitated by the ambulance men. In hospital he was put on a life-support machine, suffered two cardiac arrests and collapsed lungs.

'At this stage I was in a coma and I had a most horrific experience. I was in a tunnel and sensed 1 was travelling towards a brightish light hidden behind a bend in the cave. By the way, I'd better point out that I felt I was simply floating - I did not have the use of my arms or legs at all.' Simon reports that he experienced no bliss and joy, as are often described in NDEs.

> That was hardly my experience! On the contrary, I felt extremely frightened and scared.
>
> As I passed round the bend in the cave I saw a giant Dracula-type of mouth opening. I say 'Dracula' because there were two monstrous fangs with blood dribbling off them. At this stage, I gained the instant impression that if I proceeded towards the mouth, it would shut and the teeth would slice me in two and kill me.
>
> Looking back now, a most outrageous event followed next. I opened my eyes and saw various unrecognisable faces around me (the hospital staff). I screamed for my mum (to whom I've always been extremely close) and she reassured me that everything was OK. I was then given a tranquilliser to put me to sleep for a couple of hours.

Again, the interesting thing here is that the hellish elements of what happened to Simon are mixed with features - the tunnel, the floating, the light - of the 'normal' near-death experience. What is particularly notable is the absence of any feelings of bliss or joy.

And yet, although so few of the stories we were told featured truly hellish experiences, several (about 15 per cent) did mention moments of terror, although the experience as a whole had been seen as positive. A likely explanation could be that when an experience includes those feelings of peace, joy, or contentment, as so many do (over 80 per cent of our sample), these are paramount, and override everything else, so that whatever else occurs is interpreted in this positive light. In the absence of these feelings the experience may be felt as neutral, or even threatening. So are hellish experiences only hellish because of the absence of positive emotions? We found several accounts similar to that of Mr Mill in the Red Fort in Delhi in which it is easy to imagine that a slight alteration in perception or interpretation could have tilted the balance and changed the whole nature of the experience.

Richard Hands' childhood experience, covered in the previous chapter, was one of the few reported which contains an element of terror, and he was also one of the few people for whom the experience held no particular spiritual significance. It is easy to see how it could have been interpreted as hellish: 'I feel drawn towards the light, but there is a terror and a feeling that I do not wish it to pull me towards it. My mother is with me in this scene, trying to pull me back from the light. There is also a wind rushing past, towards the light.'

Audrey Organ also describes a moment of terror: 'But then I went up higher and felt a great and terrible feeling of my insignificance, awe that really was awful, shrinking terror. I knew with dreadful certainty that I could never measure up to something ahead, where nothing would be missed.' Yet for her the overwhelming feeling was that it was otherwise a wonderful experience.

Are there other features in the normal near-death experience which might, with a different mental 'set', be interpreted as 'hellish' rather than 'heavenly'? The hands of Margot Grey's cook, which reached up to grab her, are a recurring feature in several of the accounts we were given. The only difference is that most accounts describe friendly hands, helpful hands, reaching out to draw the person towards the light, not grabbing, snatching, threatening hands dragging them down to hell.

'My brother, who had died a few years before, was gesticulating delightedly as I approached... my mother shook her head and waved her hand (rather like a windscreen wiper).'

'I saw my father all in white with his arms outstretched towards me and I floated towards him. But as I got near he waved his arms and gestured for me to go back.'

'Masses of people all smiling and reaching out to welcome me... my mother was smiling at me and had her hands stretched out to me. I was so happy. I was desperate to reach her. I had nearly got to her hands when I felt myself being pulled away from her.'

'I was floating on this meadow towards a tree that had its branches outstretched, like arms waiting to welcome me.'

Margot Grey's cook found herself in a 'place surrounded by a mist'. Mist is also mentioned in several of the positive accounts we received, but although it is usually seen as soft, gentle and swirling it could equally well be interpreted as steam issuing from a hell-pit. Mr Fearn's colleague in Chapter 9 'then seemed to move off into a misty area and eventually arrived somewhere that was again misty but lighter in colour, like sun shining through a field fog.' The following account has an element of panic, too:

Then everything went very dark and there was the feeling of going down a tunnel with a teeny speck of light in the distance which gradually got larger until everything was very white, very bright, but there was a softness to it. It was almost like mist gradually dispersing. As it got clearer I knew instinctively that in just a moment I would come face to face with my 'maker', as I thought of him rather than God. At that point I seemed to panic and I fought against the feeling thinking, 'No, I'm not ready.'

Nearly two years ago Mrs Villiers went into hospital for a carotid artery operation followed by a heart bypass. She says that during the operation she left her body and watched her heart lying beside her body, bumping away with what looked like ribbons coming from it to hands. In fact, this is not what happens in a heart bypass operation, as the heart is left within the chest and is never taken outside the body. However, ribbons are tied to the arteries, and if Mrs Villiers did indeed see her body at this time, it would have been a confusing picture for her to identify. Afterwards, she says:

I managed for three days to live on in great pain. Then one evening, having been removed from the Intensive Care Unit, I died. My husband noticed and in spite of the nurse saying I was sleeping was very worried. Luckily, my heart specialist looked in on his way home and all hell was let loose and back to intensive care I went. But until they managed to revive me I went through a very strange happening. [I found myself in] an enormous silver great place, rather like a hangar for aeroplanes, but going on forever, and miles away [there were] some tiny figures.

I knew I had to go back where I had come through. I called God and all my family, to no avail, and tried and tried to get back. Somehow I couldn't manage to. I was so tired I said in the end, 'No, it's no good, I shall have to stay here,' and someone said, 'No, come on, have one more try and I'll help you.' I did and got back and came round in my bed.

I feel that it must have been my dear husband who unconsciously helped me but I shall never know ... What is disappointing is that everyone talks of the lovely things when they died and were brought back. My hangar was ghastly, a real Hell if there is such a thing. It has made me much less anxious than ever to die.

For Mrs Villiers, then, there was no question of wanting to stay - on the contrary, her memory is of struggling to get back, and the 'barrier' she experienced was a barrier to her return. And yet to those of us who weren't there, it sounds a fairly neutral place, certainly not a particularly frightening one. It's hard not to conclude that it was the absence of any of the positive emotions - the peace, bliss and love that most people describe - that turned the hangar into a Hell.

There is some evidence to support this view. It has been suggested that endorphins (a morphine-like chemical released by the brain) (see Chapter 14) may be responsible for the positive feelings of the NDE. Some years ago, in the medical journal The Lancet, the case was reported of a patient who was given the drug Naloxone (which is known to reverse the action of morphine) to bring him out of a coma. The patient reported that he had been having a pleasant NDE which turned to a hellish one.

SUICIDE

In those organised religions in which Hell figures, suicide is a sin and might well be considered an entrance qualification. And yet none of the people who wrote to us about a near- death experience during a suicide attempt reported a hellish or even an unpleasant experience. On the contrary, what they experienced seemed to provide a reason for continuing to live.

It seems that the mental state in the NDE bears no resemblance at all to the person's mental state before the experience. Someone who attempts suicide might be expected to be in some emotional turmoil at the time of their experience. In real life people who are depressed tend to select only depressive images and memories. And yet if we look at the experiences described below we can see that the depressive feelings vanish when they enter the experience; there is an awareness of peace, of something beautiful; there seems to be a healing of the 'broken spirit'. Here Sheila Berry describes what happened to her fifteen years ago.

I had taken an overdose of aspirin and alcohol and had been pumped out at the hospital. It was late at night and I was put into a ward. I don't know whether you would call this an NDE but at the same time my spirit was so low I felt that I could die if I really wanted to. It could perhaps be classed as a case of broken spirit if there is such a thing.

I was lying in the dark and felt myself drifting. I felt as though I was in a warm cocoon. I became aware that I was moving down a dark country lane with high hedges. At the bottom of the lane there was a cottage with a light in the window. I wanted to reach the cottage but a voice in my head said that I had to go back. I can still remember someone taking my hand and I had a feeling of great peace and a oneness with what I can only describe as the universe. I can remember returning to the weight of my body. For some time after this happened I kept hearing the most wonderful music. I feel since that time that my life has a spiritual dimension, although I do not practise any established religion.

Anne Thomson attempted suicide in the winter of 1972 when she was very depressed.

I could cope no longer with three small children and one dreadful husband (whom I later divorced). I took a massive overdose of sleeping tablets and was not found for four hours. I was rushed to the nearest hospital by ambulance from the RAF base in Wales, where we lived at the time. I very nearly died and was unconscious for four days. On the fourth day I was slipping away. I had a cardiac arrest and the doctors and sister were working on me.

I left my body. I went up and up very slowly, not looking back at myself in the bed. The peace was beyond what I can explain; it was so beautiful, I felt so light in weight and I saw I was going towards a white light - not the white like this notepaper I write on, but a spiritual white. I almost reached this light, when suddenly I was pulling downwards very fast and did not stop till I was back in my body. I was heavy, everything seemed so dark and then came to and slowly came to realise I could not be taken as three children needed their mother.

I always did believe in God but only because it was bred into me. But since that experience I have a lot of faith towards

God and towards life beyond our lives on Earth. I firmly believe he made me well and helped me through all my time of rearing three children alone in the years that followed.

Only one of the descriptions of NDEs which occurred during suicide attempts had elements that might possibly be construed as hellish. It is one of the very few in which the feeling is one of descent, into a pit, rather than upwards, and in which the light seen is red rather than white or golden.

Although there is a 'presence', this is not perceived as friendly, but not as hostile either. In fact, the whole experience has a neutral quality - not hellish, but not positive either, except for the compassion the returning 'self feels for her body in the hospital bed.

S. Durrell:

In 1963 I nearly died from a suicide attempt. I went down into a deep pit, slowly, like Alice in Wonderland, as if I were in a lift. At the bottom it was light and quite busy and bustling.

The other people were strangers and although they didn't speak and neither did I, somehow I asked the way and I was told to follow the red light.

I moved off in that direction. Gradually I found myself in a warm, dark tunnel, alone apart from a sort of presence - not hostile, not friendly, just there. Then the red light grew dim and began to flicker and I knew I would have to go back. It was absolutely dark and I was quite alone.

My body was surrounded by a panicky crowd round the hospital bed. It seemed silly of the people to be making such a fuss. The body had been crying in its sleep and I felt a great pity for it momentarily as I returned.

I told no one about this as they thought I was a loony anyway, but the experience has stayed with me all these years and I have tried to make sense of it. If it is just an innate limbic response, well... interesting.

Chapter 14

Let's Be Rational About This

THERE seems little doubt that NDEs occur in all cultures and have occurred at all times through recorded history. We now know plenty about what the subjective experience is like, but we still have to explain how it comes about, and why.

As a scientist I shall start, in this chapter, by trying to find a scientific explanation. The scientific view is that brain processes alone can account for all the phenomena of experience. Whatever happens in the near-death experience - the thoughts, feelings, sensations of movement - all these must result from neuronal activity within the brain. The entire experience is due to changes in brain function. 'Mind' is merely a product of the brain; it certainly cannot act at a distance from it, or independently of it.

If science fails to provide an adequate explanation, then we shall be forced to consider another possibility. This is that in some way not yet understood, mind and brain are different, and mind can exist independently of brain. Such theories argue that although brain processes are necessary in the structuring of feelings and experiences, they are not sufficient. There has to be an added 'something'. But at the moment any such theory has to remain an intellectual and philosophical one; it cannot be proved in any scientific way because science has no theory to support it. As Heller said: 'Many scientific theories have, for very long periods of time, stood the test of experience until they had to be discarded owing to man's decision, not merely to make other experiments, but to have different experiences.'

THE MODEL-BUILDING BRAIN

Goethe said: 'Mysteries are not necessarily miracles.' It is very tempting to try to make the mystery of the NDE into a miracle, and the following dramatic and thought-provoking account is a powerful demonstration of how very successfully the mind can mislead us into seeing a 'reality' that has very little to do with the outside world.

Mrs F. M. B. Hover was awaiting the birth of her third child - a boy, she hoped, as she already had two daughters. Having experienced two normal births she knew what to expect. So when, at four in the morning, she was woken by severe labour pains five minutes apart, she thought, fine, time to reach the hospital and the new baby should be born in time for morning coffee. It was not to be. Coffee time came and went. So did lunch. The pain was considerable and she was given gas and air, an analgesic mixture of oxygen and nitrous oxide, long known to dentists as laughing gas. Eventually:

> The urge to push came suddenly and the nurses crowded round. 'Don't push,' the midwife demanded urgently, 'the cord is round the baby's neck.' The effort was indescribable. All my mental and physical energy was focused on not pushing. I panted desperately. I drifted out of my body. The pain had gone, my mind was clear and lucid once more. The speech of the doctor and nurses came in short bursts which I could not understand. I remember thinking it was rather like a television play when they simulate distress and unconsciousness. The baby was in distress, a Caesarean would be necessary.
>
> I watched dispassionately as they loaded my ungainly body on to a trolley and I floated along about two feet above my right ear as they wheeled me quickly down the corridor. I was not in any pain, nor was I frightened, just an interested voyeur. I watched from a distance as green cloths were draped over my body and a sort of screen placed over my chest. I moved closer, about three feet above the surgeon's shoulder. My bulge was cut and out of it was drawn a gunk-covered mess. 'It's a beautiful baby girl,' I heard quite distinctly. 'What?' I thought, 'After all that I really thought it would be a boy this time.' I floated behind the nurse as she cleared the baby's tubes and wiped the worst of the debris

from my new daughter. She weighed her, wrapped her in a towel and popped her into an incubator instead of a little cot. This done, I returned with the nurse to where my body was being clipped together with something resembling a staple gun.

Cleaned and tidied, I was transferred to an ordinary hospital bed. It was at this point that I slipped quietly back into my deeply unconscious body. I remember its warmth and the stiffness of the sheets. I slept.

Someone was calling my name from far away. I was far, far below them and I did not want to wake. I could feel the clips in my stomach and knew that with consciousness would come severe discomfort. Just a little longer in the warm pain-free dark, I pleaded as I rose slowly towards the voice.

'Wake up, you don't need this now,' said the nurse, removing the mask from my face. 'Your baby is about to be born.' I opened my eyes. Green-gowned figures stood around. 'We need you to push now.' I did and my third daughter was born at 6.05 p.m.

I had obviously passed out with too much gas and air, and it had all been a dream. It was all so vivid that I have no difficulty in recalling the details some twelve years later. If, however, I had fallen unconscious and then undergone a Caesarean operation I am sure I would have claimed an out-of-body experience. I believe the mind is a wonderfully powerful instrument which is capable of transporting its owner to many dimensions, many of which do not require a physical body. Our mind's eye is often seven feet tall if we are asked to recall a situation. It does not mean it physically leaves a five-foot-four-inch body.

As I lie down to sleep at night I often ask, 'And where shall we go tonight?' I would be less inclined to do so if I thought, like in Peter Pan, that the window might be shut on my return.

The Mechanism of Model-Building

Is it possible that the NDE is nothing more than a trick played on us by a brain disordered by drugs, pain or sickness? If we're to consider this seriously we need to know how the brain actually works, how it makes the models of the world which we call reality.

Messages about the outside world come from the sense organs and are relayed to the brain. The brain uses this information to create a model of the world, part of which appears in consciousness. But do we really 'see' with the eyes and 'hear' with the ears? The answer to this is both yes and no - and that is very important.

The messages which reach the brain are themselves quite neutral. It does not matter which sense organ they come from, the information they carry is simply in the form of coded pulses. The codes are neutral. It is the analysis of the codes that gives the sensory experience of sound or smell or colour. In the condition known as synaesthesia, these coded pulses leak from one area of brain to another and they then take on the sensory experience of the area into which they leak. Musical tones, for example, may then be seen as colours as well as heard as sounds.

So, for a sensory experience to come into consciousness it has to make its way to the appropriate analysis system in the cortex. But it is not even as simple as that. Most of the time we are quite unaware of much of what is going on around us. When we want to bring something into consciousness we have actually to switch our attention and focus on it. So the whole of our rich perceptual world is created in the cortex of the brain.

We think of any experience as a unity, but it is not like that. Each brain area contributes part of the picture of our experienced world. If the cortex is damaged in a limited way, it will produce a limited deficit in your perceived world. Think of your dog. The picture you conjure up is mainly from the memory structures in a particular area of the brain (the right temporal area and the right posterior temporal association cortex). Now think of his name. When the word 'Rover' springs to mind it comes from a quite different memory area - the left temporal memory area and the left frontal speech- naming area. When you remember the face of someone you love you are using the memory circuits and the facial recognition area in the right temporal lobe. If you listen to Mozart it is the right temporal area which makes sense of the music and the rhythm. Damage this area, and although you will 'hear' sounds, they won't seem like music. Yet another area in the left posterior temporal region - the receptive speech area - is needed to make sense of the spoken word.

To bring a complete model of the world into consciousness the brain has to be working as a whole in an integrated way. If one area is damaged then its particular function will be absent or distorted, and so too will that part of the 'world model'. If the NDE is yet another 'model', then that too should be affected by the way the brain is working, which brain areas are functioning and which may be damaged.

New brain-scanning (neuroimaging) techniques mean that we can now see the brain at work. A radioactive tracer is put into the bloodstream, and wherever the brain is working harder it takes up the tracer and this shows up as a 'hot spot'. So we can see exactly which parts of the brain are active during different experiences. Scanning shows conclusively that it is not the neural codes which reach the brain which determine sensation, but the area to which they go. In people who have colour hearing (synaesthesia), for example, the visual area can be seen to light up when musical notes are heard. The codes are neutral; the brain gives them meaning.

Imaginary Models

Do people simply imagine the NDE? Brain scanning has shown that if you imagine a sound or a visual scene, the auditory cortex or the visual cortex light up almost as they would if you listened to a real sound or looked at a real object. In other words, imagination makes use of many of the same model-building cognitive structures that are used to perceive the world in reality - and to imagine the world you need an intact brain, just as you do to perceive it in reality.

This has other implications too. It means that as far as the brain is concerned, experiences which arise from the mind are just as real as those which arise from the outside world. Clearly there are differences between an imagined model and a 'true' model of external reality, because we can nearly always distinguish between the two. There are thus brain areas which put a tag on the outside experience as 'real' so that we know they are not imagined.

Dream Models

Models are built in nearly the same way, whether in reality or in imagination. Is the mechanism used for creating the dream world any different? Surprisingly, it is not.

Imagine a dog curled up beside the fireside asleep. He snuffles. He whimpers. His legs make slight twitching movements. Ah, we say, he's dreaming that he's catching rabbits. And we are probably right. His brain may be making cognitive models of rabbits in fields, and of himself chasing them. But why doesn't the dog get up and run about the room? The reason is that in dreaming sleep, although that part of the brain which controls movement responds to the dream (hence the muscle twitches), the muscles are virtually paralysed because an inhibitory mechanism largely prevents impulses from the brain from reaching them. If that part of the brain which controls paralysis during dreaming is damaged, then the dog does indeed get up and act out its rabbit-hunt.

The same is true of man. If you are dreaming that you are playing rugby for England, the brain will issue running orders to the muscles. They twitch, but they cannot respond. This is just as well, as it means that we cannot actually act out our dreams. The man playing rugby for England cannot leap from his bed and tackle whichever piece of furniture happens to be blocking his run, any more than the dog can attempt to catch rabbits in the sitting room. And just as in dogs, if the mechanism which inhibits movement is damaged by illness, then the person really will act out their dreams. Occasionally people half wake while this inhibitory mechanism is still in operation. They'll then have the terrifying sensation of being awake but unable to move, a condition called sleep paralysis.

It is interesting that during an NDE people often describe feelings that sound very like the paralysis that occurs in dreams. 'I turned my mind but I couldn't turn my head.' 'I seemed to float through the tunnel without moving my legs.' 'I didn't move my feet, I just "floated", I suppose.' 'I tried to communicate "verbally" (not from my mouth but from my mind).'

Ella Silver: 'My mind seemed terribly clear and alert - more so than ever before. I was warm and comfortable. I seemed to be lying on my back, but when I tried to look along my body I found I couldn't move. I felt as if I didn't have a body, but was all mind... Behind my right shoulder came a very gentle golden light (like old-fashioned oil lamplight). I tried to look at it but as I said I couldn't move my head.' (During an operation.)

Isabella McLeod: 'I was immediately back in my body and aware I was being pronounced dead ... I tried very hard to move fingers, toes, anything to make the midwife aware I was alive. I felt desperate and felt I became so very tiny and crouched under one eyelid pushing as hard as I could to try and open my eyes.' (Post-partum haemorrhage.)

Audrey Organ: 'Here I was in a tunnel of glorious golden light with my dad, who had died some years earlier. We were strolling side by side but with no physical walking.' (During a tonsillectomy at the age of five.)

If these people are not dreaming, why does the brain not respond to the very vivid 'reality' of the NDE by initiating the appropriate muscle movements? In other words, shouldn't one expect people to act out their NDE? When someone is profoundly unconscious, or is under an anaesthetic, then they would certainly not be able to move, but they would not be able to build models - to experience this feeling of paralysis - either. Is it possible that when NDEs occur during consciousness a mechanism similar to the inhibitory process that operates during dreaming occurs? Linus, a neurophysiologist from New York, has shown that in dreaming sleep the firing patterns of the cells in the cortex of the brain are very similar to the firing patterns which are seen in the waking state. The major difference between the dreaming and the waking states is that during dreaming the flow of incoming sense data to the cortex is restricted.

The brain continues to make models, but these models are created not by information direct from the outside world but by both emotion and memory from the internal world. Data from the outside world does sometimes slip through - a dream may incorporate feelings of cold when the duvet slips off, for example.

In the waking state the cortex is fully reconnected to the senses, and the emotion and memory-based models are now modified by incoming sensory data. We can even consider dreaming to be the basis of experience; it is the dream models that are modified by external reality. Perhaps Hamlet was wrong when he said that we sleep perchance to dream: modern science would argue that we dream perchance to wake.

If the same cognitive structures are used in both the dream world and the real world, then if these are damaged, both dreams and reality should be affected. And indeed, this is what happens. If a stroke knocks out specific cognitive modules, the model the brain produces will have a specific defect not only in the waking, conscious state, but also in dreams. Linus records the story of a woman who had a stroke which destroyed the area of her right hemisphere, which is concerned with facial recognition. The woman lost her ability to recognise the faces of her friends, and in her dreams the people she saw were faceless.

In most NDEs people have no difficulty in recognising friends and relatives quite easily, but in a few accounts people seem unable to describe the faces of the people they meet, or they describe them as faceless. David Whitmarsh says of the people he met on his blue train that 'it was difficult to make out their features, which seemed to be shrouded in a grey mist... Then again, almost as if by magic, I was in the train compartment with the faceless passengers.' Maurice James describes 'a faceless figure who ... seemed to have human form but his face was indistinct.' Jean George says: 'There seemed to be people with me but I couldn't see their faces.' Michael Mizon found himself walking beside a companion whose 'hand covered his face', and H. T. Mill found that he was among a great number of bodies but that he 'could not clearly see any of them'.

What do we make of this? Why can't these people see faces in the NDE when they can (presumably) see faces quite clearly when they are back in real life? We know that damage to the posterior right temporal area can destroy the ability to make cognitive models of faces, so could it be that the face- building area of the brain is particularly sensitive to some destructive factor, such as lack of oxygen, which may be present during an NDE? This does not fit the current concept of unconsciousness, which suggests that unconsciousness is usually global - it affects the whole brain. It would be odd to find that one specific cognitive function, the building of models of faces, is apparently disrupted by the process of unconsciousness while the remainder of the model-building mechanism remains intact. A more likely explanation is that a psychological rather than an organic mechanism is involved.

THE PARADOX OF UNCONSCIOUSNESS

It is clear that if part of the brain is damaged then we may lose part of a faculty. But what happens in unconsciousness? By definition, if we are really unconscious we are not building models, and we can experience nothing. However, we have to be careful as we can't always assume that no memory of experience means no model-building, because in some circumstances perfectly good models are built - we just have no memory of them, so we think we were unconscious. The most familiar example of this is the alcoholic black-out.

Alcohol has a catastrophic effect on memory. Simple memory tests given to people who have had six to eight pints of beer show significant memory impairment; by ten pints the memory circuits have failed almost completely. Even though he was not unconscious at the time, someone who has an alcoholic black-out may have no idea how he got home, and mercifully little memory of his behaviour the night before.

Consciousness is maintained by a delicate global system which enables all the cortical model-building structures, including memory, to be excited and active. If this system goes down we lapse first of all into confusion and then into gradually deepening coma.

This is the real paradox of the NDE. If someone is unconscious they cannot model-build. If they build an NDE model, they cannot be unconscious. If they are in a precomatose confusional state, any models they build should also be confused. Many people are actually on the operating table, under anaesthesia or undergoing resuscitation at the time when they seem to leave their bodies and see themselves. And yet this is impossible. They are unconscious. Therefore they cannot experience anything. Of course, only a proportion of NDEs occur during unconsciousness (see the table below). But this still leaves us with a lot of explaining to do.

State of Consciousness when the NDE Started

	%
Awake	33.4
Asleep	13.3
Under anaesthesia	14.2
Unconscious	17.2
Semi-conscious	20.1
Confused	1.8

The Survival of Memories

Equally difficult to explain is the question of memory. A constantly recurring comment by people who have had NDEs is how vivid the memory of it is. So it is as well to remind ourselves just how fragile this capacity to remember is. Memory is very delicate and easily damaged. And memory does not function in unconsciousness.

When we look at possible explanations for the NDE, one of the things we need to ask is whether memory of the experience is likely to remain intact. Even if someone who was unconscious could somehow experience, if their brain could build models, these models should not be remembered.

So how is it that when an NDE occurs during unconsciousness it is remembered - and remembered so clearly - afterwards?

From the point of view of both memory and model- building, it should be quite impossible to have an NDE when brain function is really very seriously disordered or the brain is seriously damaged. But is it? One of the most extraordinary accounts we received was from David Verdegaal. This is how he describes his own remarkable journey.

Seven years ago while on a sales trip to Austria for my family firm, I suffered a massive heart-attack followed by a stroke two days later. Following the arrest I was rushed to hospital in Innsbruck. It was later discovered that it had been a full half an hour from the time of the arrest to the time they finally managed to restart my heart.

There followed a period of two weeks while I lay in a coma with my wife Jill at my side, watching and praying, after flying out to be with me. In the centre of the storm, life took on a new reality for me as I came before my Maker. The first thing was the realisation that I was dead. Feeling unworthy to meet my Maker, I begged forgiveness for a misspent life. Then I saw a light that seemed to grow brighter and brighter until its brilliance had completely encircled me, as if my very soul had been transformed and enveloped in love.

It was then that I had the sensation of being gathered up and held like a newborn child. Nestling in the warmth of this loving embrace, I knew that nothing could ever harm me again. Whether I was to live or die, I knew I should be given the strength to continue. At the time I didn't know who I was or what kind of life lay ahead, but now I had the certainty that God would be leading the way.

It was then that the Lord took me by the hand and led me through a garden where surely beauty had found its name. This was an old-fashioned, typically English garden with a lush green velvet lawn, bounded by deep curving borders brimming with flowers, each flower nestling within its family group, each group proclaiming its presence with a riot of colour and fragrance as if blessed by a morning dew. The entrance to the garden was marked by a trellis of honeysuckle so laden that you had to crouch down to pass beneath while at the other end a rustic garden gate led to the outside. It was here that my walk through was to end as I was gently led through to the other side. It was at this moment that the realisation that I was going to live came to me and I would have to face the consequences of living.

There followed two weeks as I lay in a coma in an in-between world. While in the coma I was told many things, one being that I was meant to write a book recounting my life. Although I felt this was a definite instruction, I dismissed the idea as an improbable one as I was no author and the opportunity was not likely to occur. Feeling on safe ground, I submitted to the request if the situation in the future ever made it possible.

After two weeks I emerged from the coma both blind and paralysed. From then on I was to regain my faculties step by step until three years later, although still partially sighted, there was no excuse and I finally started on the work. I joined my local training centre where I was introduced to computers. Now I could neither write nor spell, the computer became my saviour as the work could be polished up later. Since then I have plodded on at a snail's pace, at the same time regaining my memory and coming to terms with the past.

Mrs I. L. Cross, a tutor who helped David in his gradual rehabilitation and who put him in touch with us, describes him as a truly remarkable person. She says: 'His recovery, slow as it has been, is mostly due to his determination and perseverance. From being a vegetable unable to move, see or recognise people or places, he has become an articulate person and able to run in a marathon.' Remember that description of David - a vegetable unable to move, see, recognise people or places. He emerged from his coma both blind and paralysed. From this we know that he must have suffered widespread brain damage, affecting different areas of his cerebral cortex. He was paralysed and so the stroke probably damaged the parts of his brain which control movement. His blindness may have been caused by the fall in blood pressure during his cardiac arrest. Certain areas of the brain, known as the watershed areas, are particularly likely to be damaged by a fall in blood pressure. The most vulnerable of these is the visual association area.

This is the area concerned with the structuring of images in three-dimensional space and the analysis of visual scenes. Severe damage to this area will leave you essentially blind, or else able to see, but unable to make sense of what you see. Probably this was what happened to David as he was, over the course of time, slowly able to learn how to

217

see again. That part of the brain used in reading is also close to this watershed area and, as David was unable to read or write after his injury, this too must have been damaged.

So here is a man who emerges from prolonged unconsciousness, significantly brain-damaged to the point where he is virtually a vegetable. We know that in someone who is as severely brain-damaged as this, memory will almost certainly be affected as well as sight and movement. Even if we concede that in some mysterious way, a brain which is disorganised to the point of unconsciousness can retain the ability to make coherent models, these should not be remembered. I would not expect David to have memory of anything he experienced during his period of unconsciousness. Even if in some extraordinary way his brain was able to make models during this time, I would expect them to be fragmented, random and unclear. But this was not so. Not only did David retain memories, but they were coherent memories of a fantastic visual world.

Even if the whole experience occurred during the first few seconds after the heart-attack, before the brain was damaged by lack of oxygen, it still should not have been remembered. Might the experience have been part of the recovery, occurring just as he was regaining consciousness? There are strong arguments against this. As we've seen, the part of his brain which creates visual images had been damaged by then, and David's experience was intensely visual. Also his memory would not have been functioning correctly as it was to some extent damaged and thus he should not have had any clear memory of experiences.

It's also interesting to note that although anoxia has often been said to play a crucial part in the tunnel experience, David did not go through a tunnel, although he must have suffered severe anoxia.

Can science provide an answer in this case? There seems to be only one possible one, and that leaves even more questions unanswered. We have to postulate that the brain can retain the capacity for making images in unconsciousness and with the visual cortex damaged, and that when the memory circuits are 'down', memory can be retained by some other means, as yet undiscovered. These are big assumptions and undercut in a major way our present view of how the brain works normally and in unconsciousness. But then, one of the fascinating things about the NDE is that it does confound so many of our assumptions about how the brain works.

CHANGING THE MODEL

The brain is an automatic model-maker. And when brain function changes, the models change. Can we explain the phenomena of the NDE simply by saying that the experience is just another model which arises because brain function is altered?

Brain function can be altered in two ways. The first is physiological: damage or changes in body chemistry cause brain dysfunction and this in turn leads to changes in experience. For example, if you are concussed by a blow on the head, or if the blood sugar concentration of your brain drops, you will become confused and disorientated.

The second way of altering brain function is psychological. The way we view an experience, the meaning it has for us, will vary according to the setting of the experience. If you see a lion in its cage, you will experience little more than a frisson, however loud its roar. Remove the bars and the meaning of the experience is transformed; the same lion will be viewed in an entirely new light. Similarly, in the NDE one might expect the meaning of the experience to depend at least to some extent on the mental set of the person who experiences it, their expectations, their culture, and the context in which it occurs.

Changing the Model through Physiology

The near-death experiences described in this book occurred during heart-attacks, surgery and childbirth. Some were triggered by accidents or injury, others by illness. So what we are looking for are factors that may be involved in all these circumstances, and which are capable of changing or destroying the brain's capacity to build coherent and logical models of the world. Anything that can change body chemistry can do this. But these changes are also likely to affect memory, so we have to find something that will not only produce the phenomena of the NDE but also allow us to remember them.

1. Is the NDE Induced by Drugs?

The first and simplest explanation for the NDE is that the experience is due to the drugs given to patients as part of their resuscitation procedure, or to the effects of anaesthesia.

NDE-like experiences have often been reported by people using drugs such as LSD and nitrous oxide (an anaesthetic gas). Nitrous oxide has a reputation for inducing aspects of a mystical experience. Many people who have had anaesthetics associate the feeling of going under with a spinning sensation which could easily be felt as traversing a tunnel. But people who have NDEs don't usually spin through the tunnel - they are much more likely to float weightlessly along it. The following account was given by Mr James Carney. Certainly it happened while he was under dental anaesthesia, but could the anaesthetic be entirely responsible for his experience?

I had a poor education. Since leaving school at fourteen I had had labouring jobs - tree-felling, parachuting in the Army, furnace man in the iron foundries and lorry driving. My friends are mostly shipyard workers or local miners, so you will understand why I have not attempted to tell anyone of my experiences. One does not discuss the idea of afterlife and reincarnation with coalminers and shipyard workers, not if one wants to keep one's friends and sanity. Football, women and greyhounds maybe, but not the afterlife. My reading at this time was mainly the football pages of the newspapers and the odd football book. I am sorry if I have bored you with these details, but I think they are relevant.

It was about twenty-five or thirty years ago [that] I came home from the foundry with a terrible toothache. I decided I would have to go to the dentist. I had what the layman knows as 'gas'. Immediately I was under I had the sensation of leaving my body through my head. I was travelling through space and when I looked down, although I could not see my body, I could see I was attached by a light grey rope. The next sensation I had was a noise like a tuning-fork. I mentally asked the question, what was that? and it seemed that instantly I received a mental answer that I had passed through a stage of life. This happened again a few seconds later. The third time I had the answer: 'This is the third evolution.' The only evolution I had heard of previously was Darwin's, but I knew it meant a third stage of life. I was then met by a complete stranger whom I knew was so concerned and friendly that I went with him without any hesitation. We passed a man playing wonderful music. Further on I saw someone approaching and recognised a young lady whom I had courted briefly a few years before, but I had by this time forgotten her. My guide then took me a little further and I knew he was going to show me something. At this point he left me and I was immediately surrounded in this beautiful golden light. The peace and happiness was overwhelming, but I knew that if I stayed longer I would not return. I then thought of my wife and young child and knew I had to return. I then found myself in a dark tunnel. I could see the light at the end and knew I must get to it. I then woke from the anaesthetic and was filled with the feeling of compassion and concern for other human beings.

This feeling was alien to me, and I am afraid to say that in my world of having to take care of myself and survive it did not last long. I am sixty-one years old now and will never forget or deny the experience. You can imagine the delight I felt when I... realised that I was not the only person who was out of step with what is termed normal.

This experience bears so many similarities to the near-death experience that it is easy to argue that in some cases the NDE may simply be drug-induced. But as Mr Carney pointed out in a subsequent letter to me: 'The fact that the gas I was under has had about a thirty-year side effect may be lost on the sceptics.' It is certainly unusual for an anaesthetic experience to remain so vividly in memory for so long, but any very powerful experience, however it is induced, may be long remembered and have a lasting effect. I was once a subject in an experiment in which I had to perform certain tasks while breathing 40 per cent of nitrous oxide with oxygen. The world suddenly became full of meaning, and I knew that I had obtained a universal symbol which contained all knowledge. When I completed the experiment and as the mask was taken from me I called to my colleagues, I have it! The answer to all knowledge! And I held up two fingers in a V sign.

Some drugs certainly do have the capacity to disorganise brain function in such a way as to produce elements of the NDE. But only 14 per cent of our sample were being given drugs of any kind at the time of their experience. The fact that so many experiences occur when drugs are not used argues that whatever area of the brain is involved can be affected in many other ways. One of these is starving the brain of oxygen - anoxia.

2. Is the NDE Induced by Oxygen Starvation?

I have already mentioned anoxia (lack of oxygen) in the brain as a possible explanation for the tunnel-and-light phenomenon of the

NDE. At first glance lack of oxygen is an attractive explanation. In many near-death experiences - cardiac arrests for example, or any experience in which there is a sudden catastrophic fall in blood pressure - the brain is suddenly cut off from its oxygen supply. Sue Blackmore, who has written an excellent study of possible scientific explanations for the NDE, has suggested that NDEs should be less likely if anoxia has a very sudden onset - as in a sudden cardiac arrest, for example, which without resuscitation will lead to death - and more likely if oxygen decline is slow, as it may be in a long period of unconsciousness, for example, or in drowning, when the heart does not stop suddenly, but continues to pump poorly oxygenated blood around the body for a while so that anoxia develops only slowly. The table below shows the circumstances in which NDEs occurred in our series, but it is difficult to draw conclusions from these. More NDEs were certainly reported during illness, surgery and childbirth than during heart-attack, for example, but then these are more common occurrences. A properly controlled study is needed to discover whether there is a real link between gradually developing anoxia and the NDE.

	%
NDE occurred during:	
Illness	23.5
Surgery	21.3
Childbirth	14.8
Accident	9.6
Heart-attack	9.3
Suicide attempt	1.9

Another point in favour of the anoxia theory is that the temporal lobe of the brain, which is involved with the synthesis of emotion, is particularly sensitive to lack of oxygen. It can be argued that when this part of the brain is deprived of oxygen it responds by generating the very strong feelings of emotion which are often characteristic of the NDE.

But this point is less convincing when one remembers that the temporal lobe is involved with memory too. Anoxia might induce the experience, but it might also mean it would not be remembered.

Moreover, the link between lack of oxygen and brain function is a complex one. The amount of oxygen delivered to the brain cells will depend on many factors - it is not simply a matter of how much oxygen enters the lungs. It depends first of all on the oxygen level in the blood, secondly on the rate at which oxygen is being delivered to the tissues (which is determined largely by blood pressure), thirdly on the ability of the oxygen to be transferred so that it can be taken up by the cells. Finally, some brain areas (the temporal lobe, for example) are more sensitive to lack of oxygen than others. So low oxygen levels in the blood do not necessarily mean that the brain is short of oxygen. Anoxia is usually measured by taking a blood sample, so it is therefore difficult to use this measurement to predict the likelihood of the NDE.

There are other reasons why anoxia is not a convincing explanation of the NDE. Let's look first of all at what actually happens when a brain is starved of oxygen. Anyone who, instead of studying the menu or the duty-free list, has ever paid fleeting attention to the air hostess giving her pre-flight instructions, will know what to do when the oxygen masks suddenly appear dangling in front of you on a flight. Priority one is to don your own mask, even before you help the dependent child beside you put on his. This is because, deprived of oxygen at 35,000 feet, you have only a very short time before losing consciousness. Pilots in training regularly undergo acute anoxia in simulators to make sure they can get their oxygen masks on in time; those who fail to do so do not have NDEs; they either go unconscious or become so confused that they try to land their planes on clouds. Indeed, Allan Pring, whose NDE is described in Chapter 8, experienced anoxia at high altitude when he was an RAF pilot and must be one of the very few people in a position to compare the two experiences. His conclusions are clear. In his NDE he says:

> I found myself 'floating' along in a dark tunnel, peacefully and calmly but wide awake and aware. I know that the tunnel experience has been attributed to the brain being deprived of oxygen, but as an ex-pilot who has experienced lack of oxygen at altitude I can state that for me there was no similarity. On the contrary, the whole [NDE] experience from beginning to end was crystal clear and it has remained so for the past fifteen years.

Acute anoxia has often been simulated in laboratories too. A few years ago, when the training of medical students was more robust than it is today, it was common practice for them to be shown the consequences of depriving their brains of oxygen. Students were told to breathe through a carbon dioxide absorber into and out of a spirometer filled with air (a mixture of oxygen and nitrogen). While they were doing this they were given a list of numbers to copy. Now, if the carbon dioxide breathed out was allowed to build up inside the spirometer as the oxygen was used up, they would quickly be aware that they were suffocating. They would find themselves breathing deeply and rapidly in a desperate attempt to get rid of the carbon dioxide. However, because the carbon dioxide was being absorbed the students remained unaware that the air they were breathing contained less and less oxygen until finally they were breathing only nitrogen.

However, what was happening was clear to the observer, who could see the students' handwriting becoming more and more disorganised and repetitive until it finally trailed away in a straight line, and they lost consciousness. Anoxia has been induced in such experimental conditions thousands of times, in thousands of people. None of them has ever reported having a near-death experience, but yet they were all on the borders of unconsciousness.

Most important of all, the characteristics of the NDE make anoxia improbable as a principal factor. As the brain becomes anoxic it ceases to function. It becomes disrupted and disorganised, so that you become gradually confused, disorientated, your perception fragments and finally you become unconscious. You do not think clearly, you don't have insights, you don't have clear, coherent visions. In fact one of the most fascinating things about the NDE is that the experience stands out as so clear and vivid during a period when the experiencer may have been very confused, even unconscious, and of which they may have no other clear memories at all.

In summary, then, if anoxia is to be the major cause of NDEs we have to postulate a series of very unlikely events. The brain has to be able to synthesise a complex internal world and to be able to remember it, despite a lack of oxygen which is so profound that brain function is widely disrupted so that consciousness is lost.

The only way round this major difficulty is to argue that the NDE occurs either as consciousness is being lost or as it is being regained. It is unlikely that it happens as consciousness is being lost as there would not be time for the memory to be fixed within the brain (when consciousness is lost memory of the moments leading up to the event is also lost). People who have NDEs are usually certain they did not occur as they were regaining consciousness. There's also the problem that when consciousness returns it usually does so gradually, as anybody who has fainted will know. But anoxia still remains a possibility that must be considered.

3. Is the NDE Induced by Hypercarbia?

As oxygen levels in the blood fall, the amount of carbon dioxide increases. Dr Blackmore points out that the psychological effects of a build-up of carbon dioxide produce symptoms which are very similar to those of the NDE. In the 1950s an American psychiatrist, L. J. Meduna, looked at what happened when people were given mixtures of oxygen and carbon dioxide as a form of psychiatric treatment (in all the lending libraries in England there is only one copy of this book, so if you borrow it, please don't lose it). Many of his subjects reported dream-like experiences which sound very similar to the NDE. Some patients described them as being like 'real dreams'. They describe 'wonderful feelings'; bright colours and geometric patterns were seen; there was a sensation of whirling, spinning circles which pull out into a straight tube or funnel. There is an emotional charge, a feeling of cosmic importance, universality, which makes the experience pure ecstasy. 'It was a very good feeling, a feeling of discovery. I felt I knew a lot more than you. Secrets of this thing unfolded. Everything was so real and simple!' Some people had out-of-body experiences, and some relived past memories. For some people the experience has a spiritual dimension:

> I felt myself being separated; my soul drawing apart from the physical being, was drawn upward ... where it reached a greater spirit with whom there was a communion, producing a remarkable, new relaxation and deep security. Through this communion I seemed to receive assurance that the little problems or whatever was bothering the human being that was me huddled down on the Earth, would work out all right and that I had no need to worry.

It is also interesting that, just as in the near-death experience, most carbon dioxide-induced 'dreams' were very positive, but a few were so horrifying that the patient awoke in terror.

Dr Meduna pointed out that although he was giving the carbon dioxide as a therapy, it tended to produce identical phenomena regardless of the individual psychiatric needs and personalities of his patients. He suggested that all the phenomena rested on some underlying physiological function of some brain structures, which function independently of personality.

The many similarities between the experiences recounted by Dr Meduna's patients and people who have NDEs make this a very appealing theory. But in practical terms there are difficulties. No Intensive Care Unit worth its salt would tolerate a build-up of carbon dioxide in the blood of a patient who has suffered a heart-attack. It would be just as unacceptable for oxygen levels in the blood to be allowed to drop, unless there was an unavoidable catastrophic fall in blood pressure: if this happens levels of carbon dioxide in the brain would certainly rise. But we are still faced with the difficulty that catastrophic oxygen loss would accompany the carbon dioxide increase, and this would be sufficient to induce unconsciousness; brain function would then be so disturbed that it is unlikely that the brain would be able to build models or to remember them. A failing brain, by definition, produces experiences which are limited, confused and disorganised. The very opposite is true of the NDE.

There are other problems with the hypercarbia theory. As well as the sensory responses, hypercarbia produces convulsive muscle movements, in some cases so violent that the person seems to be acting out his dream-like experience. This has never been reported in the NDE. We also need to remember that the onset of many NDEs is accompanied by feelings of anxiety and stress. The immediate response to a stressful situation is to take deep breaths. Overbreathing has the effect of lowering carbon dioxide levels in the circulating blood and so in the brain. So it is difficult to argue that hypercarbia is a factor in these cases.

But what we can say is that some of the NDE phenomena can be evoked by hypercarbia. The NDE may have a different trigger, and involve a wider range of experience. But probably the same physiological structures, functioning (or malfunctioning) in the same way, may produce both kinds of experiences.

4. Is the NDE a Hallucination?

A hallucination is the perception of a reality that is entirely produced by the brain but which you believe to be completely true. Hallucinations occur when brain function is disordered because of a high temperature, or in an acute psychotic illness such as schizophrenia or depression. Drugs such as LSD can induce it, and so can withdrawal from drugs such as alcohol.

But hallucinations may also be quite normal and occur in quite normal people. It is very usual for someone who has been recently bereaved, for example, to hallucinate the person they have loved and lost. And some people quite often hallucinate just as they are dropping off to sleep or waking up. These are called hypnagogic or hypnopompic hallucinations and are absolutely normal.

It would be quite easy to categorise the NDE as a hallucination - in fact, by definition, this is what it is: a vision which the experiencer believes to be real but which has no basis in external reality. Over 20 per cent of our sample were ill, and at least some would have been running a high temperature, at the time of their NDE. But describing it as a hallucination does nothing to explain the underlying mechanism and leaves many of the same old questions unanswered. Why should everyone have more or less the same hallucination in the same circumstances? And why should it seem so real? Hallucinations experienced in a fever don't have this quality at all. Even people who have chronic schizophrenic hallucinations usually retain some awareness that their hallucination is just that.

Although some experiences may clearly be hallucinations resulting from illness or drugs, or psychological factors, as an explanation for all NDEs this runs up against the same difficulty that we've come across before. Brains which are disorganised so that consciousness is lost do not produce coherent hallucinations. One is again driven back to asking how lucid experiences can arise in the disorganised brain of an unconscious person.

ENDORPHINS - THE OPIATES OF THE BRAIN

One of the discoveries of the early 1970s was that the brain produced its own pain-killing drug in response to either pain or stress. These chemicals have the same effect as morphine or heroin, and are called the endorphins, a contraction of 'endogenous morphine' (morphine produced by the body).

They reduce the perception of pain and are thought to lead to states of relaxation.

The reason heroin (which is derived from morphine) is so addictive is that it produces wonderful feelings of warmth and calmness. Anybody who has been given a pre-operation injection of a morphine-like drug such as pethidine or omnopon will remember the feeling of euphoria it produces; nothing matters and the surgeon's knife no longer holds such terror. It has been suggested by some NDE researchers that it is the release of endorphins which leads to the feelings of ecstasy and bliss which form a part of so many NDEs. Certainly the levels of endorphins rise when you are intensely frightened or under great stress. Vigorous exercise can also produce a rise. Some athletes have reported having wide transcendental experiences after running a gruelling race, and it has been suggested that this might be due to the rise in endorphins.

There is some evidence to support the view that endorphins may be involved in the NDE. The people who have near- death experiences are often in great pain or under great stress - exactly the situations in which you would expect high levels of endorphins to be produced. So we can make a good case for the involvement of the endorphins. But it is not a perfect case. The difficulties are that injected opiates never accurately reproduce the ecstatic feelings of bliss that many people describe in their NDEs. And if opiates are the explanation, why is it that most people undergoing stress and coming near to death will have had raised endorphin levels but only a small number have a near-death experience? It has recently been found that very high endorphin levels are found in patients who have had a grand mal seizure. The levels remain high for some time after the seizure, and protect the sufferer from pain that might have resulted from any injuries sustained during the seizure. However, these very high endorphin levels do not lead to ecstatic states. On the contrary, someone who has had a grand mal seizure feels tired, washed out, exhausted, anything but ecstatic. So why should endorphins be responsible for blissful states when unconsciousness is due to other causes? Another point is that endorphins secreted as a response to stress have a sudden rise and a slow decay over several hours - probably longer than the duration of an NDE.

It looks as though even if we accept endorphins as a partial explanation, we have to argue that very special brain states are required if they are to lead to the bliss of the NDE, or, alternatively, that only some personality types respond to endorphins by experiencing bliss. And this seems very much like special pleading.

THE SEAT OF THE SOUL?

We have looked at several quite promising candidates in our search for the cause of the NDE. But all we've really shown is that they can stimulate brain activity in a way which bears some resemblance to part of the NDE. All have significant drawbacks as a total explanation. It is the brain activity itself which is really interesting, because it is this which has to underlie the whole experience. If we can find an area of brain which responds to any stimulus by producing something like the NDE, then we will be rather nearer to solving the mystery.

Some time ago I received a letter from a man who told me he thought he had lost his soul. He found that he could no longer appreciate music. He could hear the notes, but they did not form a tune and they meant nothing to him emotionally. He had clearly lost his ability for musical appreciation, and with it he felt he had lost his finer feelings. He had suffered a small stroke in the right temporal lobe - that area of the brain just behind the eyes - and this had produced the condition known as amusia: an inability to hear music as music.

About ten years ago a Swiss neurophysiologist, Dr Wieser, made a fascinating discovery while investigating a patient who was about to undergo surgery to remove an area of damaged brain tissue. To pinpoint the area, electrodes were implanted on each side of the brain, deep within the temporal lobe, alongside an area called the hippocampus (because it is shaped like a small seahorse). Wieser found that when he played his patient concordant music, electrical activity showed that the right hippocampus was active; when he played discordant tones, the left hippocampus became active. This suggests that in musically naive subjects the right hemisphere may be involved in the appreciation and synthesis of concordant music.

Rhythm is also thought to be a right temporal function and thus rhythmic concordant music, the kind of music that most people think of as 'heavenly', is most likely to be due to activity on the right-hand side of the brain. So if, as happened to my soulless correspondent, the right temporal lobe is damaged, amusia may develop. One can test this further by a neat experiment. It is possible to put either half of the brain to sleep by injecting sodium amytal (a sleeping drug) into the arteries supplying the brain. If this experiment is carried out on someone who is singing, it has been found that putting the left side of the brain to sleep affects the words, while an injection into the right side affects the melody.

So it looks possible that at least one aspect of Paradise in the NDE - the sound of wonderful music - arises because of activity in the right temporal lobe of the brain.

The first direct evidence for involvement of the temporal lobe in the NDE stretches way back to the 1930s and 1940s, to the time when the American neurosurgeon Wilder Penfield, the father of modern neuroscience, was making the first attempts to 'map' the brain. During brain operations under local anaesthetic he was able to stimulate various areas of the patient's brain with an electrical probe, and note what happened. The patients were under local anaesthesia, and so able to tell him what they were experiencing. This was not as horrifying as it sounds - the brain itself doesn't feel pain, it can only perceive pain in other parts of the body. He was able to identify which areas of the brain were responsible for movement, for sight, speech and many other functions. But he also found that when he probed an area in the temporal lobes, just above the ear, patients experienced some of the phenomena of the near-death experience: a splitting of consciousness which they experienced as leaving their body, feelings of tranquillity, hallucinations of people. A few reported having flashes of memory.

The near-death experience is usually very emotional. And it is the right side of the brain which is primarily concerned with emotion. There is some evidence that you can listen more empathically in a telephone conversation with the receiver held to your left ear (from which impulses go to the right half of the brain.) We probably also use the right hemisphere to appreciate visual emotion.

Many people who have a near-death experience say that they cannot find words to describe it. Avon Pailthorpe, for example:

> This part is very difficult to describe because all the words
> I can think of to use seem limited and therefore inadequate.
> Even 'terrific' as I just used it, I thought about for some time -
> great does not seem big enough - and I certainly don't mean
> 'terrifying', because it was the opposite of that. So the words
> I am using are only the nearest I can get to what this was,
> not a definitive description.

Words, the categorisation of experiences, are functions of the left hemisphere. If an experience is ineffable, impossible for people to categorise, it suggests that it may be arising in the right hemisphere, which is more concerned with spatial images, less with words, than the left.

There are other clues which point in the direction of right- hemisphere involvement. One is the deep feeling of unity, the loss of boundaries, both spatial and personal, which is often described in the NDE. Spatial integration is known to be a function of the right hemisphere, and loss of spatial boundaries is probably due to an alteration in right- hemisphere function. Another is that perception of time is often altered during an NDE - it's quite common for people to say that time seemed to stretch out to form an eternity. Disorientation in time and misordering of events in time is yet another right-hemisphere function. People who have damaged right temporal lobes sometimes experience speeding up and slowing down of subjective time. And a third is the tag of absolute reality which near-death experiences seem to carry - they are nearly always described as vivid, true, real; often they are felt to be even more real than everyday life. This attribution of certainty to ongoing perception is possibly a function of the right temporal lobe. A similar feeling of 'knowing' something emotionally is sometimes experienced by people who have epileptic seizures which arise from a damaged right temporal lobe. Such people quite often have feelings of deja vu and, if these arise in the right temporal lobe, the feelings have real emotion - the person knows without question that they have been there before. This too resonates with the feeling of deja vu and psychic awareness which often follow a near-death experience.

How much further does this get us? It looks as though we've identified at least one part of the brain that is involved in the NDE. But this gives us nothing like a complete answer. We know that when the temporal lobe is activated in some way fragments of the mystical experience are produced. But that is all they are, disorganised fragments. There are other aspects of the NDE - words, smells, body image - which indicate that other parts of the brain are sometimes involved. The point about the near-death experience is that it is a whole, integrated experience, not a confused, fragmented one. We don't only need to know where and how it arises, but why. And that seems to me to be by far the most interesting and important question.

Chapter 15

Mind Models

EVEN if we discover a possible mechanism for the NDE, we are still left with two puzzling facts. The first is that not everyone who is dying has the experience. The second is that plenty of people who are not dying do have an NDE - or at any rate they have an experience which is so similar as to be indistinguishable from it. Numerous people described experiences they had when they were not ill, though they may have been under severe stress or very depressed. And in a few cases experiences seem to have occurred which were either quite spontaneous or deliberately self-induced. In these people, psychological rather than physiological factors clearly precipitated their experiences. Even so, it's important to remember that even if the trigger factor is psychological, brain mechanism must underlie the experiences - they are not just generated out of nowhere.

SADNESS AND THE NDE

Change the way the brain works and you change the way you see the world. Disorders of mood can actually change the way the brain works; if you are very depressed, for example, you will tend to select sad memories and notice sad events all around you. And unhappiness seems to be a quite common trigger for the near-death experience. Take Sylvia Atkinson's story.

Eighteen years ago, when I was neither ill nor dying but deeply distressed because of the recent death of my nineteen-

year-old son, who had died of an overdose of sleeping tablets following a period of depression, I experienced what,
had I lived in Old Testament days, would, I imagine, have
been called a 'vision'.

I was lying in bed, very sad and hopeless and with the
usual feelings of guilt, when I saw the long tunnel. At the
end of the tunnel appeared Nicholas, looking absolutely terrible, as though he had been immersed in water, his clothes
appearing damp and giving the overall impression of cold-
ness-chill. He came slowly towards me and as he came nearer the light became brighter, a brilliant light surrounding
him. Nearer still and he was transformed into a figure, still
Nicholas, but of absolute beauty.

Will there come a time, I wonder, when such lovely experiences are explained? Is it the brain somehow comforting
us when we can bear no more, or is it a supernatural experience which we do not yet understand?

If Sylvia Atkinson is right in thinking that this is a 'comfort' experience, then why should it take this particular form? Mrs Atkinson was not ill, and so none of the physiological explanations we've
considered can have played a part.

It is difficult to make psychological sense of it, either. Her experience occurred nearly twenty years ago when experiences like
this were seldom discussed, so it is something she's unlikely to have
known about. We can't really argue that a tunnel to God plays any
part in our cultural expectations of death. Orthodox religious belief has certainly never suggested that God might be found at the
end of a tunnel.

Neither can we explain the brilliant, transforming light, although
there is some evidence to suggest a link between strongly positive
mood and light. People in the manic phase of a manic-depressive illness, whose mood is wildly elevated, sometimes describe seeing other
people in bliss, surrounded by haloes of light. It is possible that part of
this experience might be due to a mood change. But Mrs Atkinson's
account suggests that her mood changed after she had the experience
of seeing her son transformed. At the moment science has no satisfactory way of explaining this kind of subjective experience.

The following three experiences were also apparently triggered by
unhappiness. They all occurred at a time when the people concerned

seemed to have lost the will to live - psychologically, if not physically, they were near death.

Constance Cawthorne:

My NDE occurred forty years ago and arose because of a strong overpowering urge to get to the other dimension. I was twenty-eight years old at the time, with two children. I had been in a state of despair through seeking a meaning to life and not getting any answers. I prayed to die - and one day I did!

I travelled at terrific speed down the tunnel with a tiny light ahead which got bigger as I approached it. I felt utter joy as I knew when I reached it I would find what I had been seeking. However, before I 'passed over' I seemed to be in the presence of formless (but not faceless) spiritual beings who transferred to me the thoughts that I must go back - my family needed me, and I had not finished what I needed to do.

Mrs M. T. Gogarty:

Two and a half years ago my beloved husband died quite unexpectedly. His death was a terrible shock to me and I could not comprehend life without him (we had been married twenty-six years). However, as I was left with four teenagers to look after I tried my best to carry on with life. Then, three months later, I suddenly felt unable to cope and decided that to join my husband was all I really wanted. I became very upset when I visited his parents and cried quite a lot. They were very kind and put me to bed. I drifted off to sleep and although I could hear my daughter trying to wake me, I had no inclination to open my eyes -1 felt so relaxed and warm ...

I felt I was sitting in a dark tunnel which had a very bright light at the far end. I could look into this light without hurting my eyes and then I drifted towards it. I was so happy but then the shadow of what looked like a man, suddenly appeared in this light and waved at me to go back. I went back, but again I felt compelled to go towards this lovely light - and again I was waved back. I immediately awoke, my entire body covered with perspiration - even the face of my watch was awash - and the time stopped at 3 a.m. My sister-in-law, who was asleep in the same room, rushed to my bedside and asked if I was cold as the bedroom was at that moment very cold. She could not understand how I could be so warm without a temperature.

My own opinion is that although I was trying to leave this world, it was not yet my time to do so. However, death holds no fear for me now - it is simply the beginning of a new life.

Judith Smith:

I went into hospital for a minor operation at a time when I was very unhappy with no particular wish to live. I was in a velvety dark tunnel, incredibly soft darkness and surrounded by voices -1 could see no shapes - who were all very pleased to see me. There was a tremendous sense of peace, love, compassion and understanding. At the end of the tunnel there was a very bright luminous light and a landscape beyond, very beautiful. As we approached the light, one of the voices said 'Are you coming or staying?' and I knew that if I went I would die. I thought about it - certainly there was no fear - but I said, 'No, I haven't finished my life yet.'...

The experience was incredibly vivid, and I lost all fear of death. When the surgeon came round I asked him if there had been anything odd about the operation and what drugs they had used (I wanted to find out if it was drug-induced) and tried to tell him, but he just gave me an odd look and walked away. After that I tried to find someone who had had the same experience but everyone thought I was crackers, so I haven't told anyone about it for many, many years.

There may well be 'life after life', or it could be the way the brain shuts down? Either way, death is something to look forward to, when it comes.

So once again, all our scientific planks have been knocked away. We can't explain these experiences by suggesting the cause may be drugs or brain damage, too little oxygen or too much carbon dioxide.

All that we are left with is an overpowering, life-numbing sadness. These brains are certainly capable of making models. But why should the models they make be almost identical to the NDE?

IS IT ALL A DREAM?

Most people who have NDEs remain convinced that what happened to them was not a dream. But this is still a possibility we have to consider when we are looking at experiences like these in which people are not ill and no physiological explanation seems possible. We have seen that during dreaming, brain physiology is highly organised, and this makes it unlikely that NDEs occurring when the brain is damaged and malfunctioning are simply dreams. Can we also argue that even when the brain is functioning normally there are psychological aspects of the NDE that make dreaming an unlikely explanation?

The first difficulty is that if the NDE is only a dream, it is odd that so many people experience the same, or at any rate very similar dreams. There are a few dream situations which most of us will have experienced - flying dreams, dreams in which you are trying to run but cannot, dreams in which you are walking naked through a crowded place, for example. But these dreams do not really have a common pattern. They are much more related to the dreamer's individual thoughts, experiences, what is happening to them in their everyday life than the NDE seems to be.

We do know that we can to some extent 'dream to order'. People undergoing psychoanalysis, for example, tend to produce the kinds of dreams they have discovered that their analysts like to interpret. So could it be that if death is very much in our minds we will fulfil our own expectations by dreaming about the NDE? This is certainly a possibility, but most of the people who had these experiences knew nothing of NDEs at the time they had them.

Dreams, on the whole, do not have the tag of absolute reality which is such a hallmark of the NDE. They have their own peculiar logic: one scene transforms itself into another and the relationship between the dreamer and the dream is not always clear - is the dreamer an onlooker or is he part of the story? The sense of person is not always well defined in a dream, but is strongly emphasised in the NDE. Dreams, whether good or bad, often leave an aftertaste, but seldom one which lasts more than a day or so. The strong and lasting feelings of peace and bliss mentioned so often by people who have had NDEs do not seem to have their counterpart in the dream world.

One striking difference between NDEs and dreams is that dreams are not remembered, or at any rate, memory for them is not nearly as efficient as it is for events in the waking state. And this is as it should be - if dreams were remembered as clearly as real-life events it would be easy to become confused and unable to distinguish between a dream world and the real world. Indeed, the few people who do remember their dreams very well sometimes do have genuine difficulty in deciding what is real and what was only a dream.

Finally, I think we also have to accept that subjectively, the NDE does not feel like a dream. Everybody knows what a dream feels like; the people who described these NDE experiences remain convinced that what happened to them was not a dream.

A MODEL INDUCED BY A FEAR OF DEATH?

In extremis we will go to any lengths to comfort ourselves. So it is quite reasonable to suggest that the NDE might simply be our response to the threat of impending death; a fantasy that our brain creates to persuade us that death is not the end, but the beginning of some new and exciting existence.

If this is true then it has to be said that as a strategy it works extraordinarily well. Almost everyone who has a near-death experience says that they lose their fear of death afterwards. But as an explanation it is not so persuasive. Why does it seem so real? Why isn't it more consistent than it seems to be with a person's own belief system or religion? Even people who believe that death is simply a snuffing-out and who have no particular wish to believe in an afterlife sometimes have the experience. Why should so many people create the same scenario, making their way into the next world through a tunnel and into the light? Why does it happen even when catastrophe renders the person unconscious before they have had any chance to realise how near to death they actually are? Finally, if we are simply looking at a comfort measure, why does anyone have hellish experiences? These are certainly rare, but it seems to me they would be unlikely to occur at all if this explanation really held true.

An alternative view might be that the experience is genetically programmed into us so that death, when it comes, is not only tolerable but welcome. But here again this begs more questions than it answers. Why doesn't everybody have it, and why should it occur at inappropriate times when death is by no means imminent?

DISSOCIATED STATES

It is clear from many accounts that the NDE can be triggered by pain or panic. So it's reasonable to ask if what is happening is that the brain is somehow opting out, finding a way out of an untenable situation. We know that there are psychiatric conditions, known as dissociated states, in which the brain does seem to switch off in this way, insulating the person from very painful emotional or physical feelings.

The two most common of these dissociative states are derealisation and depersonalisation. Derealisation means that you feel normal but the world feels unreal. It's as if you are in a dream world, something which is clearly comforting if there is a very strong outside threat. In a state of depersonalisation you yourself feel unreal, although the world seems real. It is rather as if you are outside yourself, looking at yourself acting in a play but without experiencing any of the feelings an actor should feel.

Everything people tell us about near-death experiences makes them seem quite different from dissociated states. Those who have near-death experiences are clear that what happened to them had no dream-like qualities. Nearly everyone comments on the intense reality of the experience - even if you are out of your body you still remain real and the world still seems real. Pain is absent, but feelings of peace and tranquillity, even of extreme bliss, are generated. In a dissociated state it is much more likely that relief from pain is bought at the price of feeling nothing.

It seems unlikely to me that the NDE is a dissociated state, or that it is any form of escapism, of the brain simply shutting down through fear of death or destruction. It has quite different features, and it seems much more probable that it must have a quite different mechanism.

A MYSTICAL EXPERIENCE IN A
TRANSCENDENT REALITY?

We set out to test the NDE for 'reality' in a scientific way. But I think we have to conclude that we haven't managed to explain everything.

There are aspects of the experience which simply don't fit into our scientific paradigm and which seem to be inconsistent with a physical or even a psychological phenomenon. There remains the possibility which we raised in Chapter 2, that the NDE is a mystical experience, and that it originates in a transcendental reality.

One way of testing this is to look at some experiences in which it seems very unlikely that there is either a physical or psychological mechanism at work. Mrs Frances Barnshey was one of the few people who described an experience which seems to have arisen quite spontaneously.

I was in bed, recovering from 'flu, reading. I began to feel very relaxed and peaceful. I've never felt like that either before or since that experience. I put down my book as I could hear my husband and two children moving about downstairs, getting tea ready, and I remember thinking, 'Lovely, there's going to be a cup of tea in a minute,' and just at that point I felt myself shoot up out of my body, through the crown of my head at the most terrific speed, like being fired from a rocket. I was out in space, no dark tunnel, and I thought, this is how the birds must feel, so free. I was actually like a kite on an endless string, which I could feel attached between my shoulder blades. I couldn't see any kind of body belonging to me, I seemed to be mind and emotions only, but I felt more vital, more myself than I've felt in my life at any time before or since.

I found myself travelling towards this tremendous light, so bright that it would have blinded me if I'd looked at it here, but there it was different. I reached the light, which was all round me. I saw no one and heard no one, but I knew I wasn't alone, and I felt this wonderful love enfolding me and *understanding* me. No matter what my faults, what I'd done or hadn't done, the light loved me unconditionally. I so *wanted* to stay there, but I was told neutrally that this couldn't be, I had to go back, and then I felt this cord on my back - the biblical silver cord? - pulling me back and the next thing I knew was that I was back in my body and my son was coming into the bedroom with my cup of tea. The experience is as vivid in my mind as it was when it happened. I've always believed in life after death, though I no longer belong to any form of organised religion, preferring to find my own path, but if I needed anything to confirm my belief in another plane of existence, that experience certainly did. I feel so grateful to have had it.

Mrs Barnshey was neither ill nor unhappy when she had her experience. She did not believe she was near death, neither did she want to die. So it is difficult to find a physiological explanation for her experience, or to argue that it was due to stress. In fact it seems to have had no clear precipitant except possibly the 'flu. Even so, it shows many major features of the NDE, the out-of-body experience, the darkness (tunnel), the light and the love.

At this point let's remind ourselves of the characteristics of a mystical experience. Bucke, a nineteenth-century Canadian psychiatrist, was one of the first Western scientists to try to define it, and he listed nine features which he believed categorised its main elements. These were:

1. Feelings of unity.
2. Feelings of objectivity and reality.
3. Transcendence of space and time.
4. A sense of sacredness.
5. Deeply felt positive mood - joy, blessedness, peace and bliss.
6. Paradoxically. Mystical consciousness which is often felt to be true in spite of violating Aristotelian logic.
7. Ineffability. Language is inadequate to express the experiences.
8. Transiency.
9. Positive change in attitude or behaviour.

Does all that sound familiar? Although the NDE tends to have its own specific visual imagery - its 'storyline', if you like - the feelings evoked, the sense of unity, love, peace, the timelessness, the feelings of ineffability, are all described too by people who have mystical experience. As we mentioned in Chapter 2, surveys have shown that mystical experiences are really very common. About one third of the population will have a 'weak' mystical experience at some time in their lives - saying, for example, that at times they feel in the presence of some power greater than themselves. Some surveys have produced even higher rates of occurrence: a study of students at Nottingham University (a city whose claims to fame are founded more on lace and outlaws than on spirituality) indicated that as many as 65 per cent of them had had this kind of experience.

A social survey in 1988, conducted by the National Opinion Research Centre, University of Chicago, found that more than two thirds of Americans say they have had at least one mystical experience. Five per cent say they have such an experience 'often'. Are they getting commoner with each succeeding generation? Or is it that the climate makes it easier for people to admit to these experiences - the more aware people are of them, the larger the sympathetic audience for other people who want to talk about their own experiences? Perhaps surprisingly, this survey found that although mystical experiences were more common in those whose lives have some spiritual dimension, for example, people who practise prayer or meditation, those who were active church- goers or members of a synagogue were less likely to report them. This may be because some churches frown on these experiences or because churchgoers may cease to attend after an experience of this nature simply because it was so profound that anything the church can offer seems less interesting.

Deeper mystical experiences such as Bucke described are rarer, but still not uncommon. Probably they happen to about 10 per cent of the population - very close to the estimated rate of near-death experiences amongst people who have been resuscitated in an Intensive Care Unit. When something occurs so commonly we can assume that it is a normal part of human experience, mediated by brain structures common to everyone. This sudden precipitation into a different form of consciousness is what Yeats is describing in 'Vacillation':

My fiftieth year had come and gone,
I sat, a solitary man,
In a crowded London shop,
An open book and empty cup
On the marble table-top.

While on the shop and street I gazed
My body of a sudden blazed,
And twenty minutes more or less
It seemed, so great my happiness,
That I was blessed and could bless.

In all religions there are specific esoteric methods, for example meditation, which, when practised, lead to the experiencing of a transcendent reality. Although there has been little scientific research on the effects of meditation on the brain, what evidence there is suggests that this and similar practices in some way modify brain activity.

William of Occam's proposition that the simplest explanation is usually the best is as valid today as it was in the fourteenth century. It is logical to assume that one brain mechanism underpins both NDEs and mystical experiences, rather than to argue that one of them - the NDE - has quite a different explanation. There is a strong case for suggesting that changes in the function of the right side of the brain - the right temporal lobe - might be involved, not only (as we've just discussed) for the NDE but for all other mystical experience. People who have damage in the right temporal lobe often report fragments of the mystical experience. And in a research study I carried out some time ago I found a relationship between mystical experience, psychic ability and changes in temporal-lobe functioning. Clearly a unitary cause is the most likely.

If we accept that the NDE is a form of mystical experience, it explains at least some of the things that have puzzled us. It explains why not everybody who is near death has one, and why there is no common cause. From many of the accounts I received it is abundantly clear that you do not have to have been resuscitated - you do not even have to have been near death - to have a near-death experience. Numerous people have described experiences they have had when not actually near death - in childbirth for example, when in great pain, or ill and feverish, or under anaesthetic; or when they are intensely depressed or frightened. Some researchers believe that although no single feature of the near-death experience occurs only in near-death conditions, near-death NDEs can be distinguished from NDEs in other situations. Psychiatrists Gabbard, Twemlow and Fowler Jones suggested that someone who actually is near death when he has his experience is more likely to hear noises during the early stage of the experience, more likely to experience the tunnel and to see a brilliant light, more likely to see his own body at a distance, and more likely to sense other beings, especially dead friends. He is also more likely to feel that the experience has some purpose or mystical significance, and that it has changed his life in some way. A similar, later study by a group at the University of Virginia, Owens, Cook, and Stevenson, suggested that those who are actually near death are significantly more likely to report an enhanced perception of light, and to have enhanced cognitive powers (for example, speed and clarity of thought, vivid colours).

243

However, if the NDE is indeed a mystical experience I can think of no logical reason why these non-near-death experiences should be any different from those in which the experiencer is quite definitely on the threshold of dying. Reading through some accounts of people we know not to have been near death at the time of their experience, I found it very difficult to distinguish these accounts from 'real' NDEs. The same phenomena, the same feelings of peace and joy are described; the aftermath of the experience (usually a loss of any fear of death) is the same, and the experiences are no less significant and valuable to the person concerned than they are if he or she actually has been snatched right from the jaws of death. The table below shows what happens if we use the criteria suggested by Gabbard, Twemlow and Fowler Jones to analyse some of these accounts - the drug-induced experience of Mr Carney (covered in Chapter 14) (F), Mrs Barnshey's spontaneous experience (E), and the four experiences (A,B,C,D) recounted at the beginning of this chapter which seem to have been triggered by unhappiness.

	Noises	Tunnel	Bright light	See physical body	Sense other beings	Purpose/ mystical
A 4/6		•	•		•	•
B 4/6		•	•		•	•
C 3/6		•	•			•
D 3/6	•	•	•			
E 4/6		•	•		•	•
F 4/6	•	•	•		•	

These seem to me to be indistinguishable from the real thing.

The only element which is consistently missing from each account is the vision of the experiencer's own body from a distance. This does not seem particularly significant because we know that the out-of-body experience is one element which can, and often does, occur in isolation, in people who are not near death at all (see Chapter 3).

As a comparison, I analysed accounts from six of the people who had been very close to death at the time of their NDE. All of them were unconscious. Two (David Verdegaal and H. N. Smith) had had heart-attacks; two (Mary Errington and Ella Silver) were unconscious during an operation; Michael Mizon had received a severe head injury in a car accident, and David Whitmarsh had been electrocuted. The total number of features scored by these NDEs is rather less than in the six analysed above. And once again, the light is the only constant feature.

	Noises	Tunnel	Bright light	See physical body	Sense other beings	Purpose/ mystical
DV 3/6			•		•	•
HS 2/6			•		•	
MM 4/6	•	•	•		•	
DW 3/6		•	•		•	
ME 3/6	•	•	•			
ES 3/6		•	•		•	

So what we see is that a set of very similar experiences can be triggered off in many different circumstances, and sometimes can simply arise spontaneously. Whatever the circumstances, such experiences seem to be equally valuable and equally significant to the person who has them. And that the experiences are so similar and seem to have such similar significance argues powerfully for the fact that whatever it is, the near-death experience is not simply the product of a confused or dying brain but a mystical experience which may happen at any time to anybody.

Clearly there must be brain structures which mediate the NDE and they are probably the same structures which mediate any mystical experience. It would be a simple and likely explanation to suggest that these structures can be stimulated in many different ways, from either psychological or physiological causes. If this is so, then the form of the experience would have to be defined by these brain structures. This would explain the roughly similar content of the experiences, and would also allow for the experience to be modified by culture and experience.

But the major question still remains unanswered. How is it that this coherent, highly structured experience sometimes occurs during unconsciousness, when it is impossible to postulate an organised sequence of events in a disordered brain? One is forced to the conclusion that either science is missing a fundamental link which would explain how organised experiences can arise in a disorganised brain, or that some forms of experience are transpersonal - that is, they depend on a mind which is not inextricably bound up with a brain. This is a possibility that we shall look at further in another chapter.

If this theory is right, if the NDE is a natural part of human experience, but one which originates outside the human brain even if it is mediated through it, then the only way to validate it is through experience.

Chapter 16

The Dying of the Light

THE certainty of death is the only certainty we have. It terrifies us, because we cling to permanency and death marks the end of everything we think we know and love. It fascinates us, too. Bartlett's Familiar Quotations has nearly eleven columns of entries on death and dying, compared to six on the soul and only a single column on immortality.

This century is the first in which death has not been for most of us in the West a common, everyday, domestic occurrence. In the past, not only did people die younger, they usually died at home, with their families around them. Death was part of everyone's experience. Now we prefer to hand it over to the state to deal with rather than handle it ourselves. Granny is much more likely to die in an ordinary hospital ward than at home. And many of us will never have had any personal experience of death until our own parents die.

Medical advances have given us the power to prolong life, but have taught us nothing about how to die. If anything, death seems to threaten us more than it ever did. We treat it as an embarrassment, outrageous, something that shouldn't happen, or at least not to us. Or at least not to those we love.

We tend to share Dylan Thomas's view that death is something to be fought every step of the way:

Do not go gentle into that good night,
Old age should burn and rave at close of day;
Rage, rage against the dying of the light.

It is only recently that people have felt able to say freely that they have, for example, cancer, without resorting to euphemisms and evasions. Outright admission that you were a cancer sufferer was acknowledging the unthinkable - that you were going to die. People now feel the same way about AIDS. Death is thought of as something we have to shield each other from, not help each other through. We don't find it easy to find the right thing to say even to someone who's been recently bereaved, let alone to someone we know is terminally ill. To those of us who are not near death, or who have never lived through the death of someone they love, it seems that the prospect of death must be so painful as to be unbearable. And in the face of someone else's unbearable pain, it's instinctive to draw back. It's always hard to leave someone you love, and the dying are going away forever.

So it is no wonder that the near-death experience has so captured our imagination. It seems to hold a double promise: that dying is not such a terrible experience after all, and that there is an afterlife, possibly even one in which we will be reunited with those we love.

DOCTORS AND THE NDE

Doctors do not always feel so positively about the near-death experience, even, perhaps especially, when they meet it on their own territory. The medical profession has its own hang- ups about death. When your business is to save life, death is a reminder of your fallibility. This may be why some doctors find the near-death experience difficult to deal with. It is easy to imagine how a surgeon might feel if a patient under his or her care announces that he has died during an operation, or how threatening it would be to an anaesthetist to be told by a patient that he has seen every detail of the operation.

Occasionally I have encountered some of these attitudes myself when I have been trying to set up research programmes into the near-death experience. The head of one Intensive Care Unit refused to allow me to question any of his patients - it would be pointless, he said, because in his unit they could have no experiences; they were properly anaesthetised and unconscious. Clearly he felt that if one of his patients reported an NDE, it could only be because of his own professional incompetence. But such attitudes are becoming rarer as the NDE becomes more accepted by both lay people and professionals.

It's not only because they see it as a threat to their professional competence that many doctors are uneasy about the NDE. Doctors are scientists; they fight disease using scientific methods, and may be mistrustful of the NDE because it seems so outside the realm of science. They may think that if they acknowledge that a patient has in fact been near death, this will distress them. Moreover, doctors are no more immune than anyone else to uncertainties and fears about their own death. The NDE may force them to reexamine some of their own beliefs, not always a comfortable process. As several letters show, a few professionals clearly do find the near-death experience hard to accept, and their diligent search for a rational explanation is probably as much to reassure themselves as their patients. As Jane Dyson reported: 'Doctors and nurses to whom I have spoken just put it all down to the effect of drugs, bright hospital lights or torches being shone in my eyes, but I know it was more than that, something which I cannot explain. But I hope one day to speak to someone else who has "nearly died" if they have any after-effects which they cannot understand.'

Peter Horrocks:

> I looked down on myself in the bed below. I was in no way frightened but I remember thinking that it was important to rejoin my body but finding it difficult to do so until someone came into my room and broke the spell. I do not recall being apprehensive that I would not be able to do that. On the third and last occasion that this happened, however, a nurse came into my room and I not only remained where I was on the ceiling, but I told her so. She said something like, 'Don't be silly,' and with some relief I found myself back in bed, feeling rather foolish.

Mrs Jean Giacomozzi: 'I remembered the doctor removing the cotton wool plug. When I later saw this doctor I told him everything. Although he seemed rather shocked at my story, he had no explanation as to how I knew so much about the events of the previous night.'

Ella Silver: 'The next day I... told the sister. I thought she would scoff but she didn't. She listened very quietly with her hand on my shoulder. She told me they had been very concerned about me because they could not pull me out of the anaesthetic. I had been out for hours and my pulse was very low. I felt the sister believed me, strangely enough.'

Gillian McKenzie:

> When the surgeon came round to see me I asked if I'd died.
> He made some comment that it was the anaesthetic and I
> was hallucinating. I didn't say any more because I knew he'd
> think I was nuts. But if it was really only drugs and halluci-
> nations, why didn't the doctors say, yes, we know about that,
> we've had other patients describe that. But they didn't, and
> I felt very much alone. There was no one I could discuss
> it with. It was the reaction of the medical staff which wor-
> ried me most. I was sure they would think I was peculiar,
> although I knew I wasn't.

We mustn't forget that although the NDE is a positive experience
for most people, it's also a puzzling one. People often want to talk
about what has happened to them. But usually they are afraid of being ridiculed, so unless doctors and nurses give them an opportunity
to do this, and are accepting and sympathetic, they won't find it easy
to do. For anyone whose experience has been less than positive, it's
even more vital to be able to talk about it.

> When I was thirteen years old I had a major heart operation.
> I was recovering in a small cold room. I seemed to be on
> ice I was so cold and uncomfortable. I do not know to this
> day whether I was having a hallucination but there was a big
> window and I saw Jesus with two child angels either side
> floating down to me. I apparently left my body and floated
> up to them looking down at me ... I got frightened and said
> I wasn't ready to be an angel and I didn't want to go. That
> was it. I eventually recovered from the operation but never
> told anybody about this in case they thought I was mad.
> Since then my life has been full of ups and downs and
> I often think about it and feel guilty for not going when
> my time came. I feel that I rejected God and since my life
> on Earth has been to prove to me Hell is here and Heaven
> waits. At times I get so depressed and have actually tried
> to kill myself.

Perhaps if Ms Stella Ash, who is quoted above, had been given the
chance to talk to someone about her feelings at the time, she might not

have been haunted by this childhood experience throughout her later life. Counselling the dying is a skill still not always taught in medical schools, but there are now voluntary courses for doctors, nurses and other professionals who work with the dying which include discussion of the NDE. Professionals who have an awareness of what it involves should be sensitive to the needs of patients who perhaps want to talk about what has happened to them, but are unsure of how their disclosures might be received. Without this awareness doctors may be tempted to regard their patients as confused or disorientated, and as Melvin Morse has said, 'Words like these lead physicians to medicate the visions right out of a dying patient.'

Surgeons are not usually famous for their sensitivity and so it is especially heartening to hear how Allan Pring describes the reaction of his surgeon when he told him what had happened during a routine operation. This operation was in 1979, and it is quite possible that this surgeon had never heard of near-death experiences, very probable that he had never encountered anyone who had had one. And yet he found the time to listen to his patient, and the sensitivity to take what he said seriously. It is easy to imagine how emotionally destructive it would have been if the surgeon had dismissed the whole experience as an anaesthetic reaction of no importance or significance.

When I recovered consciousness I was in quite an emotional state and when the surgeon made his rounds I gave him a detailed account of my experience. I assured him that had I not chosen to return then he would have had a corpse on his hands. He was intrigued and we discussed the matter at some length the next day when I had fully recovered from the anaesthetic ... The surgeon detailed a young doctor to make some notes of my story.

I suspect that the extremely busy young man thought I was deranged. One of my sons, a newly qualified doctor working in another hospital nearby, visited me on several occasions. He was rather concerned because giving a detailed account of my experience caused, and still causes me to become emotionally upset. The tears are a mixture of terrible sadness and extreme happiness.

Letting Go

The accounts we have given in this book are mostly from people who have been 'near death'. Unfortunately, it is in the nature of death that there are no survivors; no one who can tell us what death

251

is actually like. We may assume that when people are near death and are then resuscitated, their experience is much like the real thing, but it is only an assumption. The interesting thing about the following account is that it seems to confirm at least one aspect of the NDE - that it is often the pull of family and friends which seems to draw the dying person back from the brink. From Mrs B. L.

Wills' account, her dying brother did indeed feel this 'tug of love' from the living which so many people describe. Perhaps this story also shows us that the living have an important part to play, and that it may be easier to leave this life if those we love are loving enough to let us go.

> The day my brother passed away, I was with him all day, together with his wife and sister-in-law. During the day he got out of bed to go to the bathroom and chatted to us, asking us to thank the various people who had helped him during his lifetime. Then various comments he made during the day made us realise he was travelling on a journey. He asked us time and time again to let him go - to me it seemed our spirits were wanting to hold him, so we told him we would let him go, and I started to pray to God that he might take him into his safekeeping.
>
> When the end came it was so peaceful, the room seemed full of angels and we were not sad, but happy.

You are almost guaranteed a reaction when someone discovers that you are working on a book about the NDE. Sometimes it is fascination, sometimes disbelief. But over and over again, people (even when they have just been expressing extreme scepticism) will say something like, 'But I can tell you something very odd that happened to me once...' or, 'Let me tell you about something my grandmother once told me...' They don't recognise what happened to them as bearing any relation to the near-death experience. The friend who told us this story was very surprised indeed when it was suggested that what she'd experienced was, in essence, exactly what happens to people in the NDE.

> It was a very, very painful, very long labour. And at one point I found myself thinking, I just can't be bothered with all this any longer. I felt I was just slipping away from it all.

I wasn't really aware of my husband or any of the people around - they didn't count. It was only me. My husband could see something was happening to me, I looked so awful, and he was frantic and shouted at me, 'Jen, come back.' It was his voice that brought me back, I'm sure. But I really didn't want to come back.

To me this suggests that there are probably many people who certainly wouldn't think of themselves as having had near- death experiences but who may at least have started on that journey. This raises the possibility that the NDE may be a spectrum of experience, and that this feeling of 'slipping away' is simply the initial stage. Mrs Hover, whose experience during the birth of her third child is described in Chapter 14, also wrote about another experience she had when, some years ago, she was ill in hospital. She did not suggest that this was a near-death experience, but simply felt that it had given her some comforting insight into what it might be like to die.

The next week passed in a haze of pethidine. I had never been so ill for so long. There was a time when I thought I might die. The interesting thing was that there was a peace and calmness in that thought that I had not anticipated. I remembered the death of my own mother and the anguish it caused me, but I also remembered her own peace and resignation at that time. She seemed untouched by our sadness.

I had not made a will and my affairs were not orderly. If I had died there would have been a great deal of grief but at that time it did not matter. I had made my peace with myself and my God and the world was no longer of any concern.

A week later I was better and horrified to realise that I had not seen or even thought about the children for a week. Normality returned, but now I have no fear of dying. I know that it will be a peaceful experience even if the prelude to it is unpleasant. I do not believe in an afterlife, just death, a sleep from which there is no awakening. This, however, does not make me fear the experience.

Facing Up to Death

Probably the main reason we fear death so much is that we don't know what it will be like. So it is valuable to be reminded that even without an NDE, one's view of death may be transformed simply by having come face to face with it. I certainly find it comforting to think that death may simply be a peaceful drifting away, a gradual fading of all earthly attachments. We fear it because our point of reference is now, because we are so aware of all we would be leaving behind.

Whatever our views on the next life, we do not want to be dragged kicking and screaming away from this one. But death might not seem so threatening if we could bring ourselves to believe that it won't be like this, that at the point of death, nothing matters any more.

Our fear of death and love of life mean that we seldom prepare either for death itself or the process of dying. Ask your friends how many of them have made a will which is up to date and takes into account changing family circumstances. Probably not many. We know we should do it; our reluctance to take practical steps is at least partly because we're reluctant to face up to our own personal extinction.

Most of the esoteric literature and the view taken in the Christian Church is that we should be ready for death at any moment, for we don't know when that moment is. The saint has no possessions (literally no attachments); each day he rolls up his sleeping blanket and tidies away his cooking utensils, sets everything in order and is mentally prepared for his own death that day.

Our own view is more likely to be that when death comes, we'll be prepared to face it. In fact, when the time comes we have no option but to face it. But it's odd that while we make quite serious preparations for marriage, parenthood and retirement we are reluctant to prepare for death when we are in full health. If you were to drop dead tomorrow are your relationships in good repair, or would your survivors have the additional burden of guilt or anger to cope with? Have you made a will, and do your family know how and where you would like to be buried or cremated? Finally, do you have some personal philosophy which (if you are given any time for reflection before you go) will make it easier for you to die in peace? When you are with someone who is dying, the main requirement is that you be there, not that you do anything.

Make sure his or her surroundings are both peaceful and cheerful, and try not to take over completely, making all the decisions, removing from your friend or relative every vestige of control over what happens to him.

Should you talk about death to the dying? Take your cue from them, but don't go to great lengths to avoid the issue. At a time like this people are treading so delicately, being so careful not to say the wrong thing, that it is easy for many of the right things to go unsaid. And later, when you realise that there isn't going to be another chance to say them, this can be yet another source of grief. If there is unfinished business, rifts in the family or relationships that are strained, it's important that everyone has the opportunity to try to heal them, to say 'I am sorry,' or '1 forgive you.' This is not only so that the dying person can let go in peace, but so that the people left behind can have a peaceful and guilt-free parting.

It is always worth remembering that we may have a very limited picture of what the dying person can experience. Even when someone appears to us to become unconscious, as is very likely in the terminal stages of an illness, he or she may be able to hear more than we imagine he can, feel our touch even though he does not respond. Holding his hand, talking to him, may give him more comfort than we realise. We can't ever know this for certain, but we can at the very least draw comfort ourselves from knowing that we tried to round off his life with a loving farewell.

Melvin Morse has suggested that we need to make the deathbed more crowded with people, less crowded with machines, and this is something we'd do well to keep in mind - if the choice is open to us. It's natural to demand a miracle when someone we love is dying; whatever the financial or emotional cost, if there is any way they can be dragged back to life, we want it. But high-tech around the deathbed is sometimes more concerned with the feel-good factor of the relatives, who need to know they have done everything they can, than with the peace and comfort of the dying.

It is a pity that we have got out of the habit of dying at home. Given the choice, most people would prefer this, and so too would their families - provided they can be given sufficient support. And yet there is a steadily increasing trend towards hospital deaths. In Scandinavia, 90 per cent of deaths take place in hospital. In England and Wales, in 1975, 58 per cent of deaths took place in hospital; by 1987 this figure had risen to 63 per cent.

Dying at home is rather like childbirth at home - you can create your own conditions, and retain at least a small measure of independence and control. Friends and family can come and go as they please. Hospital, however good the staff are at providing the necessary medical and nursing support, cannot always answer the emotional and social needs of the dying patient and his family. Many junior doctors and nursing staff feel that their training did not equip them to care for the dying, and in any case, on an acute ward staff are often too busy to sit and talk with a dying patient. It isn't always practical for relatives to be with him all the time; quite often the person dies alone. In one's own home there is none of the sense of isolation that may be inevitable in hospital. Pain is one of the fears that most of us have about dying. But with modern techniques, control of even severe pain need not be a problem for the person who wants to die at home. Motorised syringes can inject a slow and continuous dose of pain-killers under the skin. Relatives of cancer patients need not feel they are coping alone, with the help of specially trained Macmillan Nurses, who will visit the homes of people dying of cancer, bring the expertise of the hospices into the home, and thus allow many more people to die at home.

There's no doubt, though, that unless there is a lot of family support, nursing a terminally ill patient at home can be a huge emotional and physical load. If an illness is at all protracted, it is hard for one carer to cope alone. A hospice, set up especially to care for the dying, and also to help their families, may be the best solution. Hospices are experts in pain control, but it isn't only their expertise in giving the right amount of medication which benefits the patient. Experience in hospices has shown that in a quiet and supportive atmosphere people don't seem to feel pain to such an extent and require less analgesia.

If there is one common theme amongst the experiences described in this book it seems to be that they take away the fear of death. If I had a patient who was afraid of dying, or who was angry or depressed at the prospect of death, I wouldn't hesitate to talk realistically to him or her about the near-death experiences others have had if he indicated that he would find this helpful; or to arrange for him to talk to someone who has had such an experience.

There are doctors who believe that it can be therapeutic to encourage patients to have a 'pre-death' vision, by a process akin to guided meditation. Dr Morse describes how Dr Gardner, a psychologist at the University of Colorado Children's Hospital, helped a thirteen-year-old dying of leukaemia to find an image that would help him deal with the anxiety of death. 'The boy chose an eagle, which could soar through the air - away from his pain-filled body - to a place of peace and love.' One of the questions we really are no nearer to answering is why some people have NDEs while others, in an apparently identical situation, do not. All we do know is that it seems to have nothing to do with belief - however strong your faith, it doesn't earn you an NDE. And one of the dangers of regarding the NDE as some kind of proof that there is an afterlife is that disillusionment can be strong if the proof fails to materialise. People who have a strong religious faith may feel this faith shaken if they recover from a near-death situation but have not had an NDE.

Some people have suggested that there is a risk that in talking about the NDE to the dying we may be holding out false hopes; that for many, dying is not going to be either a pleasant or a positive experience. After all, proponents of natural childbirth are sometimes criticised because they give too rosy a view of childbirth. Women who have taken on board the full package and believe it will all be as simple as falling off a log are shocked and outraged when, however faithfully they follow instructions, childbirth turns out to be both painful and extremely hard work.

I don't think that is a risk we need take too seriously, provided we are careful to make the distinction between the process of dying and death itself. After all, this is a distinction that the people who have had the experience are themselves very clear about, as this account emphasises.

> I also know that I am in no way afraid of death. I don't want to die and I am certainly concerned about the possible method of dying ... The 'dying' part of all my experiences has been very unpleasant, that is the rushing or falling down that black tunnel, the fighting to keep away from that nasty oblivion and then the complete surrender to it because it is too powerful to overcome. But then the incredible reward of emerging into that brilliant white light, so white that one cannot find a word that could adequately describe its brilliance.
>
> Also, a wonderful feeling of wellbeing, of tranquillity, love and happiness. No sadness, no remorse, no fear, not even the missing of loved ones who are so very important to us in this life. Just total peace.
>
> I am not a religious person and I am certain I will never become one, despite these experiences, as I now have my own ideas as to what life (and death) may be about through them. Also, I sincerely believe that this 'other life' awaits us all and that the real truth of our existence will be simple to

understand from whatever great power out there which allowed us this life in the first place.

So perhaps we should not be too preoccupied with what the NDE means to us, whether we believe it offers proof positive of a soul or the possibility of an afterlife. All we have to do is to accept what it means to the people who have actually experienced it and allow for the possibility that any one of us might experience it too.

Chapter 17

What the Dying Tell Us

S EVERAL years after I had first come across the near death experience, I was sent this account, by Pauline Drew, of something that happened the day before her mother died.

"Suddenly she looked up at the window and seemed to stare intently up at it... .....She suddenly turned to me and said "Please Pauline, don't ever be afraid of dying. I have seen a beautiful light and I was going towards it.... it was so peaceful I really had to fight to come back." The next day when it was time for me to go home I said "Bye mum, see you tomorrow." She looked straight at me and said "I'm not worried about tomorrow and you mustn't be, promise me." Sadly she died the next morning....but I knew she had seen something that day which gave her comfort and peace when she knew she had only hours to live."

The account intrigued me firstly because it contained so many elements of the NDE – the experience of light, the feeling of peace, the feeling that Pauline's mother had been shown a glimpse of another reality from which she was reluctant to return and the abolition of any fear of death, and secondly because of the suggestion that after this experience Pauline's mother somehow knew she was going to die the following day. This made me think that we should perhaps not look at the near death experience in isolation as something that occurs only as life is almost extinguished, but as part of a continuum – the process of dying - and that part of this process might be a preparation for death itself, beginning in the hours or even days before death.

As happened with the NDE, once we became aware of these end of life experiences we found them everywhere. If I mentioned them in a lecture there were always people in the audience who were eager to recount similar experiences in their own family. And whenever we talked to our own friends and family yet more strange stories emerged – from the sudden intense feeling of disaster that struck our daughter's best friend at the moment her father was dying, 4000 miles away, to the odd and inexplicable behaviour of a friend's cat after the death of the aunt on whose lap he liked to sit.

These deathbed visions have a long anecdotal history. There are many stories of early Christian martyrs and saints who were visited by Christ, Mary or another saint to warn them of their impending death and accompany them into heaven. One of the first written records of such a vision was by the 8th Century English historian Bede, who wrote of a dying nun who was visited on her deathbed by a recently deceased holy man. He told her that she would die at dawn, and indeed she did. Towards the end of the 19th Century, psychical researchers Gurney, Myers and Podmore, published Phantasms of the Living, which included accounts given by normal, apparently sane people who claimed to have seen apparitions of dead friends or relatives.

However, it was not until the 1920s that these odd apparitions aroused any serious scientific interest. The first attempt at a systematic scientific study of them was made by Sir William Barrett, a physics professor at the Royal College of Science in Dublin. His interest in the topic was aroused when his wife, an obstetrician, told him what had happened when she was called to deliver the baby of a young woman, Doris, who was dying of a haemorrhage. Lady Barrett described how, as Doris lay dying, she began to see visions:

> "Suddenly she looked eagerly towards part of the room, a radiant smile illuminating her whole countenance. 'Oh, lovely, lovely' she said." When asked what it was that she saw she replied 'Lovely brightness, wonderful beings.' A moment later she exclaimed:
>
> 'Why, it's Father! Oh, he's so glad I'm coming; he is so glad. It would be perfect if only W. (her husband) would come too.'

Lady Barrett then described how Doris spoke to her father again, saying, 'I am coming', and turning to Lady Barrett added 'Oh, he is so near.' And then she added, looking rather puzzled, 'He has Vida with him, Vida is with him.'

It was this last remark that made Sir William take the story seriously. Vida was Doris's sister: they had been very close, and although Vida had indeed died three weeks earlier, Doris, because of her delicate condition, had not been told. The fact that Doris had seen her sister, who as far as she knew was alive and well, in this 'other place' and in the company of the father she knew to be dead, convinced Sir William that he could not simply dismiss the incident as insignificant. He began to collect similar experiences and his book, *Deathbed Visions*, published in 1926, concluded that these experiences were not merely a by-product of a dying brain, but could occur when the dying patient was lucid and rational.

The first comprehensive and objective study of these visions was made by Karlis Osis and Erlendur Haraldsson (1977)). In 1961 Osis conducted a questionnaire survey of 5000 physicians and 5000 nurses, asking about the hallucinations they had observed in terminally ill patients under their care. He analysed the 640 replies and categorised two types of hallucinations; visions of nature or landscapes, and apparitions of people, usually dead relatives or friends who had come to help the dying in their transition to the next life. (Osis 1961). Together with Professor Erlendur Haraldsson, Osis carried out two further surveys, one in the United States in 1961-64 and one in India in 1972-73. One of their most interesting findings was the apparent cultural bias in the travelling companions seen in these 'take-away' visions. In the United States survey the most common apparitions were of dead relatives and friends, while religious escorts were much less frequent. However in the Indian experiences the reverse was true; it was religious figures such as the "yamdoot" – the messenger sent by the God of death - who were the most frequent take-away companions, while apparitions of dead relatives or friends appeared far less often.

But despite the wealth of anecdotal evidence about the phenomena that are reported to occur at or around the time of death, the medical profession has been slow to recognise them. Plenty of scientific papers have been published about palliative care and pain control, but very few about the mental states during the dying process, or about the visions reported at this time by dying people, perhaps because this area is of little interest to the medical profession who feel that at this point they cannot control the process and are no longer involved. There has been little research into the experiences themselves, or the way carers respond when patients try to talk about these phenomena, or whether hearing about the experiences influences the carers' work in any way. We wanted to know how common the experiences were, whether we could find any rational explanation for them, and the impact they have both on the dying person and on the family or professional carers. In an attempt to answer these questions we have interviewed carers in a palliative care team, two hospices and a nursing home in the UK and three hospices in Holland. (Brayne et al 2006, Fenwick et al 2007, Brayne et al 2008)

We also have data from Dr Una MColville, a Palliative care physician in Ireland, who gave our questionnaire to an Irish Hospice, making altogether over 110 carer interviews.

When we started to look at these experiences more seriously, we realised that once a climate had been established in which it was accepted first that they did indeed occur, and second, that it was permissible to talk about them, it became clear that they were quite common. A wide range of phenomena are associated with the dying process, but those that seem to occur, or at least to be reported, most often are these.:

Death bed visions

Perhaps the most commonly reported of these end of life experiences are visions, usually of dead relatives, or someone to whom the dying person was emotionally close. The visions are usually seen in clear, or only moderately impaired, consciousness and their purpose seems to be to help the person through the dying process. They are almost always comforting and seem to provide a spiritual preparation for death.

> "My dear Mother died last year and unfortunately we were not with her. When the Nursing Home rang to tell me she had passed on the nurse said" I wouldn't normally tell anyone this but as I know you well I will. About half an hour before your Mum died she said to me "You see that lady sitting in my armchair, it's my sister. She's waiting for me". I found this very very comforting."

Sometimes not only does the visitor appear in the room, but the dying person describes journeying with them to an intermediate reality that they perceive as being more real than the real world, and interpenetrated by light, love and compassion. Here both relatives and strangers may be seen, and nearly always are felt as a comforting presence, there to help with the dying process and holding out a promise of the possibility of a continuation of consciousness.

The mother of a 32 yr old woman dying of breast cancer described to me what happened in the last two to three days of her daughter's life…

> "She was conscious of a dark roof over her head and a bright light. She moved into a waiting place where beings, her grandfather amongst them, were there to help her and told her everything would be ok. She moved into and out of this area, and was adamant that it was not a dream."

Deathbed coincidences

One of the most interesting, and indeed inexplicable, of these end of life experiences is the deathbed 'coincidence', in which a person has a sudden realisation that someone they are emotionally close to has died, and discovers later that this did indeed happen at the time they felt this strong intimation of the death. Often the two are far apart, and the one who has the experience may not even know that the other is ill. Often this happens either in a dream or on a sudden awakening from sleep and a vision of the dying person is seen which seems to convey the message that they have come to say goodbye and to give reassurance that all is well with them.

> "I was only a child of 11 years old when she died but during the night of her death I became awake (I don't know what made me wake up) and saw my Nan at the end of my bed… I can remember feeling very sleepy and wondering why I was awake during the night and why Nan was by my bed and asking her what was the matter.
>
> Nan began to tell me that she was going away and that meant that I wouldn't be able to see her for a long long time, but that I wasn't to worry because she would be alright where she was going because it was a lovely place. I asked if I could come and visit her there but she said that wouldn't

be possible but she would still be able to see me ...would watch over me and would always be there for me if I ever needed her. I said something like 'ok nanny, that's nice' she said 'I love you' and I said 'I love you too' and with that she told me to lie down and go back to sleep .... so I did.

In the morning my parents said that they had some very sad news to tell me and went on to start to explain that nanny had died. I replied that I already knew that...because nanny came to tell me she was going away but it was alright because she was still going to look after me and that I was not to worry."

Less often the contact takes place when the person is fully awake and then it's more usual for them not to see a vision but to feel a strong sense of presence of the person or occasionally to experience an uncharacteristic and inexplicable burst of grief or an intense feeling of unease, which they only later discover occurred at the time of the person's death. Occasionally the feeling of unease seems to be a premonition of the death itself.

My father had lung cancer, but a long way from dying, so we all thought. One night in December, three days before my daughter was born, so I was very large and only just squeezed behind the steering wheel! I had this great panic to get to my Father, although I had not had any reason to go with such urgency. I arrived at my parents' house after a hour's journey, and my Father was walking about, and very surprised that I had arrived so late, and without letting them know I was coming. Within two hours my Father had died!!!! He took to his bed, and I sat with him holding his hand, not for one moment realising these were his last moments with us. I always felt I was meant to be there with them.

Something leaving the body

The perception of something leaving the body around the time of death is a little discussed phenomenon, reported consistently by professional carers and, most importantly, relatives, but usually only when they are directly asked about it. The accounts are very varied, but central to this experience is a form or shape which someone present may see leaving the body, usually from the mouth, chest or through the head though we have also had accounts of something leaving through the feet. Sometimes it will hover above the body before rising to disappear through the ceiling and it is often associated with love, light, compassion, purity and sometimes with heavenly music. Not everyone who is in the room sees the vision, its appearance is transient and its perception is sensitive to interruption - people coming into the room or talking often make it disappear. Those who have had the experience, particularly if it is associated with love and light, feel enormously comforted, a feeling which may go on for many days after the death and more importantly, the experience remains a comfort over many years.

Light around the body

In most religious and mystical traditions, light holds a special significance. As we've seen, light is a predominant feature of the near death experience and always its qualities are described positively – it is said to be warm, loving, peaceful, compassionate, and also compelling, so that people feel drawn towards it. When one compares the experiences which are reported by the dying with the near death experiences of people who survive, there seem to be far more similarities than differences. It is logical to conclude that the two sets of experiences are related, that they form part of a continuum. Light is often seen, not only at the time of death but in the days or even weeks before death. Mrs. Judith Wilson who used to work in an old people's home commented:

> "I have witnessed several people who spoke of a bright light a few days before death. They all said it was beautiful and some said they could see people within the light. All of these people passed peacefully.

What is especially interesting, however, about light at the time of death is that occasionally people who are sitting with the dying do see the light, as though they are somehow sharing the same vision. This is a phenomenon often reported by carers or relatives as well as by the dying themselves. The light is usually described as bright and white and associated with strong feelings of love and compassion which at times permeate the whole room. It is often describes as emanating from or surrounding the body, and it usually lasts over the time of the death process.

265

"Suddenly there was the most brilliant light shining from my husband's chest and as this light lifted upwards there was the most beautiful music and singing voices, my own chest seemed filled with infinite joy and my heart felt as if it was lifting to join this light and music. Suddenly there was a hand on my shoulder and a nurse said "I'm sorry love. He has just gone." I lost sight of the light and music, I felt so bereft at being left behind."

Several other strange events associated with the time of death were told to us – mechanical failures, such as clocks that are reported to stop at the time of death (as in the old song about grandfather's clock), reports of odd animal behaviour or of some animal or bird being seen from the sickroom that has special significance for the dying person.

These stories were as varied as they were fascinating, but three points were made again and again in the accounts we received. The first was how comforting these experiences had been to both the dying person and those who witnessed the phenomena. The second was the conviction that what had happened was not a dream, or wishful thinking, or a figment of the imagination, or a drug induced hallucination. And the third was the sense of relief our correspondents felt at being able, often for the first time, to talk freely about the experiences which had had such a powerful effect on them. (Fenwick and Fenwick 2008)

Looking for a cause

The carers we talked to in all our studies felt confident that deathbed visions are not drug-induced. Many, probably most, of the patients in their care were on some kind of medication, and the staff were well aware that some of these drugs did indeed induce hallucinations. But they insisted that drug induced hallucinations were of a quite different quality from a true end of life vision, and had a quite different effect on their patients. (Betty 2006).

As for coincidences, are they indeed simply that – coincidences? For the people concerned the emotional impact of the experience is so great that it remains a lasting source of comfort; whether it is dismissed by others as 'simply coincidence' is irrelevant. The fact that it happened is enough.

On this basis alone we can differentiate them from the ordinary coincidences of everyday life that we are all familiar with. Neither do they seem to have much to do with religious faith or expectations. The woman who told us the following story added that she was not a Christian, nor was she from a religious family, and that she had no absolute belief about life after death.

> My mother recently passed away. At the exact time of her passing she came to visit me in a dream. She was anxious and frustrated that she had not been able to say goodbye to me in person and seemed a bit worried that death was an ending. There was a grey looking ghost/angel by her, and she found that frightening. I then had another angel come who seemed connected to me and he said that he would take her - I then told her that she was fine and that there was life after death and we could say goodbye right now.
>
> She then relaxed. Then there was an AMAZING feeling of love and peace and rightness. I can't explain it in words. Then she left. I only found out the time of her death later the next day. It was a loving and special experience and made my moms passing more acceptable, so I have no worries now!

One can never altogether dismiss the rational explanation of coincidence. But very often the person who has the experience has no knowledge that the other person is ill or dying, and the timing is so precise that it seems much more rational to consider the alternative, unscientific explanation that there is somehow a linking of minds at this final moment of departure.

Implications of end of life experiences

End of life experiences suggest that the dying process is taken care of, that the dying are often more aware at the end than was previously thought and that the support of family at this time is of enormous value. The phenomena themselves are fascinating, however we try to explain them, but not everyone will experience them.. However, everyone is going to die, and what we should be aiming for is to make sure that as far as possible, everyone has a 'good death'.

What exactly do we mean by a 'good death?' A 'good death' should simply mean that the person has died as he or she wanted to die. For some this might mean at home surrounded by their family, for others it might mean a hospice with professional carers. Some people wait to die till they are alone, others seem able to hold onto life till someone they particularly want to say farewell to has arrived at their bedside. For most people a 'good death' probably means dying with an untroubled mind, with conflicts and misunderstandings resolved. For everyone it probably means that death should be as quick and as painless as possible. The real barriers to a good death are those of unfinished business such as family conflicts, and unresolved personal issues such as guilt or hate, and the most effective tool in helping those we love experience a peaceful and a 'good' death, is to help, if we can, in the process of reconciliation.

Many health care workers who are involved with end of life issues realise that if they are to help their patients 'die well' they need a better understanding of the dying process, and further education or training to deal with its existential issues. We are now very good at making sure that when people die they are as comfortable and pain-free as possible. What we are not so good at is catering for and teaching others to care for the spiritual needs of the dying. Virtually everyone who has witnessed an end of life experience and seen its effects recognises what a comfort they can be both to the dying person and to their family, and the part they can play in enabling patients to die a peaceful death. It's now much more generally recognised and accepted that end of life experiences are indeed 'spiritual' in the sense that they have profound meaning and personal significance to the patient. (Fenwick et al 2010, Fenwick and Brayne 2011), and that giving those patients who have these experiences the opportunity to talk about them and have them validated is a necessary and important aspect of terminal care.

Chapter 18

Beyond the Grave

'THERE is something beyond the grave; death does not end all, and the pale ghost escapes from the vanquished pyre,' said Sextus Propertius (c54-c7 bc). One human strategy for coming to terms with the fact that we do not live forever and making the idea of death more tolerable is to conceive the notion of a soul which survives the body, or of a continuing life following this transient earthly one. However slim the evidence for it, most of us cling, like a child with its comfort blanket, to a faint belief in this 'pale ghost', and welcome any sightings, however fleeting, which reinforce this inner conviction. Even if we accept that the NDE tells us something about the process of dying, does it do anything to confirm the continuation of personal consciousness after death?

FINDING A DIFFERENT FRAMEWORK

So far we've taken a largely scientific, and therefore a rather limited view of the NDE. We've been looking at mechanism, and almost everything we have said has been based on the assumption that the NDE takes place in or is constructed by the brain. We've confined 'mind' to the brain because, scientifically, as we saw in Chapter 2, we have no other option. When the brain dies, the mind dies; the scientific view does not allow for the possibility of a soul, or for any form of personal survival after death.

It is only by looking at some non-scientific views that we might find a wider explanation of the NDE, one that could help us interpret the

NDE on another level, as part of the spectrum of mystical experience, and to decide whether there's any meaning behind the mechanism, and perhaps even allow for the possibility of the soul or the continuation of personal consciousness. At the moment most of these views are simply theories, with little or no evidence to back them up. But the history of science tells us that science changes across time, today's heresies sometimes become tomorrow's orthodoxies. So we are entitled to look at the NDE in the context of a wider framework, in the hope that science may eventually catch up with speculation.

Most of the NDEs we've looked at so far have been reports of personal experiences. But suppose these experiences can be shared by other people who are close to the dying person? We can of course explain this reasonably enough by saying that people who are very close to each other, who have lived together for a long time, are living in a common framework and do tend to share the same thoughts and the same emotions. But if we accept for a moment the idea that mind need not be confined to the brain, then a much more literal sharing of experience becomes a distinct possibility.

This is a story that was told to me by the niece of an old lady who was an old family friend. Some years ago the old lady lay peacefully dying, at home, in her own bed. Her niece, who was looking after her, was sleeping in a room just along the corridor. She left the doors of both rooms open so that she could easily hear her aunt if she called. During the night the niece woke and saw light outside her door. Thinking that a light had been left switched on, she got out of bed and saw that the light was streaming from the door of her aunt's room. As she entered the room she saw that the light was surrounding her aunt. As she watched, the light slowly faded and her aunt died.

When I was told this story it reminded me of a letter I had received from a mother who was at the hospital bed of her dying child. She too had described seeing a light full of pure love shining from and surrounding her child as he finally died. Now, one has to think very differently about a light which can be seen only by the dying person and one which seems to emanate from them which others can see. I decided to look back over the letters I'd received to see if anyone else had experienced similar phenomena when people they loved were dying.

This is how James Bell described what happened to him and his family while they were with his father, just before his death.

It was in the small hours of the morning. We were all sitting with my father, who was suffering from cancer and had been given a short time to live. There was a small speck of light on a wall, straight in front of the bed. This light was darting at random across the wall, and we all saw it. The funny thing is, my dad had had an injection after which he would normally sleep for a time. But this day he was sitting propped up by pillows, watching the wall. After a time the wall changed colour; it went from being dark, as the room was dark, to a bright colour. Then a figure appeared on the wall. It looked like a monk, someone with a long cloak which covered the head and face. At this I went and stood at the end of the bed. Within a short time my mother, sister, brother, could all see a mist forming from my head down the right side of my body, as if the figure that was behind me was not a big person and I was in the way. My sister came up to me and ran her fingers between the mist and me. She kept saying, 'Who is it, Dad, who is it?' For myself, I could feel a presence which, when I tried to feel it, was like a cobweb on my arms and back of my hands and neck. I went across to touch my dad's hand but he just lifted himself and pushed me away. I tried again but this time he was really mad and gave a fierce shout at me ... he waved his hands as if to say, get out, go away. Then the doctor came in to settle my father, and at this everything disappeared. The next night at the same time we all looked out for this light but nothing happened. Sadly my father died.

These accounts seem to show that the NDE may not be just a private experience, but part of a common world that we can all experience. Other stories I've been told show that the relatives of the dying are sometimes involved with the process in a very special way.

I was with my sister who was thirty years old and dying of cancer. She was twisting her hands and her knuckles were almost white. I knew she was terrified of dying, she said so many times while she was ill. She was trying to tell me what she could see. So I said I could see something as well and I would tell her what I could see and she could say yes or no. I could see this beautiful gold light at the end of a tunnel; she agreed, so I held her hand and down we went together. She was afraid but I told her it was all right, I was with her and I wasn't afraid. It seemed as though we were almost floating but the main thing was the light at the end of the tunnel was getting bigger and brighter. We travelled on and then all of a sudden it seemed as if I went into a plate glass window but looking across at my sister she just went through into the garden. She looked back at me and called me and said our gran was there. I could see a few of my relatives around the edge of the garden, which was raised ground with a white fence around. The people were on the other side. The flowers were beautiful and the grass reflected the gold from the sunshine. My sister was standing with her arms up above her head, turning around in circles and calling me to come. I said I can't, they won't let me through. With that it was almost like a gust of wind took me backwards and the next thing I knew with a big thud my body started to move. I then looked at my sister who was quite quiet. This was around 11 a.m. and she passed away about 8 p.m. that night.

How do we interpret that story told to us by Mrs Barbara Sherriff? She and her sister were evidently close; they may have had shared beliefs, but is it possible they could have had a shared, telepathic experience? For the first time, scientific experiments carried out by Jacobo Grinberg- Zylberbaum in Mexico (detailed later in this chapter) have indicated that telepathy between two people in a loving and empathic relationship may indeed be a reality.

Another interpretation is possible. Mrs Sherriff also mentions that she is a healer, and it may be that she was using her intuitive healing ability to share her own vision with her dying sister, using it as guided imagery to help her through her fears.

It is interesting, too, that like many people who wrote to us, Mrs Sherriff had had one previous out-of-body experience. This, and her ability as a healer again seems to suggest that there may be a kind of clustering - that perhaps people who have NDEs are, as a group, more likely to have psychic experiences too. A very similar story was told to us by Ms M. P. Cockerton.

Twenty years ago I lost my mother. I was with her very near the end, and had a wonderful - well, I didn't know what it was other than a 'vision', that's what I've called it ever since. I wasn't dreaming (I was by her bedside in hospital at the time) and it wasn't my imagination running riot. What I saw was a wonderful place, I don't know if it was a garden or what, I only know it was beautiful and that there was a hill down which came my auntie who had died several years previously. (She was my mother's youngest sister, to whom she was very close.) She held out her hands to my mother and they went away together. I really can't describe what peace of mind it gave to me.

It is interesting to compare this with Sylvia Atkinson's account in Chapter 15 of what happened to her after the death of her son. Both think of what they saw as a 'vision'; for both the experience was deeply comforting. Of course one can look on these visions simply as images thrown up by the mind in response to stress. But for both women the meaning and the value they held went far beyond this. These experiences could suggest a different reality and a different model of the universe, one in which there is an interconnectedness between people both before and after death. But unless mind and brain are separate it is difficult to see how this can be.

This idea of interconnectedness after death appears again in this incident, described by Mrs B. Wills. It happened at the time of her husband's death twelve years ago, when he was fifty-one.

My husband had said he would find some way of reaching me, should anything happen. I assured him I would not be afraid. He had to go into hospital a few hours before he died, and about 5.30 a.m. I was partly awake when I felt something heavy land on the bed, come up over my body and kiss me. That was the time my husband's heart stopped beating, according to the sister.

Henry Maj tells a very similar story:

My father worked as a coal miner. He is very stolid in his beliefs and has a down-to-earth approach. Black is black, white is white and nothing in between. One evening, when she was fifty-four, my mother had a heart-attack, and an ambulance collected her from home. My father, upset, went to the toilet and reported that whilst there the door was rapped rapidly and repeatedly. Wondering who was there and realising that someone must be knocking to convey a report on my mother's deteriorating condition, he quickly opened the door to find only an empty stairwell. He felt that he knew my mother had died and she had, in fact, died on the way to hospital in the ambulance. I realise that my father must have been in an emotional state, and I know this is a subjective opinion, but, as I have often said to my brothers and sisters, if my father said something had happened, then it had, and it would probably not have been emotively engendered.

My mother knew she was going to die, and she had told us of visions she had had of a 'white' lady and a train at a station to take her away.

What are we to make of these stories? Were they manifestations of out-of-body experiences? Are they an indication that there is something - let's call it a soul -which leaves the body at death? Even if we accept this it is hard to believe that a disembodied soul is capable of landing heavily on a bed, let alone rapping at a door. It is easy to dismiss the timing in each case as coincidence. And yet the possibility that someone at his moment of death may somehow be able to reach out and touch the mind of the person he loves has to be considered.

Finally, an account from Ms Helen Springfield. This is a description of what she experienced while she was waiting at home while her mother was in hospital having an operation.

My mother entered hospital in 1986 for major heart surgery. Unfortunately, complications set in and she was returned to theatre. I was later informed that following the second bout of surgery her heart was very weak and tired, and it was only medication and the heart and lung machine that was keeping her going. I found myself watching my mother for the rest of the day and I saw her mother and father (long since passed over) around her. During the afternoon the family were called to her bedside as they had withdrawn the medication, leaving her on the support machine only. I stayed at home, but was still able to watch my mother clearly. I could still see her parents and other long-dead members of her family. I could see rays of orange, purple and gold around her. I watched my mother with her parents on either side of her walk down a tunnel, surrounded by a silver light. She turned and looked at me and I felt compelled to look at the time. It was 4 p.m., and just as a mother is attached to a baby by the umbilical cord, I could see a shaft of gold light with orange running between my mother and myself, and as she turned she called to me - it was so loud she could have been standing in front of me - and she reached out her hand to me. I could see myself take her hand and I saw her walk back through the tunnel towards me. Later in the day I spoke to my father on the phone and asked what had happened at 4 p.m. and he told me that mother's condition had started to change and stabilise and at 4 p.m. my father and the rest of the family went into the hospital's chapel and lit a candle in prayer.

Yet again the same images, the light and the tunnel, appear. Let me remind you again that the imagery of the NDE was not widely known in 1986. In parapsychological terms this experience would be called remote viewing, which means Ms Springfield was able to 'see' what was happening at a distance. Unfortunately, there is a useful piece of the jigsaw missing. We are not told whether Ms Springfield's mother did indeed share this experience with her, or whether it originated in her mind alone.

If we accept the subjective experience of the people who gave these accounts, then we have to accept that what happens to the dying person can in some way affect those around them; that the NDE can sometimes be a shared experience rather than just a personal one. One mind seems to be affecting another mind directly - and this is not something that is built into or can be accounted for by any of the scientific theories we've looked at so far. We have to look for some quite different theory of mind.

The first possibility is that mind may have a non-local effect - an influence beyond the brain, mediated by some physical principle not yet defined by science. This would mean that brain processes can affect, at a distance, other minds (telepathy) and physical matter (psychokinesis, or PK).

Recent work in the area of parapsychology has produced preliminary results which, if they are confirmed, might provide some persuasive evidence for non-locality of mind The most convincing experiments are the Gansfield experiments, which have examined mind-reading ability in a state of sensory deprivation and Bob Jahn's set of experiments in America, which have shown the ability of minds to influence a random number generator, or to affect the way balls fall in a large pinball machine. The experiments conducted in Mexico by Dr Jacobo Grinberg-Zylberbaum, raise the possibility that information can be transferred directly from brain to brain between empathic individuals, are also persuasive. None of these experiments so far provides cast-iron proof, but they are being taken seriously enough for other researchers to try to replicate them.

However, even if non-locality of mind is eventually accepted as proven fact, this does not imply the possibility of soul or the continuation of individual consciousness after brain death. Personal consciousness depends on memory, and unless there is some evidence that memory is not locked within the brain, but can be stored outside it, it is difficult to argue that individual consciousness can survive the death of the brain.

THE POSSIBILITY OF SOUL

A view which goes a step further is that mind and brain are quite separate; that mind can exist independently of a brain and memories can be stored beyond the brain as well as within it. This is the kind of theory we would have to adopt if, for example, it could be shown that information about the physical world can indeed be acquired by someone who is having an out-of-body experience, which is not available to him through his sense organs. It would also allow for an existence of personal identity beyond the brain and so beyond brain death. Now we are into soul territory.

It is the medical profession who are in the best position to fill in some of the remaining pieces of the near-death puzzle. Many of the most convincing cases of out-of-body experiences during the NDE occurred in either the operating theatre or the Intensive Care Unit. And yet we've seen how very difficult it is to get more than simply anecdotal evidence to support claims that people did actually see things when out of their body that they could not otherwise have seen.

There are many cases in which at first glance it seems that this must have happened. But nearly always, when they are examined in detail, it proves hard to substantiate the claims that are made. One of these has become so well known that it is often quoted to 'prove' that information really can be acquired by someone who is out of his or her body. This was a case concerning a woman, Maria, who was brought into a Seattle hospital after a cardiac arrest. Maria told her social worker she had seen various things while she lay there, her own body from the vantage-point of the ceiling, the view from outside the emergency room, and a shoe, described in great detail, which she had seen on a third-floor window ledge at the north end of the hospital building. She described the shoe as having a worn patch by the little toe and the lace stuck under the heel. Doubtful, the social worker went in search of the shoe - and found it, exactly as Maria had described it. Convincing? Of course. The only problem is that no one who has tried to follow up this story has ever actually been able to find this particular woman and talk to her. So we still have to regard it as hearsay rather than hard fact. *(Authors' note: since this book was written the social worker in question has been traced and has verified the story).*

If we want to verify such claims we have to enlist the cooperation of hospital staff. To begin with, it is their observations and records which can show how close a patient actually came to death - they know those who are, so to speak, most 'at risk' of having an NDE. They may be able to tell us how long a patient was unconscious and how low his blood pressure was, so that we can gain some idea of the degree of hypoxia and hypercarbia.

With the cooperation of medical staff it would be possible to set up simple tests in a hospital theatre or Intensive Care Unit to test whether or not people who have NDEs can really gain information when outside the range of their bodily senses. The scientific argument runs like this. During an NDE, although the patient believes he is on the ceiling, he is still lying on the bed, his ordinary senses gathering information in the normal way. From this the brain creates a world which places him on the ceiling. This is straightforward. The alternative explanation is that the patient really is viewing the room from a vantage-point on the ceiling. If this is truly so, then he should be able to gain information that he could not get access to when lying on the bed below.

It should not be impossible to test this. For example, objects might be placed on a shelf close to the ceiling, which can be viewed only from the ceiling and not from below. Provided nobody is told what is up there, the only way a patient could identify them correctly is if he has actually been out of his body near the ceiling. If this did happen, it could only mean that the patient could gain information by direct use of his mind, not only through his senses.

Charles Tart, an American scientist, has suggested a clever twist to this experiment. What he has proposed is that instead of an ordinary article being put near the ceiling, a visual illusion should be put there - an ambiguous image which is only recognisable when the eyes and brain are working together. Eye movements are vital to produce accurate perception. The eye is continuously making rapid flicks and tremors, very slightly changing the position of the image on the retina, so that the retinal cells are continually stimulated. If the eye movements cease, the image changes and is gradually lost; colours fade, corners and planes disappear and lines begin to merge. It is this continual movement which makes the perfectly static black and white figure shown left look as if it is in perpetual motion.

Supposing this was the image placed at ceiling level. If the patient were to report that he had seen it as we see it, with this slightly shimmering, shifting effect, then we'd know that he had been using normal eye and brain mechanisms. But if, on the other hand, he saw only the simple black and white pattern, then we might have to assume that mind was somehow or other short-circuiting all brain processes in obtaining this information.

To my knowledge, no one has yet tried the illusion experiment. However, at the moment, several teams are carrying out similar experiments using real objects. If there are any positive sightings, this would have dramatic implications. It would indicate that mind and brain are separate. Science would then have to reformulate its ideas concerning consciousness and the relationship of mind to brain. And if mind is separate from brain, then the possibility that mind may in some way survive the death of the body is something that science would have to take seriously. We might have to give the near-death experience a much more literal interpretation than we have given it so far.

We might, for example, suggest that at some point during the dying process mind and brain separate. We also have to assume that mind can retain memory (otherwise there could be no memory of the objects seen on the ceiling). Mind, with its retained memory, disappears down the tunnel and enters a phase of consciousness which it interprets as light. Because mind contains memory, it will interpret any experience it comes across just as it has been interpreting experiences in this world, using this life's memories. We'd therefore expect such experiences to show both cultural and individual differences, which we already know they do.

But what happens when mind has spent some time in this condition? We have to predict that if mind contains an experiential system and a memory system then it will gradually acquire an additional bank of memory and experience and so be able to construct experiences of a quite different reality.

However, at the moment this theory is not a strong contender for scientific acceptability because there are no known physical principles whereby mind can exist or memory be stored outside brain processes. We have to look to totally non-scientific frameworks to support it.

TRANSMISSION THEORIES

We've been assuming that everything is created within the brain. An alternative view is that everything is transmitted *through* the brain. Transmission theories have been popular for a long time, but there has never been much evidence to support them.

William James was one of the strongest exponents of the transmission theory. He described in his book *Human Immortality* (1898) the idea that beyond the 'veil of reality' in this world, and particularly beyond the brain, there is a transcendent reality in which the soul may live. He argued that it is the brain which transmits through it and modifies the beam of consciousness. He pointed out that there is no specific test which will allow us to determine whether the brain creates consciousness or whether it transmits, through its functioning, the beam of consciousness. 'In strict logic, then, the fangs of cerebralistic materialism are drawn. My words ought consequently to exert a releasing function on your hopes. You *may* believe henceforward, whether you care to profit by the permission or not.' He sums up by saying: 'All abstract hypotheses sound unreal; and the abstract notion that our brains are coloured lenses in the wall of nature, admitting light from the supra-solar source, but at the same time tingeing and restricting it, has a thoroughly fantastic sound. What is it, you may ask, but a foolish metaphor?' He goes on to elaborate the strength of this view and it is as relevant to our science today as it was almost one century ago. Science still does not understand the conversion of the objective world outside to the subjective world of meaning.

In its simplest form, a transmission theory states that mind and brain are different and are linked together in some way. Sense data is transformed by the brain for transmission to an external mind. Mind in its turn can will an action which is transmitted to brain and so is able to initiate brain processes and thus actions. Although memories are held partly within the brain, a large part of memory is stored external to the brain, and in this personal identity is located.

The attraction of transmission theories is that they allow for the concept of survival of personal identity after death, and thus give a meaning to life beyond the purely biological and cultural. They try to explain something that many people feel intuitively - that human beings, besides being individuals, are part of a greater whole. But once again we come up against the difficulty that at present there is no known mechanism which would link brain to mind in this way, or which would allow memory to be stored outside the brain.

Another weakness of transmission theories in general is that even if they are correct, they are difficult to test. A transmission theory would argue that as mind is transmitted through the brain, disturbances in brain function will produce disorders of mind because their transmission is interrupted.

But a similar argument can equally well be used if it is argued that mind is located in and is a function of the brain. Then too a disorder of brain function will produce a disorder of mind. There is no experiment which can easily distinguish between these two possibilities.

Several people have suggested possible transmission mechanisms, and it is interesting to look at these. But we have to remember that at the moment they are entirely speculative.

Sir John Eccles, one of this century's most distinguished neurophysiologists and a Nobel laureate, has suggested that there is an interface between brain and mind. Here the 'dendron' (a hypothetical region of the nerve cell processes of the brain) links with the 'psychon' (the hypothetical atom of mind). However, so far nobody has managed to identify dendrons or psychons, so the theory remains just that, a theory.

The theory of morphic resonance is biologist Rupert Sheldrake's attempt to explain how memory might exist independently of an individual brain, and could be accessed by other brains. He postulates the existence of 'morphogenetic fields'. A morphogenetic field is part of the structure of the universe, existing everywhere at once. It is thus possible for matter to be influenced by this field at the same time in widely separate areas. He suggests that information relating to a pattern of behaviour can be transmitted from the brain to this morphogenetic field. The transmitted information modifies the field and the field in its turn modifies other similar brains so that they become more likely to reproduce this particular piece of behaviour. He uses this morphic resonance theory to explain, for example, how it is that when rats in one part of the world learned to run through mazes, other rats in other places seemed to acquire this ability simultaneously, and why scientists working in different places and not in contact with each other often tend to make the same discoveries at more or less the same time. Dr Sheldrake believes that experiments which he and other workers have carried out have produced some evidence for his field theory, but so far the scientific world is not convinced.

Another field theory has been postulated by Jacobo Grinberg-Zylberbaum. His theory suggests that the electromagnetic fields which are produced in the brain by the passage of nerve impulses in some way interact with the fabric of space. This interaction allows the transmission of an effect from one brain to the next. However, the transmission is strongest when the two people are in similar states, for example in people who have strong empathic feelings for each other. He has produced some evidence in support of his theory, as he has shown that the response of one brain to tone pips can be transmitted to another (out of earshot) brain. All this theory suggests is that mind can influence activity in the world beyond the brain, in its present form it offers no explanation or evidence for the existence of *memory* beyond the brain.

There are other field theories which postulate a remote but constant link between minds. Jung's concept of the collective unconscious is one such theory. Jung suggested that part of the mind exists beyond individual brains and is a reservoir of human experience inherited from ancestors, independent of time and place. This would certainly be an explanation for the fact that the same images (archetypes), crop up again and again in NDEs, dreams, religions, myths and fables. Jung's theory might provide an explanation for this story I was told by a Japanese woman.

Shortly after the death of her mother she dreamt that she was standing in the middle of the river, on the left bank of which stood her father; on the right, her mother. Her mother beckoned to her father to come across and join her. But he did not, and finally, she turned and walked away. Now, in Japanese Buddhism the symbolic divide between this world and the next is a river. There has been some research into Japanese near-death experiences, and as might be expected, the river is a recurring motif in many of these. However, this woman had been brought up a Christian, and at the time she had her dream she had no knowledge of Japanese Buddhism, and no memory of ever being told about the symbolism of the river.

So here once again, we have an appealing theory, but with the insurmountable difficulty that there is no way known to science by which memory can be held anywhere except within the brain.

AFTERLIFE HYPOTHESES

Finally, we have to ask if it is possible that the near-death experience provides proof of one of mankind's longest-held, strongest-held beliefs, that the 'pale ghost' does indeed escape the funeral pyre and survive the death of the physical body.

A bewildering variety of views of the afterlife is held by different people in different cultures. In nearly all religions, there is a belief in the survival of some aspect of man after death, usually with a parallel belief that actions in this life have a consequence beyond it, via karma or the soul. In Judaeo-Christian thinking, the soul is a divine aspect of God which is in each one of us - the 'image of the Creator'. The body surrounds the soul and transmits to it knowledge of those actions and thoughts which are carried out here on Earth. The soul is thus part of the individual's life on Earth but after death it separates from the body and progresses.

Sogyal Rinpoche, in his book *The Tibetan Book of Living and Dying*, discusses the interesting parallels between the Tibetan view of dying and life after death and the near-death experience. Tibetan Buddhism suggests that at death the soul separates from the body and for a period of forty-seven days lives a disincarnate existence before being born again. The quality of the birth in the next life will depend on the quality of the life previously lived. The Tibetan tradition refers to two states, the *bardo* (or state) of dying, and the *bardo* of becoming - the state you go into after death. The momentary release of mind from body which seems to occur in the NDE, and the experiences it then goes through, show extraordinary similarities to the experiences of the 'mental body' in the *bardo* of becoming. In the *bardo* of becoming the dead are able to see and hear living relatives, as if in an out-of-body experience. *The Tibetan Book of the Dead* describes the mental body as being 'like a body of the golden age', able to travel anywhere and with the power of clairvoyance. And just as happens in the NDE, other beings are met in the *bardo*, and different realms are visited.

There is, however, one major and significant difference between the two states. The Tibetan teaching is that the *bardo* is a state entered into only after physical death, as the person is being 'reborn', while those people who have near-death experiences are only near death - they do not actually die, though they may briefly appear to be dead. The interpretation of the Tibetan masters is that whatever happens in the NDE happens within the natural *bardo* of this life - that people may perhaps be standing on the threshold of the bardo, but they have not entered and returned. The analogy Rinpoche himself suggests is an attractive one. Could it be, he suggests, that when they experience the light 'just before its vast sun rises, they catch a strong glimpse of the first rays of dawn?' The strength of any theory which allows for the existence of the 'pale ghost' is that it also allows for personal responsibility. Intuitively, most people want to feel that the world has a meaning. A purely mechanistic and deterministic view of the world, seen only through the eyes of science, removes any possibility of personal transcendent values. We need a wider view to encompass the instinctive belief that we matter, that we are part of a greater whole, and that our actions carry a personal responsibility and have consequences for us or for the universe at some future time. In the last resort, without a soul we are merely mechanical entities responsible only to our biology and to our culture.

However, when we are looking at the NDE it is probably a mistake to look for literal truth, rather than psychological or spiritual truth. Is it even worth speculating about whether the NDE sheds any light on what happens after death? Speculation is all it can ever be. We can believe, or not believe in life after death, but none of us can really know. What we do know, beyond any shadow of doubt, is that we die, and what happens as we pass from life to death is something that legitimately concerns us. It's possible that the NDE can show us something about the process of dying. But if it does hold a key, it is less likely to be the key to the secrets of life after death than the key to the secrets of life itself. We have seen that the NDE is both timeless and independent of death, that it seems to be part of the spectrum of normal human experience. Even if we don't look to it for proof of an afterlife, it may tell us about the structure of mind, the boundaries of human experience, even about the universe itself. For many people the NDE is a profound spiritual experience. It makes them value life without clinging to it, appreciate each day as though it was their last.

Again and again in different situations we come across the imagery and the experience of the NDE. Very similar experiences also happen to meditators in the various Buddhist traditions. The OBE is common, and the approach of a disc of living light, sometimes seen as if down a long tunnel, is very often reported by meditators using the Buddhist Vipassana practice. Ms Dorothy Bailey described a tunnel- and-light experience of her own which she had during a retreat, a week of intensive Vipassana meditation in 1967.

I was floating in the air and could see landscape below, and wanted to get to another place. The knowledge was given to me that if I dived down through one of the factory chimneys that were standing around, that was the route. I looked down and there was the black opening in front of my feet. I was standing on the rim of a chimney. Remembering my diving training I took up the classic position on the rim with my toes curling over the edge and then dived through.

The body felt weightless but I was conscious of a graceful acceleration. I was in this dark tunnel (not falling but travelling horizontally) with the walls beginning to flow by at some speed. The darkness began to bear in on me and I looked ahead to see if I could see. Then, when travelling fairly fast, a small pinpoint of golden light appeared in the distance. With the speed of travel the point expanded until I saw it was a disc, expanding at an ever- increasing rate as I accelerated and accelerated towards it. Suddenly I realised it was the end of the tunnel and the beautiful other place was to be found through it. I mentally glimpsed it. Yet the golden disc seemed to be on its own and vibrant with light. It grew at an ever-increasing rate and I knew I was travelling too fast. It was inevitable and imperative that I entered and immersed myself in this living light to get to the desired place, the beautiful land outside, but I felt I was travelling too fast to hit it at the right time. It was important to reduce the rate of my approach. The disc was now filling half the total scene. The light from it made the brick walls rushing by visible, and I was amazed and a little afraid of the speed. 'I must reduce speed, it will have danger in it to hit the light at this moment (I am impure, things to clean up). Later on, yes, most definitely, but not yet.'

So I pressed my heels and elbows out sideways to act as brakes and pressed them hard against the walls. The light filled all my vision to 180 degrees, warm, living. Then I 'woke up' (though it was not a dream), whole- minded and peaceful.

Before she had this experience, Ms Bailey had spent a long time in intensive meditation, sitting still and watching her breathing, and it is very likely that she was becoming sensorily deprived. This may well have altered her brain function in some way - we know that people who are sensorily deprived do have expanded visual imagery. It's just possible that prolonged Vipassana meditation also alters the carbon dioxide environment of the brain, but I suspect that it's unlikely to do this sufficiently to produce true hypercarbia. But whichever mechanism we suspect, why should it produce these particular experiences - the tunnel and the light? It is as if there is some basic mind structure underpinning everyday experience which can be activated in many ways. The really interesting question then, is, what is this mind structure and what is its purpose? The function of meditation is to still the discursive mind by clearing away the clutter of our everyday cognitive structures. Many meditation practices are also designed to enhance emotional experience. The tunnel, the blackness, is non-experience. In this state the basic feature of mind can surface and this is composed of strong positive emotion and white light.

If this interpretation is correct then this tunnel-and-light experience is not dependent on the full elaboration of cognitive structures, but is beyond the realm of ideas. It may be that we are able to experience this aspect of mind only when our basic cognitive model-building brain is silenced, for example by meditation, or by fear, or in unconsciousness, or in those rare moments of transcendence, the mystical experience. If this is indeed so then we could argue that in any of these conditions the bedrock of experience is perceived. This interpretation also contains the implication that the fundamental structure of the universal mind is unconditional love, without form and composed entirely of light, outside time and universal. As one pulls away from this basic ground state then the clutter of cognitive structures becomes apparent and sensory images - sounds, scents, people, buildings, flowers and gardens - are included in the experience. These features are probably secondary and thus culturally determined.

However, we may finally have to accept that however hard we look for a logical and scientific explanation that lies behind near-death experiences, we may never find it. Even if we could fully explain their mechanism, would we be satisfied? I suspect not. I think that many, perhaps most of us, would continue to look for a meaning beyond them that wasn't simply mechanical. Perhaps we should just accept and value these experiences for what they are, experiences which are enormously meaningful and powerful to those who have them, which can change attitudes towards both life and death in a positive and often a permanent way, and lead those of us who don't have them to ask far-reaching and universal questions about our nature. Allan Pring, whose own experience (dealt with in Chapter 8) was an event so powerful that its memory can still reduce him to tears, has this to say:

> For my part I believe and accept that the truth of NDEs will never be known. At least not this side of the grave. As far as I am concerned what happened to me made complete sense ... religion does not come into it but I have seen enough to understand why the concept of an almighty God came about in the minds of intelligent men...
>
> I suspect that all religions of the world have the basic answers. For my part I am not religious, nor do I believe in God or any divine mysterious force either benign or malevolent towards man. But from what I have learned I would recommend that every human being seriously considers the possibility that death is not the end of everything.
>
> There is no end but there are endless consequences.

It is human nature to want to know the reason why. This is why interpreters of dreams, from Joseph to Jung, have commanded such a following. We do not like to believe that an experience which makes a powerful emotional impact might be essentially meaningless. This devalues the experience and so, by implication, devalues us because we set so much store by it. We want to believe that we have meaning in a wider sense - that we are more than brain function, more than just a speck in creation, and that finally, personal consciousness will continue in some form or another. We want to believe that when we enter the light we are coming home, that we do indeed touch the inner reaches of a universe that is composed of universal love.

If we have never personally had such an experience we can only theorise. And while theories are fine, and fun and even useful, I believe that we can learn more about its true significance by listening to the people who have been there, who have had first-hand experience of what the rest of us can only talk about. So let me give the last word to Maurice James, someone who has been there, and who seems to me to come as close as it is possible to get to the truth in the light.

> Part of me thinks of my experiences as being a physical-psychological-drug phenomenon, but part of me also believes the experience to be of a much deeper significance and that I was very fortunate and blessed to have had the experience.
>
> I do know that at times when I catch the eye of a robin or blackbird in my garden I feel as I look into the eye that the eye has knowledge that I have.
>
> Whatever it is, it's just over the horizon and one day I'll travel there. Today and the sense of being alive are only a minute part of this greater time and timelessness. One thing is for sure, and that is that death has no fears for me.

Bibliography/References

Barrett, Sir William 1926 *Deathbed visions*

Betty LS. 2006. Are they hallucinations or are they real? The spirituality of deathbed and near-death visions. *Omega.* 2006; 53: 37-49.

Blackmore, Susan, *Dying to Live.* Grafton 1993.

Brayne S, Farnham C, Fenwick P. 2006. An understanding of the occurrence of deathbed phenomena and its effect on palliative care clinicians. *Am J Hosp Palliat Care.* 2006; 23:17-24.

Brayne S., Lovelace H. Fenwick P. 2008. Nurses and Care Assistants End-of-Life Experiences and the Dying Process in a Gloucestershire Nursing Home as Reported by Nurses and Care Assistants. *Am J Hosp Palliat Care* ; 25; 195 – 206

Feng Zhi-ying and Liu Jian-xun, Near-Death Experiences Among Survivors of the 1976 Tangshan Earthquake. *Journal of Near-Death Studies* 1992 II (1), pp.39-48.

Fenwick, P., Some Aspects of the Physiology of the Mystical Experience. *Psychology* 1983, Survey No.4. ed. Nicholson, J. and Foss, B., pp.203-23. Leicester. British Psychological Society.

Fenwick. P and Fenwick E. 2008 *The Art of Dying.* Continuum

Fenwick P, Lovelace H Brayne S. 2010. Comfort for the dying: five year retrospective and one year prospective studies of end of life experiences. *Archives of Gerontology and Geriatrics* 2010. Sep-Oct;51(2):173-9. Epub 2009 Nov 13

Fenwick P, Brayne S. 2011. Deathbed Visions and Coincidences End-of-Life Experiences: Reaching Out for Compassion, Communication, and Connection. *American Journal of Hospice and Palliative Care* 2011, Feb;28(1):7-15. Epub 2010 Aug 27

Gabbard, Glen O. and Twemlow, Stuart W, Explanatory Hypotheses for Near Death Experiences. *Revision* 1981, Vol.4, No.2. 68-71.

Gabbard, Glen O, Twemlow, S. W. and Jones, F. C. Do Near-Death Experiences Occur Only Near Death? *Journal of Nervous and Mental Diseases* 1981, 169:19-27.

Grey, M. *Return from Death*, Arkana, London 1985.

Greyson, Bruce, Near-Death Experiences and Personal Values. *American Journal of Psychiatry* 1983, 140:5 618-620.

Greyson, Bruce, The Near-Death Experience Scale. *Journal of Nervous and Mental Diseases* 1983, Vol.171, No.6., pp.369-375.

Greyson, Bruce, The Psychodynamics of Near-Death Experiences. *Journal of Nervous and Mental Diseases* 1983, Vol.171 No.6., pp.376-381.

Gurney Myers and Podmore *Phantasms of the Living*

Kubler Ross, Elizabeth, *On Children and Death*. Collier Books 1983.

Lorimer, David, *Whole in One*. Arkana 1990.

Meduna, L. J., *Carbon Dioxide Therapy*. Charles C.Thomas. Springfield, Illinois.

Moody, Raymond, *Life after Life*. Atlanta, Georgia, Mockingbird 1973.

Morse, Melvin, *Closer to the Light*. Souvenir Press 1990.

Morse, Melvin, *Transformed by the Light*. Piatkus 1992.

Morse, Melvin, Venecia, David, Milstein, Jerrold, Tyler and Donal, C., Childhood Near-Death Experiences. *American Journal of Diseases of Children*, November 1986, Vol.140, pp.1110-1114.

Noyes, R. 1972, The Experience of Dying. *Psychiatry* 35: 174-84.

Noyes, R. and Kletti, R. 1977, Panoramic Memory: A Response to the Threat of Death. *Omega* 8: 181-94.

Noyes, R. and Slymen, D. 1979, The Subjective Response to Life-Threatening Danger. *Omega* 9: 313-21.

Osis K and Haraldsson E. 1977 *At the Hour of Death*. Hastings House.

Osis, K. 1961. *Deathbed Observations by Physicians and* Nurses. New York. Parapsychology Foundation, Inc.

Owens, J. E., Cook, E. W., Stevenson, I., Features of "Near-Death Experience" in Relation to Whether or Not Patients Were Near-Death. *The Lancet,* Nov. 1990, Vol.336, pp.1175-1176.

Pasricha, Satwant and Stevenson, I., Near-Death Experiences 390 Bibliography/References in India. A Preliminary Report. *Journal of Nervous and Mental Diseases* 1986, Vol.174, No.3., pp.165-170.

Pasricha, Satwant, A Systematic Survey of Near-Death Experiences in South India.

Penfield, W. 1955, The role of the temporal cortex in certain psychical phenomena. *Journal of Mental Science* 101: 451,Äî 65.

Rawlings, M., *Beyond Death's Door.* Nashville, Thomas Nelson 1978.

Ring, K . *Life at Death: A Scientific Investigation of the Near-Death Experience.* New York, Coward, McCann and Geoghegan 1980 and New York, Quill, 1982.

Ring, K. and Rosing, C.J., The Omega Project: An Empirical Study of the NDE-prone personality. *Journal of Near-Death Studies,* 1990, 9:211-19.

Ring, Kenneth. *Life at Death. A Scientific Investigation of the Near-Death Experience.* New York, Coward 1980.

Roberts, Glenn and Owen, John, The Near-Death Experience. *British Journal of Psychiatry,* 1988, 153: 607-617.

Stevenson, Ian and Greyson, Bruce, Near-Death Experiences. *Journal of the American Medical Association,* 1979, Vol.242, No.3, pp.265-267.

Index

S

T

Paperbacks also available from
White Crow Books

Leo Tolstoy—*My Religion:*
What I Believe
ISBN 978-1-907355-23-3

Leo Tolstoy—*On Life*
ISBN 978-1-907355-91-2

Leo Tolstoy—*Twenty-three Tales*
ISBN 978-1-907355-29-5

Leo Tolstoy—*What is Religion*
and other writings
ISBN 978-1-907355-28-8

Leo Tolstoy—*Work While*
Ye Have the Light
ISBN 978-1-907355-26-4

Leo Tolstoy with Simon Parke—
Conversations with Tolstoy
ISBN 978-1-907355-25-7

Vincent Van Gogh with
Simon Parke—*Conversations*
with Van Gogh
ISBN 978-1-907355-95-0

Howard Williams with an
Introduction by Leo Tolstoy—*The*
Ethics of Diet: An Anthology
of Vegetarian Thought
ISBN 978-1-907355-21-9

Allan Kardec—*The Spirits Book*
ISBN 978-1-907355-98-1

Wolfgang Amadeus Mozart
with Simon Parke—
Conversations with Mozart
ISBN 978-1-907661-38-9

Jesus of Nazareth with
Simon Parke—*Conversations*
with Jesus of Nazareth
ISBN 978-1-907661-41-9

Thomas à Kempis with Simon
Parke—*The Imitation of Christ*
ISBN 978-1-907661-58-7

Emanuel Swedenborg—
Heaven and Hell
ISBN 978-1-907661-55-6

P.D. Ouspensky—*Tertium Organum:*
The Third Canon of Thought
ISBN 978-1-907661-47-1

Dwight Goddard—*A Buddhist Bible*
ISBN 978-1-907661-44-0

Leo Tolstoy—*The Death*
of Ivan Ilyich
ISBN 978-1-907661-10-5

Leo Tolstoy—*Resurrection*
ISBN 978-1-907661-09-9

Michael Tymn—
The Afterlife Revealed
ISBN 978-1-970661-90-7

Guy L. Playfair—*If This Be Magic*
ISBN 978-1-907661-84-6

Julian of Norwich with
Simon Parke—*Revelations of*
Divine Love
ISBN 978-1-907661-88-4

Maurice Nicoll—*The New Man*
ISBN 978-1-907661-86-0

Carl Wickland, M.D.—*Thirty Years*
Among the Dead
ISBN 978-1-907661-72-3

Allan Kardec—
The Book on Mediums
ISBN 978-1-907661-75-4

John E. Mack—*Passport*
to the Cosmos
ISBN 978-1-907661-81-5

All titles available as eBooks, and selected titles available in Hardback and Audiobook formats from www.whitecrowbooks.com

9 781908 733085